Financing Patterns for Infrastructure Projects

Published by
ACADEMIC FOUNDATION
in association with

Institute of Public Enterprise

ABOUT THE AUTHORS

Amareshwar Mishra (M.A. (English); MBA and LL.M) started his career as a lecturer and then switched over to banking (UCO Bank). Working in different capacities, he retired as General Manager (Corporate Credit). He was awarded best urban trophy for performance twice while he was the regional head and was made Convenor for mid-market segments and agriculture lending as well as Parliamentary committees of the bank. He has also worked in IIFCL as Chief General Manager (Credit). Presently, he is visiting professor of business schools across India. He has published numerous articles in various journals/bank's house journals and law journals and other periodicals.

R.K. Mishra is ONGC Subir Raha Chair Professor on corporate governance and Senior Professor and Director, Institute of Public Enterprise (IPE), Hyderabad. With PhD from the University of Rajasthan and a visiting fellow at London Business School, UK, he studied for International Teachers programme at SDA Bocconi, Milan, Italy. He has been a management consultant to PWC, DFID, Adam Smith Institute, ADB and Centre for Good Governance. He has supervised more than 50 doctoral researches from several universities and his areas of interest include corporate governance, international management, technology management, PPP and corporate restructuring.

Financing Patterns for Infrastructure Projects

AMARESHWAR MISHRA
R.K. MISHRA

ACADEMIC FOUNDATION
NEW DELHI

www.academicfoundation.com

First published in 2013
by

ACADEMIC FOUNDATION
4772-73 / 23 Bharat Ram Road, (23 Ansari Road),
Darya Ganj, New Delhi - 110 002 (India).
Phones : 23245001 / 02 / 03 / 04.
Fax : +91-11-23245005.
E-mail : books@academicfoundation.com
www.academicfoundation.com

in association with

Institute of Public Enterprise, Hyderabad

Disclaimer:
The findings/views/opinions expressed in this book are solely those of the authors and do not necessarily reflect the views of the publisher.

Cataloging in Publication Data--DK
Courtesy: D.K. Agencies (P) Ltd. <docinfo@dkagencies.com>

Mishra, Amareshwar.
Financing patterns for infrastructure projects / Amareshwar Mishra, R.K. Mishra.
p. Cm.
ISBN 9788171889884

1. Infrastructure (Economics)--India--Finance. 2. Finance, Public--India. 3. India--Economic policy--1991- I. Mishra, R.K., 1948-, joint author. II. Title.

DDC 363.60954 23

Typeset by Italics India, New Delhi.

Printed and bound by The Book Mint, New Delhi.
www.thebookmint.in.

Contents

List of Tables, Figures and Boxes

Tables

Figures

Boxes

Abbreviations

ABS	:	Asset Backed Securities
ADB	:	Asian Development Bank
ADT	:	Average Daily Traffic
ATS	:	Associated Transmission System
BOLT	:	Build, Operate, Lease & Transfer
BOOT	:	Build, Own, Operate & Transfer
BOT	:	Build, Operate & Transfer
BoP	:	Balance of Plants
BPLR	:	Banks Prime Lending Rate
BTG	:	Boiler, Turbine and Generator
BTO	:	Build, Transfer & Operate
CA	:	Concession Agreement
CCI	:	Cabinet Committee on Infrastructure
CCPS	:	Compulsorily Convertible Preference Shares
CDR	:	Corporate Debt Restructuring
CEA	:	Central Electrical Authority
COD	:	Commercial Operation Date
CP	:	Concession Period
CSFs	:	Critical Success Factors
CTU	:	Central Transmission Utility
CWC	:	Central Water Commission

DEA	:	Department of Economic Affairs
DER	:	Debt Equity Ratio
DPR	:	Detailed Project Report
DSCR	:	Debt Service Coverage Ratio
DSRA	:	Debt Service Reserve Account
EBIT	:	Earning Before Interest and Taxes
ECB	:	External Commercial Borrowing
EMP	:	Environmental Management Plan
EPC	:	Engineering, Procurement & Construction
ESSF	:	Environment and Social Safeguard Framework
FIs	:	Financial Institutions
FM	:	Force Majeure
FRR	:	Facility Risk Rating
FSA	:	Fuel Supply Agreement
FSR	:	Facility Risk Rating
FTA	:	Fuel Transport Agreement
GCB	:	Gross Calorific Value
GSI	:	Geological Survey of India
IDFC	:	Infrastructure Development Finance Company
IIFCL	:	India Infrastructure Finance Company Ltd.
IPO	:	Initial Public Offer
IRAC	:	Income Recognition and Asset Classifications
IRR	:	Internal Rate of Return
ITA	:	Income Tax Act
JNNSM	:	Jawaharlal Nehru National Solar Mission
KYC	:	Know Your Customer
LCN	:	Lending Confirmation Notice

LDO	:	Lease, Develop & Operate
LGD	:	Loss Given Defaults
LIA	:	Lender Insurance Advisor
LIE	:	Lender Independent Engineer
LLC	:	Lender's Legal Counsel
LOA	:	Letter of Assurance
LTOA	:	Long Term Open Access
MCA	:	Model Concession Agreement
MIS	:	Management Information System
MoCA	:	Ministry of Civil Aviation
MoU	:	Memorandum of Understanding
NHAI	:	National Highway Authority of India
NHB	:	National Housing Bank
NHDP	:	National Highway Development Programme
NII	:	Net Interest Income
NOF	:	Net Owned Fund
NPV	:	Net Present Value
O&M	:	Operation & Maintenance
PAT	:	Profit After Tax
PCD	:	Partly Convertible Debentures
PD	:	Probability of Default
PGCIL	:	Power Grid Corporation of India
PIM	:	Project Information Memorandum
PLF	:	Plant Load Factor
PMDO	:	Pooled Municipal Debt Obligation
PMS	:	Project Management Services
PPA	:	Power Purchase Agreement

PPP	:	Public Private Partnership
PPPAC	:	Public Private Partnership Appraisal Committee
PTC	:	Pass Through Certificates
RAM	:	Risk Assessment Management
RAP	:	Resettlement Action Plan
RBI	:	Reserve Bank of India
RFP	:	Request for Proposal
RFQ	:	Request for Quotation
ROT	:	Rehabilitate, Operate & Transfer
SEB	:	State Electricity Board
SEBI	:	Securities and Exchange Board of India
SIDBI	:	Small Industrial Development Bank of India
SIPS	:	Special Incentive Package Scheme
SLR	:	Statutory Liquidity Ratio
SMA	:	Special Mention Account
SPV	:	Special Purpose Vehicle
SWOT	:	Strengths, Weaknesses, Opportunities & Threats
TEC	:	Techno-economic Clearance
TNW	:	Tangible Net Worth
TOL	:	Total Outside Liability
TRA	:	Trust & Retention Account
UMPP	:	Ultra Mega Power Projects
VFM	:	Value for Money
VGF	:	Viability Gap Funding
WACC	:	Weighted Average Cost of Capital
WPI	:	Wholesale Price Index

Foreword

India has carved out a significant position in the world economy and is inching towards becoming a powerful growth centre. The nation's GDP growth rate has consistently exhibited steadiness, with the international trade having increased sharply. Infrastructure sector has a significant contribution in this context and the development outlook of the sector is very encouraging.

The huge funding requirement for present and future infrastructural development in the country indicates the need to develop the insights in traditional funding methods as also relatively new models for public project finance and this throws up the 'knowledge' challenge. This book on 'Financing Patterns for Infrastructure Projects' by Shri Amareshwar Mishra and Dr R.K. Mishra represents a systematic colloquium aiming towards better analytical understanding of the factors, tools and techniques to carry out assessment of infrastructure projects while financing. Such a compendium of knowledge on infrastructure project finance is an excellent initiative to facilitate better and systematic understanding of the issues surrounding project finance, associated risks, concession arrangements and financing methodologies. The publication serves to clarify financial, structural and some legal issues pertaining to infrastructure projects in order to qualify for financial assistance. Further, it intends to provide the necessary iterative approach to deal with the various alternatives to evolve a financially bankable project.

The body of work contained in this book is the essence of the knowledge and practical experience of Shri Amareshwar Mishra and Dr. R.K. Mishra.

I am sure this will provide a great deal of knowledge to facilitate the infrastructure sector practitioners to comprehend the real and analytical perspectives and present the infrastructure projects proposals in a complete form, elucidating the market conditions and financial features. It is my hope that the book will draw the attention of universities, not only to stimulate greater dissemination of information amongst students to take up infrastructure studies but also amongst infrastructure practitioners in financial institutions.

—S.K. Goel
Chairman and Managing Director,
India Infrastructure Finance Company Limited

Preface

This book is a compendium of work to consider and carry out a detailed assessment of infrastructure projects with a view to enable a better understanding of the factors, tools and techniques employable in financing such projects.

The aim of the compendium is to enable insights into the various interactions between the financial institutions (FIs), project promoters, regulatory institutions and the government. Further, the necessary linkages between the various partners engaged in the implementation and execution of projects such as engineering and procurement contractors, suppliers, public agencies, accounting firms, escrow bankers, lenders engineers, etc., are also highlighted.

The body of work contained in this book is the essence of the knowledge and practical experience gathered in the course of three decades journey in the banking sector, financing medium to large corporates and infrastructure projects. Modelled with a comprehensive focus on the practical issues facing the infrastructure projects in terms of existing regulatory guidelines, policies/programmes of Government of India (GoI), state governments and other authorities, market requirements and operational considerations, the book collectively discusses the key issues holistically and suggests checks and balances in line with constructive requirements to make credit proposals meaningful for considerations of FIs. The objective of the book is to facilitate the infrastructure sector practitioners to comprehend the whole gamut of exercise in the real and analytical perspectives and present the infrastructure projects proposals in a complete form elucidating the market conditions and financial features. In short, this is a work aimed at assisting and enabling infrastructure practitioners to fully understand and play the game within the field rules.

I owe a debt of gratitude to a number of people, who have assisted me in writing this book. It would have been an impossible task to write it and endure the challenging times, without the love and support of my family and friends. They have all played a major role in bringing this book to a completion. I know that I owe each one of them a huge debt of gratitude.

I am especially indebted to Shri Sanjeev Gupta, Managing Director, NEXGEN; Dr E.S. Rao, CGM, IIFCL; Shri P. Jaishankar and Shri M. Nagaraj, GM, IIFCL; Shri A.K. Sharma, DGM, UCO Bank and Shri Arun Gupta, AGM, UCO Bank, for meticulously reading through a number of drafts of this book and for the helpful suggestions, advice and constructive comments.

I am very thankful to Mr Sanjay Kumar and Miss Shivani Mishra of IIFCL for helping me with secretarial assistance in coming out with the book.

— Amareshwar Mishra

1 Introduction

To keep the pace of economic growth of our country, investment in infrastructure development and its upgradation has become the only commercial viable proposition. Rightly said that there are three I(s): Inflation, Inclusion and Infrastructure, which are key components of Indian economic growth. All the three I(s) are the areas of national priority, however, the driving force for the growth in the coming years is reported to come primarily from infrastructure.

Infrastructure is an enabler—an enabler of trade, an enabler of great economic growth, an enabler of better quality of life and also the critical enabler of successful regional integration. It represents the wheel of economic activity as shown in Figure 1.1.

Figure 1.1

Infrastructure and Development

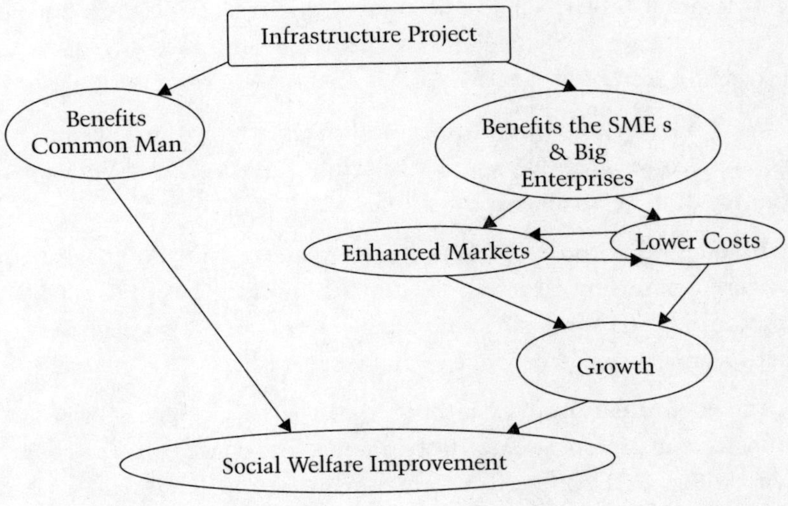

The role of infrastructure is substantial, significant and frequently greater than that of investment in other forms of capital. Therefore, it is said that infrastructure services are used in the production process of nearly every sector. Economic return of infrastructure investment varies not only by sector but also by its design/location and timeliness. The effectiveness of investment, whether it provides the kind of services valued by users, depends on characteristics such as quality, reliability and quantity. It is essential to match supply with what is demanded. The efficiency with which infrastructure services are provided is also a key to realising potential returns.

To increase the momentum of economic growth, the government has taken several initiatives for promoting infrastructure development like processing of public private partnership (PPP) projects which are carefully structured for safeguarding user and government interests with a view to ensure efficient services at competitive costs. The committee on infrastructure was constituted to initiate policies that would ensure time bound creation of world class infrastructure and develop structures that maximise the role of PPPs and monitor the progress of key infrastructure projects to ensure that stipulated targets are realised.

With the change of time and pace of infrastructure development, the committee on infrastructure was replaced by a Cabinet Committee on Infrastructure (CCI) which has been given the task of deciding financial, institutional and legal measures required to enhance investment in infrastructure sector.

With a view to streamlining and simplifying the appraisal and approval processes for PPP projects, the Public Private Partnership Appraisal Committee (PPPAC) had been constituted.

To meet the emerging issues and constraints, an institutional framework comprising an inter-ministerial committee has been established for the purpose of appraising/approving projects and also suggesting the changes required in existing policies and systems.

The government in the month of March 2012 specified 29 sub-sectors as infrastructure, in an attempt to harmonise the concept in the country's economy. The CCI approved a framework that categorises these sectors under five categories.

Box 1.1

Master List

Transport: Roads and bridges, ports, inland waterways, airport, railway tracks, tunnels, viaducts, bridges, urban public transport

Energy: Generation, transmission, distribution, oil pipelines, storage facility, gas pipelines

Water Sanitation: Solid waste management, water supply pipelines, water treatment plants, sewage collection, treatment and disposal system, storm water drainage system, irrigation

Communications: Telecommunication

Social and Commercial Infrastructure: Education institutions, hospitals, certain hotels, structure special economic zones (SEZ), tourism facilities and agriculture markets, fertiliser, terminal markets, soil testing labs

The CCI has also cleared the creation of an institutional mechanism to update the master list and for revisiting the sub-sectors outside the list. This, it said, would be done by a committee headed by the secretary to the Department of Economic Affairs (DEA).

A government release said, 'Harmonization of existing definitions of infrastructure sectors will facilitate a coordinated approach, among agencies providing support to infrastructure, and, thus spur infrastructure development in a more optimal manner.'

The new list of infrastructure sub-sectors will guide all the agencies responsible for supporting infrastructures in various ways. However, each financing agency will, therefore, be free to spell out its reasons and draw its own list of sub-sectors out of the master list, which it intends to support with adequate justification for inclusion/non-inclusion of specific sub-sectors from the list.

Financing of Infrastructure Projects

Infrastructure projects require debt of longer maturity. Such debt is usually not available because of the following constraints:

i. Absence of benchmark rates for raising long-term debt from the market.

ii. Asset-liability mismatch of the tenor of debt in case of banks and financial institutions (FIs).

iii. High cost of long-term debts.

Infrastructure investments are often complex involving time consuming systems and procedures, approvals, and also followed by long term contracts/concession and assessment of demand over the life of the investment impacting revenue and validity of investment/large capital assets/long gestation period and mostly non-recourse finance and cash flow driven in terms of operating activities, investing activities and financing activities. They also focus on the mix of debt and equity used in showing the optimality of capital structure and also long term solvency position.

Infrastructure lending is different from the conventional project financing, primarily because most infrastructure projects are in the nature of PPPs and evaluation of projects requires a careful understanding and analysis of the complexities and risks inherent in such partnerships. Ownership and operations of infrastructure projects are separable and a variety of models exist to meet the specific characteristics of projects and regulations. A typical example is an electricity generation project which the private sector builds, owns and operates (BOO) for a certain point of time (called the concession period), and finally transfers it back to the government. This concept is called BOOT (build, own, operate and transfer). For a road project, the private sector may be invited simply to build the facility, operate it during the concession period and transfer the facility back to the government without actually ever owning the same. This concept is called the BOT (build, operate and transfer). In this case, the ownership of the road remains with the government and the private sector recovers its investment and returns thereon by charging a levy on the users of the road during the concession period.

Infrastructure projects are typically implemented in a special purpose vehicle (SPV) which is a distinct corporate entity incorporated with the objective of implementing and operating the project. This ensures that the risks associated with the project are ring-fenced and do not flow back to the sponsor entities. Project sponsors take out equity stake in the SPV depending on the project cost, sponsors' ability and objectives, as well as the project lenders requirements; the minimum stake could be in the range of 20 to 30 per cent of the project cost. Infrastructure projects are financed generally through a higher debt to equity ratio (DER) if off take is assumed by bankable activities. For example, in Indian road projects where private company would construct, operate and maintain the road during the concession period and would earn an assured annuity from the National Highways Authority of India (NHAI) irrespective of the actual level of traffic, lenders may be willing to consider higher DER up to 4:1. In power projects, where off take was assured to an extent of a certain plant load factor (PLF) by the concerned State Electricity Board's (SEB's), lenders prefer DER of 2.33:1. For large conventional projects where the project and also the lenders are exposed to pure market risks, DER would rarely exceed 2:1.

Keeping the above facts in view, it is required that credit decisions in infrastructure projects have to be rule based. Credit scoring has to be based on credit history and customer data. Collections have to be algorithmic and structured. Surrogate measures have to be used for credit assessment. More so, financing infrastructure projects depend on good governance, a predictable regulatory regime and a hassle free, rules-based business environment. Lenders are making major long term commitments, large sums of money, long gestation and long operation period needing as much as predictability and consistency as possible. Not just over 2 or 3 years but over 10, 20, 30 years. The more this can be assured, the less the risk and the easier and more attractive it will be for the lenders to come in and lend the money. Hence, infrastructure lending requires high quality financial analytics, projections, sector expertise, financial debt structuring, contract design and evaluation of projected cash flow patterns. It is true that structures and processes in various sectors in infrastructure have to vary. As such process discipline is the underlying foundation on which the expertise can be executed.

$1 trillion spend is estimated for infrastructure development under the Twelfth Five Year Plan, and about 50 per cent is expected to come from the private sectors. The recent budget has also taken a note of this front. The doubling of allocation in infrastructure debt fund through allocation to National Highway Development Programme (NHDP), India Infrastructure Finance Company Limited (IIFCL), National Housing Bank (NHB) and

Small Industrial Development Bank of India (SIDBI) coupled with full exemption from basic custom duty for equipment for road and highway construction are likely to boost infrastructure sectors. Major schemes such as credit guarantee and direct transfer of subsidy are likely to change growth environment. One year extension of sunset clause on text incentive for infrastructure projects under Section 80 of Income Tax (IT) Act is also a welcome step. Achieving infrastructure development as estimated requires coordinated efforts at various levels. All stakeholders—policymakers, regulators, public and private providers, resource holders, equipment providers, banks, foreign institutional investors (FIIs) and end users need to act in concerted manner to build the country's future. This fact is also evident from Figure 1.2.

Figure 1.2

Country-wise Analysis of Infrastructure Spend

Per cent 100%=INR 220 lakh crore

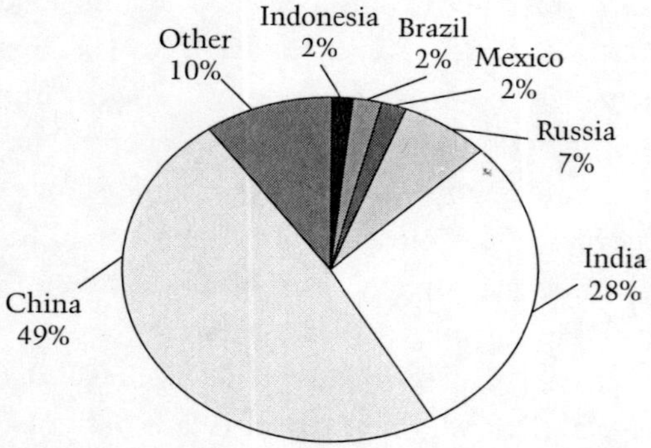

Notes: * Total demand for infrastructure across emerging market nations will be INR 220 lakh crore over the next decade (2008-2017).

* China accounts for INR 108 lakh crore (49%) and India for INR 63 lakh crore (28%).

* Majority of infrastructure spending will occur in electricity and roads.

• India would be the second largest emerging market destination for infrastructure spend over theXIth & XIIth Plan period.

In our country, banks have dominated infrastructure finance in recent years. They have also exhausted their prudential limits in terms of sector, borrower and project exposures. More so, the Reserve Bank of India (RBI) has also rightly been concerned about asset-liabilities mismatches and concentration risks which has put flow of fund to infrastructure project on hold. Our country has also tapped multilateral lenders as other countries like Brazil, Chile, Korea have but with our country reaching the peak of exposure to World Bank lending. While infrastructure needs remain large, this pool is unlikely to grow quickly in medium term. Hence, large insurance companies and pension and provident funds would have to be allowed to diversify into bonds issued by insurance company. Here an important concern would be the exposure to the credit risk of infrastructure bond which needs to be arrested.

2 Public Private Partnership (PPP) Projects

I

What is PPP?

PPP is an arrangement between a government or statutory entity or government owned entity on one side and a private sector entity on the other, for the provision of public assets and/or related services for public benefit, through investments being made by and/or management undertaken by the private sector entity for a specified time period, where there is a substantial risk sharing with the private sector, and the private sector receives performance linked payments that conform (or are benchmarked) to specified, predetermined and measurable performance standards.

The shift from public sector projects to PPP requires a significant change in governance and mindset. It involves a shift from project construction, operation and maintenance (O&M) by the public sector to a 'hands off' approach, where the focus shifts to quality of service delivery at competitive costs. Instead of taking day-to-day decisions relating to implementation and operation, the PPP relies on a comprehensive contract for delivery of predetermined outcomes.

PPP projects normally empower the concessionaire to use the public assets for building infrastructure projects and also to levy and collect user charges for the use of such public assets. They are public projects in which private capital is being deployed for the benefit of the economy and the users. In case services of requisite standard are not provided to the public, it would give rise to legitimate criticism of the government, which always remains responsible and accountable for delivery of services to the users.

PPP reduces the burden on state resources for development of the project and enhances innovativeness, management skills and efficient delivery system for the private sector.

In PPP projects, there is annuity as well as the toll system. In annuity system, the investor gets the return only in the form of annuity (which may be yearly or half yearly) during the concession period. The right of toll revenue belongs to the government. This option may be used when the investors are not willing to take the operating risks.

Provision may be made for a bonus for the early completion of the project as well as the early completion of annuity if completion is delayed for reasons other than the fault of the government.

The Need for PPPs in India

India is amongst the fast growing economies of the world. To keep-up the pace, in view of rapid industrialisation, increasing organisation, tightening environmental law and regulations, rising income levels and increasing demand for better utility services from the public and also increasing food requirement in line with the rising income levels, Government of India (GoI) has to accelerate PPP projects despite the fact that it is plagued by budgetary constraints and is finding it difficult to meet the growing demands of infrastructure services. PPP presents a new and innovative financing method in which private sector investment is utilised through a mutually beneficial arrangement. Since huge financial requirements of infrastructure projects cannot be met either by public sector or private sector alone, PPP has become a logical, viable and necessary option for the two to work together. Secondly, funding in infrastructure is characterised by large upfront and usually sunk costs with long gestation periods before revenues are generated. These aspects necessitate long term commitment from both the parties to be documented in a well structured contract which PPP provides. Thirdly, PPP yields the expected social and economic benefits ensuring the quality services at a most competitive price. Another equally important feature is that in PPP the move is on output based contracting than input, where focus is not on the creation of an asset but on the procurement of services associated with the asset so created.

In brief, the following factors have emerged as instruments for PPP in our country:

i. Poor operational and financial performance of state owned entities.
ii. Significant portion of the population has remained unserved.
iii. Service from state owned entities (SOEs) is often unreliable.
iv. Pressure for infrastructure sector reforms has risen in the context of a major global economic crisis leading to slower growth.
v. Inability of state sectors to finance maintenance and new investments.
vi. Private investment removes or reduces the fiscal stress on governments.

Figure 2.1

Public Private Partnership

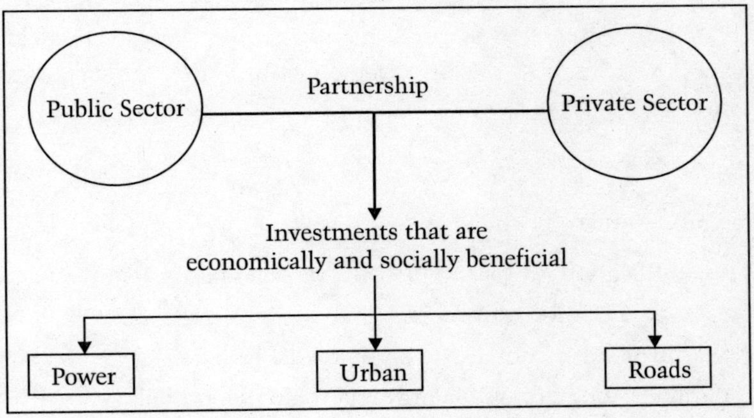

Benefits from Infrastructure PPPs

i. Deeper domestic capital markets.
ii. Broadened politcal support.
iii. Stronger customer support.
iv. Improved service quality, efficiency and competitiveness.
v. Efficient risk allocation.
vi. Access to foreign capital and expertise.
vii. Improved investor perceptions.

When Should PPP be Used?

i. The public sector environment is suited to supporting PPPs.
ii. The project is suitable to being carried out as a PPP.
iii. The potential barriers to successful project implementation have been identified and can be overcome.
iv. Project must be commercially viable for the private sector and offer value for money (VfM) for the public sector.

Procurement Process for PPP

The private sector companies shall be selected through a transparent and open competitive bidding process. The criteria for bidding shall be the amount of viability gap funding (VGF) required by a private sector company for implementing the project, where all other parameters are comparable.

The government or the statutory entity proposing the project shall certify that the bidding process conforms to the provisions of this scheme and conveys the scheme to the empowered institution for the disbursement of the grant, if any.

Process of PPP Projects

The process involves the following stages:

i. Identification (or selection) of the project and its approval.
ii. Pre-qualification of bidders.
iii. Issue of bid documents to pre-qualified bidders.
iv. Submission, receipt, opening and evaluation of bids.
v. Award.
vi. Signing of agreements.
vii. Financial close.

This process is done through a committee called Standing Committee for PPP. The said committee proposes a preliminary report mentioning the appropriate costs of the feasibility reports. The feasibility report indicates:

i. Estimate of costs.
ii. Volume of demand.
iii. Sensitivity analysis.

It also lays down:

i. Potential, legal and technical issues.
ii. Extent of land acquisition.
iii. Scope of rehabilitation.
iv. Environmental effect of the project.
v. Likely level of the user fee.
vi. Duration of concession period.
vii. Public acceptability.
viii. Degree of government support.

The Standing Committee shall study the feasibility report and prepare an assessment report which will throw light on the proposed PPP mode and requirement of government report which will be put forth for consideration and approval of a high powered committee. If approved by the high powered committee, the approval of the competent authority along with the approval of the Finance Department shall be taken to proceed further. The detailed project report may be prepared and shall be routed through the Standing Committee and then to the high powered committee.

Preparation of Pre-Bid/Bid Documents

The concerned department shall set up a duly constituted pre-qualification, evaluation and award committee. The committee shall take steps to get all documents ready for the bidding process. Documents shall consist of:

i. Instruction to bidders.
ii. Minimum design and performance standards and specifications.
iii. Draft agreement.
iv. Form of bid.
v. Forms of performance security.
vi. Other documents, as may be necessary.

Typical Documents for PPP Projects

Substantive Documents

i. Concession agreements.
ii. Manual of specifications and standards.
iii. Rules for user charges.

Process Documents

i. Request for quotation (RFQ) for pre-qualification of bidders.

ii. Request for Proposal (RFP) for financial bids.

iii. RFP for selection of consultants.

Issues in Financing in Infrastructure Projects under PPP

PPP projects for financing are considered if they are bankable through proper structuring and engineering. The choice of the project to be put under PPP framework requires to be supported by well researched analysis as PPP projects also have a number of issues as shown below. Thus, those issues need to be arrested. For example, a concession agreement reflecting the partnership's true trust should clarify the rights and duties of both the parties in unambiguous terms. It should be flexible enough to ensure smooth operability and amicable resolution of differences to benefit the project. Land acquisition is equally the core, contentious and time consuming issue to be dealt seriously and timely. Revenue uncertainties reflect poor income generation which is a product of volume, demand and price. These have considerable importance and weigh heavily on the minds of private investors before they decide to participate in the project. In fact, one of the vital clearances required before undertaking the project is environmental clearance separately for construction and operation activities. Detailed investigation of such requirement is necessary, since non-compliance may culminate in the contract's termination at a later stage. Sometimes Government actions affect the ability of project to generate earnings. These arise from the direct and indirect actions taken by the government to provide effective and efficient governance to the country or from some political considerations. To evaluate the regulatory issues, the private investors have to examine the socio-political climate, the independence of the regulatory framework, its empowerment and functioning, bureaucratic mind set, etc.

Project Level Constraints

- Issues in the concession agreement.
    - o Limitations on assignment of concessions/licenses to other parties.
    - o Dispute resolution, recourse, arbitration and exit clauses.

  - o Restriction on end usage, tariffs, escalation clauses, termination payments.
  - o Land acquisition problems.
  - o Often stalls the project altogether.
  - o Rehabilitation and resettlement.
  - o Disagreement over compensation for the acquired land.
  - o Political sensitivities affect the land acquisition process.
  - o Uncertainty in revenues.
  - o Lack of expected traffic in road/port/airport projects.
  - o Reluctance to pay tolls, taxes and usage charges, especially for water projects.
  - o Weak payment mechanisms.
- Environmental Issues.
  - o Environmental issues outside the commercial aspects can delay project closure.
  - o This may lead to opposition from various parties, such as the government, non-governmental agencies, citizen groups, etc.
- Creditworthiness of the customers (especially government agencies).
  - o Government agencies are often loss making due to heavy subsidies offered.
  - o Strained cash flows and weak financials of municipal and local bodies.
  - o Lack of credit ratings.
  - o Corporate governance and disclosure issues.
- Policy and regulatory issues.
  - o Policy changes during the investment period.
  - o Delay/lapse of licenses and clearances.

Institutional Constraints

- Many project sponsors and developers are relatively new infrastructure players.

- o Structuring projects to make them bankable is often a time-taking process.
- o Asset-liability mismatch.
- o PPP projects have a long payback period, often greater than 10 years.
- o Risk-averse financiers look at shorter investment horizons of 5-7 years.
- o Underdeveloped corporate debt markets prevent issue of long term bonds.
- o Inadequate financial structuring.
- o Lack of sync between project cash flows/risks and financing.
- o Very few financial institutions (FIs) which are dedicated to financing infrastructure projects.
- o Lack of local knowledge.
- o Foreign investors not aware of all local operational issues, leading to a high risk premium being demanded.

Project Characteristics Affecting the Choice of PPP

i. New ('Greenfield') or existing ('Brownfield') assets.
ii. Ownership flexibility.
iii. Lifetime of the asset and scale of capital costs.
iv. The nature of the service to be provided and the supporting infrastructure assets.
v. Cost recovery options.
vi. Stability of demand for the services required.

Forms of PPP

There are various forms of PPP in use depending upon the degree of involvement and assumption of public and private sectors in the venture. Distinctions in the form lie in terms of ownership, capital investment, tenure and risk bearing. There may not be any straight jacket model which can claim its universal applicability. Many hybrid forms can be developed on the level of authority and the length of commitment as seen below:

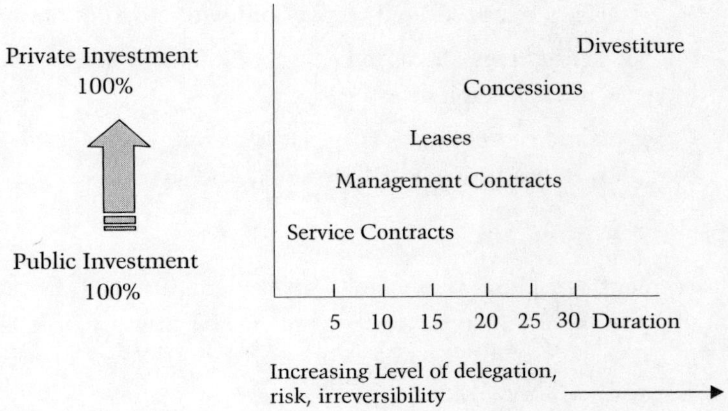

Spectrum of Private Participation

Model	*Ownership*	*Management Expertise*	*O&M*	*Capital Investment*	*Commercial Risk*	*Tenure*
Service Agreement	Public	Public and private (limited to selected task)	Public and private (limited to specific activities)	Public	Public	3 to 5 years
Management Agreement	Public	Private	Private	Public	Public	5 to 10 years
Lease	Public	Private	Private	Public shared private (limited to working capital)	public shared private	5 to 15 years
Concession	Public	Private	Private	Private	Private/ shared	15 to 25 years
Divestiture	Private	Private	Private	Private	Private	25 years

Service Agreement

Service agreement is activity based. It tends to secure private sector participation for performing specific tasks. Public sector sells system ownership to the private sector and retains regulatory authority as detailed hereunder:

i. Public agency employs private entities to assist in running specialised activities of their utility.

ii. Public agency retains overall responsibility for O&M of the system.

iii. Public agency bears all commercial risk, finances fixed assets and provides working capital.

iv. Compensation to contractors on basis of lump sum, fixed fee, or cost plus, or on the basis of a physical parameter.

Management Agreement

Management agreement is 'general management' oriented. It transfers responsibility for the O&M of a government owned utility to the private sector. The objective is to enhance a utility's technical capacity and efficiency in performance.

i. Private entity

   a. Takes over the O&M of a particular part of the utility.

   b. Operates it according to mutually agreed performance standards.

   c. Normally collects revenue on behalf of the public agency.

ii. Public agency

   a. Retains responsibility for the overall system, including expansion and major rehabilitation.

   b. Set payment terms that rewards efficiency and good operation against present standards and future targets.

   c. Payment to private company is based on agreed rates for specified items which can also include profit sharing.

Lease

Under a lease arrangement a government owned asset is leased to a private firm to be operated and maintained for a fixed period of time. Private sector pays for the use of the system, the public sector operates the system as given hereunder:

i. Does not cover the funding of the overall capital investment for rehabilitation and expansion.

ii. Remains the responsibility of the government.

iii. Private sector builds a facility and operates it for a given period.

   a. Contractor would be responsible for any repairs.

   b. Contractor will cover working capital requirements.

   c. Ownership of facility is with the public entity.

Concessions

Under this arrangement the government or public authority grants a concession or franchise to a private firm to design, construct, finance, operate and maintain a utility's assets for a certain period, say 15 to 30 years, or even beyond.

i. Concessionaire finances the investment costs.

ii. Concessionaires get revenue from users/customers, on a predefined tariff formula to allow for agreed upon costs.

iii. The government may still provide a subsidy in kind or cash.

iv. At the end of the contract, the concessionaire must hand over the system back to the government (in case of build operate and transfer (BOT)).

Divestiture

Divestiture relates to the process of the sale of assets or shares of a state-owned entity to the private sector. It is similar to concession in certain ways as it gives the private operator full responsibility for financing, building and operating the utility but unlike a concession, legal ownership gets transferred to the private operator. Under a concession arrangement, the government ensures that the utility's assets which the government continues to own, are used well and returned in good condition at the expiry of the concession period where as under divestiture the government performs the task of regulation only because in theory the private company, on its own, shall be concerned with maintaining the assets in perfect conditions. In the divestiture model, the private operator gets an added advantage. As an owner of the assets it can raise funds from financial institutions (FIs) on more competitive rates on collateral of these assets. Thus in divestiture, public sector sells system ownership to the private sector and retains regulatory authority.

Table 2.1

Forms of Concessions

Model	*Description*	*Application*
Build-operate-transfer (BOT)	Private investors are provided with a concession to finance, build, operate and maintain a facility. During the concession period, the investor collect tolls from the users as return to their investments. After the end of the concession period, the facility is transferred back to the public authority.	Developing highway networks, power plants, utilities sectors, port terminals.
Build-own-operate (BOO)	Similar to BOT model without transfer of ownership.	Telecommunications projects, waste water treatment plants, power plants.
Build-transfer-operate (BTO)	The private parties build a facility and transfer it to the public authority just after construction.	In controversial projects with high public opposition for private participation.
Build-operate-lease-transfer (BOLT)	This is similar to a BOT project, except that the transfer is carried out over the years by lease adjustments.	Developing power plants, utilities sectors, port terminals.
Lease-develop-operate (LDO)	In this case the public authority retains ownership of the facility under a lease arrangement. The lessee finances development and oversees the operation.	Airport facilities.
Rehabilitate-operate-transfer (ROT)	Private investors rehabilitate and operate a facility during a concession period and transfer it later to the public authority.	Retrofit sewage and water systems.

Table 2.2

Characteristics of a Typical PPP Mode in Water and Sanitation Sector

Modes/ Features	*Asset ownership during the contract*	*PPP duration*	*Capital investment focus and responsibility*	*Private partner revenue risk and compensation terms*	*Private partner role and involvement*
Distribution or operations concessions	Public	Long (e.g., 15-30 yrs.)	Brownfield Private	High user charges	Design, finance, construct, manage, maintain, transfer.
BOT—bulk water supply system	Public	Long (e.g., 15-30 yrs)	Greenfield (bulk water infrastructure) Private	Medium-high (could have a Take or Pay Agreement) bulk water charges from urban local bodies (ULB)	Design, finance, construct, manage, maintain, transfer.
BOT—water supply distribution system	Public	Medium (e.g., 8-10 yrs)	Greenfield Private	Medium Capex reimbursement by ULB+ user charges+ operator fee for O&M from ULB	Design, finance, construct, manage, maintain, transfer.
BOT—water supply distribution system and sanitation network	Public	Long (e.g., 15-30 yrs)	Greenfield/ Brownfield	High user charges	Design, finance, construct, manage, maintain, transfer.
Performance based management contracts	Public	Medium (e.g., 5 yrs)	Not the focus Public	Low/high predetermined fee/revenue share, performance based	Management of all aspects of O&M
Service management contract-metering billing and collection	Public	Short (e.g., 3-4 yrs)	Only towards metering Private	Low recovery of investment in meters fixed annuity for O&M from ULB	Minimum Capex, management, maintenance of meters, billing and collections.

Table 2.3

Characteristics of a Typical PPP Mode in Bus Rapid Transit System (BRTS) Sector

Modes/ Features	*Asset ownership during the contract*	*PPP duration*	*Capital investment focus and responsibility*	*Private partner revenue risk and compensation terms*	*Private partner role and involvement*
Rolling stock (buses)					
Cost plus contract	Private (could also be public)	Medium (e.g., 5-7 yrs). Could also be based on the distance covered	Greenfield (Buses) Private	Low reimbursement of actual operating cost including management fee from public entity, based on performance standards	Acquisition of buses, operating buses including provision of a driver and maintenance of buses, providing workshops and parking facilities.
Gross cost contract	Private (could also be public)	Medium (e.g., 5-7 yrs). Could also be based on the distance covered	Greenfield (Buses) Private	Low reimbursement of pre-specified operating cost based on performance standards. Operator however faces a cost escalation risk.	Acquisition of buses, operating buses including provision of a driver and maintenance of buses, providing workshops and parking facilities.
Rolling stock (buses)					
Net cost contract	Private (could also be public)	Medium (e.g., 5-7 yrs). Could also be based on the distance covered	Greenfield (Buses) Private	High ticket collections (bus tariff fixed by public entity. In case of non-profitable areas of operation, subsidy is payable by public entity to private operator. In case of profitable routes, premium paid by private operator to public entity.)	Acquisition of buses, operating buses including provision of a driver, collection of revenue and maintenance of buses, providing workshops and parking facilities.

Table 2.4

Characteristics of a Typical PPP Mode in Road Sector

Modes/ Features	*Asset ownership during the contract*	*PPP duration*	*Capital investment focus and responsibility*	*Private partner revenue risk and compensation terms*	*Private partner role and involvement*
BOT-Toll	Public	Long (e.g., 15-30 yrs)	Brownfield/ Greenfield Private	High Toll revenue	Design, finance, construct, manage, maintain and collect tolls.
BOT-Annuity	Public	Long (e.g., 15-30 yrs)	Brownfield/ Greenfield Private	Low Annuity revenue/ unitary charge	Design, finance, construct, manage, maintain.
BOT-Shadow toll	Public	Long (e.g., 15-30 yrs)	Brownfield/ Greenfield Private	High shadow toll revenue	Design, finance, construct, manage, maintain.
Performance based maintenance contracts	Public	Medium (e.g., 5 yrs)	Not the focus Public	Low Predetermined fee, based on performance	Management of all aspects of O&M.

Table 2.5

Characteristics of a Typical PPP Mode in Solid Waste Management Sector

Modes/ Features	*Asset ownership during the contract*	*PPP duration*	*Capital investment focus and responsibility*	*Private partner revenue risk and compensation terms*	*Private partner role and involvement*
Management contract (waste collection and/or transportation)	Public land fill site and treatment plant private-vehicles and equipment	Medium (e.g., 3-10 yrs)	Not the focus Public	Medium Take or Pay arrangement	Full responsibility for collection of waste and transportation to land fill site.
BOT-(waste treatment and/ or disposal facilities)	Public	Long (e.g., 25-35 yrs)	Brownfield/ Greenfield Private	Medium Take or Pay arrangement	Design, construction, O&M
Build-own-operate-transfer (BOOT) (waste treatment and/or disposal facilities. Could also include a waste to power facility.)	Private	Long (e.g., 25-35 yrs)	Brownfield/ Greenfield Private	Medium in case of Take or Pay arrangement. High in case of user charges	Design, construction, O&M

Table 2.6

Characteristics of a Typical PPP Mode in Ports Sector

Modes/ Features	*Asset ownership during the contract*	*PPP duration*	*Capital investment focus and responsibility*	*Private partner revenue risk and compensation terms*	*Private partner role and involvement*
Opex based (operations of existing facilities with minimum Capex)					
Management contract	Public	Medium (e.g., 5-10 yrs)	Not the focus public	Low-medium Fixed fee basis of performance based payments	Management of specific port support operations.
O&M concession	Public	Long (e.g., 30 yrs)	Brownfield private	High tariff from port operations	Minimal refurbishment/ expansion O&M of port asset.

Accounts and Audit

The concessionaire shall maintain the books of accounts keeping record of all receipts (all realisable fees and other revenues derived/collected by it) income and expenditure payments (including payments from the escrow accounts). It shall provide: balance sheet; cash flow statement; profit and loss account; and copy of report by statutory auditors.

Any claim or document provided by the concessionaire to the authority in connection with or relating to receipts, income, payments, costs, expenses, accounts or audit, and any matter incidental thereto shall be valid and effective only if certified by its statutory auditors.

In the event of there being any difference between the findings of the additional auditors or the concurrent auditors, as the case may be, and the certification provided by the statutory auditors, such auditors shall meet to resolve the differences and if they are unable to resolve the same, such dispute shall be resolved by the authority by recourse to the dispute resolution procedure.

China and India: A Comparision

Today, while China's economy may be 4 times larger than India's, our PPP market is 10 times larger than that of China's. In fact, India is today the world's largest PPP market. Just look at PPP investment in India in infrastructure.

Period	*Approximate infrastructure sector investments*	*Estimated PPP %*	*Estimated PPP*
10th plan	222	25	56
11th plan (estimate)	500	37	185
12th plan (projections)	1000	50	5000

The government has taken huge efforts in creating the enabling environment for PPP. The efforts relate to enacting new legislation like—the Electricity Act 2003, the amended National Highways Authority of India (NHAI) Act 1995, the Special Economic Zone Act 2005 and the Land Acquisition Bill. Also the creation of new institution like regulatory authority in telecom, power and airports, implementation authority like the NHAI, FIs like Infrastructure Development Finance Company (IDFC), India Infrastructure Finance Company Limited (IIFCL) and so on. A slew of model concession agreement across sectors created the template for private participation. Innovative financial intervention like VGF, annuity model and stimulation of debt for infrastructure have also added fiscal punch. The Planning Commission, the Department of Economic Affairs in the Ministry of Finance and the Prime Minister's Office have played a stellar role in making PPP happen. Many states too—notably Punjab, Gujarat, Maharashtra, Karnataka, Delhi and Tamil Nadu—have built significant capacity to deliver on PPP.

A study report (the 2011 infrastructure scope report) of the Asian Development Bank (ADB) shows that India stands in the same league as developed economies like Korea and Japan on implementation of PPP projects. The report says that PPP development in India has been driven by strong political will and advancement in public capacity and processes. India has also performed well in enhancing its operational maturity or the ability to implement infrastructure projects. While India is behind China in operational maturity, it is ahead of the rest of the countries in Asia Pacific. With 614 projects in water, electricity and transportation reaching financial closure between 2000 and 2009, China has the highest number of projects followed by India with 261 projects. The report also adds that India has utilised technical and financial support of multilateral agencies, including ADB and World Bank for the development of public sector expertise.

Sector-wise PPP Initiatives Undertaken in India

In this context the PPP initiatives taken place in India under the different sectors showing GoI's commitment to move forward to infrastructure growth in the planned manner are given as under:

Highways

i. Four laning of the Golden–Quadrilateral and NS-EW corridors (NHDP I and II).

ii. Four laning of 12,109 kms (NHDP III).

iii. Two laning of 20,000 kms (NHDP IV).

iv. Six laning of 65,000 kms (NHDP V).

v. Other highway projects (NHDP VI).

Railways

Indian railway has initiated a number of measures to attract private sector investment in the following areas:

i. Introduction of completion in container movement.

ii. Dedicated freight corridor.

iii. Development of railway stations.

iv. Development of logistic parks.

v. Mumbai sub-urban metro project.

Ports

An investment of approximately Rs 68,835 crore is envisaged from PPPs. GoI has encouraged private sector participation in port development and operations. Foreign direct investment (FDI) up to 100 per cent is permitted under the automatic route for port development projects. International operators are invited to submit competitive bids for building and operating port terminals on a revenue share basis. Foreign players including Maersk (JNPT), PND (JNPT and Chennai), Dubai ports and port of Singapore Authority (TUTICORIN) have already established themselves in the Indian port sector. Some of the noteworthy private initiatives is—Pipava Port/Gangavaram Port/Simar Port/ Gopalpur Port/Mundra Port/ Dharma Port and Kirtania Port.

Civil Aviation

Private participation for development and modernisation of metro projects—four metro airports at Delhi/Mumbai/Bangalore/Hyderabad—has been widely acclaimed.

Telecom

Broadband services: The competition in this sector has been quite intense and as a result, the consumer and the economy have benefitted significantly from private participation.

Power Sector

i. Since 2003, 30 private power projects with a total capacity addition of 22,038 MW have achieved financial closure.

ii. In 2008-09, the private sector contributed 883 MW of the total capacity addition of 3454 MW.

iii. Inter-state transmission systems: The first public-private joint venture, namely, The Tala Transmission System with route length of around 1,200 kms was developed in 2006-07 through a joint venture between Power Grid Corporation and a private entity at a cost of Rs 1,100 crore. Private participation through PPP mode in intra-state transmission systems has also been initiated with RFQs having issued further evacuation of about 27,500 MW in the state of Haryana.

Urban Infrastructure

A number of water supply and sewerage project involving an estimated cost of Rs 1,684 crore are being implemented through PPP mode in Maharashtra/West Bengal/Tamil Nadu.

Metro Rail Projects

PPP initiatives have been taken for provision of metro rail system in different cities—Delhi Metro, Hyderabad Metro, Mumbai Metro, Bangalore high speed project.

The above initiatives of GoI shows its commitment towards PPP.

II

Financing of PPP Projects

Government has adopted the PPP mode to promote mainly infrastructure projects due to several reasons, the main reason being huge funding requirements and also the constraints in realising the same. The project requires formulating a complex financial package which involves financial viability, addressing contractual agreement and risk allocation among the two parties to achieve successful financing. The technique of financing of PPPs is closely linked to 'project finance'. The term project financing basically deals with the financing of an economic unit. The lender looks initially into the cash flows and earning of that unit as the source of funds from which a loan will be repaid to the assets of the unit as collateral for the loan. The PPP structures are typically more complex than traditional public procurement of assets due to the number of parties involved and particularly the mechanism to share the risks. In project finance, lenders and investors rely either exclusively ('non recourse') or mainly ('limited recourse') on the cash generated by the project to repay their loans and earn a return on their investments. This is in contrast to corporate lending where lenders rely on the strength of the borrowers' balance sheet for their loans. The financing structure is designed to optimise the cost of finance for the project and allocation of risks between the public and private sectors as agreed in the PPP contract.

Benefits of Project Finance for PPP Projects

Benefits for Public Authority	*Benefits for Private Investors*
• Lowered project cost.	• High leverage.
• Creates more competitive markets for projects.	• Risk spreading and limitation.
• Control and due diligence of the project which is also monitored by the lenders.	• Long-term finance.
• Transparency of financing.	• Increased borrowing capacity.
	• Keeping small debts off balance sheet.

In a PPP model the private-sector consortium forms a special company called a 'special purpose vehicle' (SPV) for each project, to develop, build, maintain and operate the project for the contracted period. In cases where the government has invested in the project, it is allotted (but not always) an equity share in the SPV. The consortium is usually made up of project sponsor(s), building contractor, a maintenance company and bank lender(s). It is the SPV that signs the contract with the government and with subcontractors to build the facility and then maintains it. The SPV has no other assets other than the project assets. These projects are characterised by non-recourse or limited-recourse financing where lenders are repaid from only the revenue generated by the projects. (A non-recourse loan means the loans secured by the project assets and paid entirely from the cash flow rather than from the general assets of the sponsors. A limited-recourse finance means a debt in which the creditor has limited claims on the loan in the event of default. It is in between secured bonds and unsecured loans).

Figure 2.2

Typical Model of a PPP Project

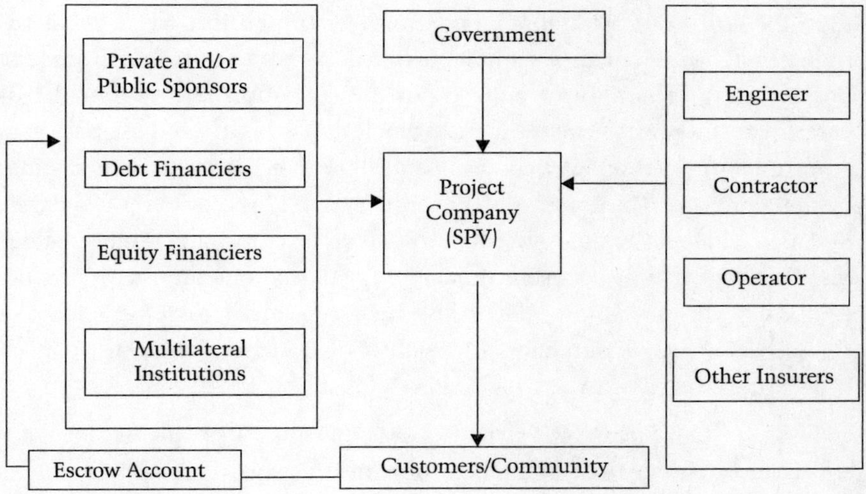

Source: UNESCAP

The financing of a project will be made of different amounts of debt and equity, the source and structure of which will vary depending on the project. The debt financing will generally be provided by the government sponsor, and equity financing is by the private sponsors, in exchange for ownership in the SPV. For debt financing, the investment needs of the project are met by the budgetary provisions. The VGF scheme of the GoI provides financial support in the form of grants to infrastructure projects undertaken on PPP mode which is generally 20 per cent of the project cost. These grants are either one time or deferred basis, and are strictly restricted for the purpose of making the projects commercially viable. GoI has also requested the World Bank to help bridge the critical shortfall in infrastructure financing. Historically, the World Bank has a long association with India in building infrastructure—be it the railways, national highways, state highways, or water systems—and has developed considerable expertise in these areas. World Bank support helps in increasing the availability of long-term finance for infrastructure PPP projects in India and also help the IIFCL to stimulate the development of a long-term local currency debt financing market for infrastructure in India.

Sources of Project Finance for PPP Projects

Equity: Equity is subscribed by the parent companies sponsoring the SPV and by its shareholders, who view the project as an attractive investment opportunity. Contractors for construction, maintenance, operations and supply of equipment are also normally persuaded to participate in equity. Government agencies such as the NHAI and state government undertakings may also contribute to equity to a limited extent in some projects. Currently, foreign firms, particularly those from Malaysia, Japan and Indonesia, are investing in BOT projects in India. Equity holders get their returns only after all other project obligations are met. Thus the equity holders may gain profit or lose their expected return, depending on the success or failure of the project. Equity holders carry the highest risk and it is natural that they expect high returns (about 20%).

Debt: Debt capital is necessary for most PPP projects as the concessionaire may not be able to provide the entire investment in the form of equity. The sources of debt are the commercial banks, FIs and multilateral organisations. Commercial banks in the past have been providing debt instruments with short tenure of less than seven years, to be in tune with the normal deposit tenures. FIs are willing to advance funds for longer duration. Multilateral agencies, such as the World Bank, the International Finance Corporation (IFC) and the ADB, provide funds for road development on long-term (20 to 30 years) basis, but they insist on government guarantees. A promising source of debt funds is the insurance sector, whose appetite for long-term assets matches with the needs of infrastructure projects for long-term debt. Debt from these lenders is termed as 'senior debt' to denote that, in the case of project default, the lenders of senior debt will have the first right to the cash flow and assets of the project over the providers of equity and mezzanine capital. Debt can also be mobilised by issue of bonds, including deep discount bonds, with duration to match the debt repayment period for the project. Tax-exempt infrastructure bonds are permitted by government for this purpose.

Loan Syndication: It is a loan offered by a group of lenders called as a syndicate who work together to provide funds for a single project. The loan may involve fixed amounts, a credit line or a combination of two. Typically there is a lead bank or underwriter of the loan, known as the 'arranger' or 'lead lender'. The lead lender may put a proportionally bigger share and performs administrative duties among other syndicate members.

Mezzanine Finance: Mezzanine finance is investment with some qualities of debt and equity, and so it carries a risk profile intermediate between debt and equity. This may take the form of subordinated debt or preference shares with regular interest. Mezzanine capital ranks below the senior debt and carries a higher rate of interest than senior debt. It is normal to persuade the contractors/suppliers to subscribe to mezzanine capital. The concessionaire may be able to secure a larger senior debt on favourable terms in view of the mobilised mezzanine capital.

When the financial viability of an otherwise desirable project is weak, the government may assist the SPV by providing a subordinated debt and/or a guarantee to award a bridge loan for debt-servicing in case of a shortfall in revenue in the early part of the operation period.

Receivable Financing: This is based on lending against the established cash flow of a business and involves transferring a cash flow stream to an SPV similar to a project company. This cash flow may be derived from the general business or specific contracts which give rise to the cash flow. The SPV then borrows against this cash flow, without any significant recourse or guarantee to the owners of the original business, who are able to raise funding off–balance sheet, as well as reduce the business risks.

Securitisation: Funds are raised in the bond market by process through which the issuer creates a financial instrument by combining its other financial assets and then marketing repackaged instruments to investors. This process can encompass any type of financial asset and promotes liquidity to the firm. PPP projects are quite suitable for securitisation because of their low risk.

Financial Structure

Careful analysis of financial structure is required to establish the right financing structure for a PPP project. As expected return on equity is higher than return on debt, the relative amount of debt and equity in capital structure have important implications on the cash flow of the project. Higher proportion of debt requires larger cash flows for debt-servicing, which will be difficult in the initial years of project operation when earnings are generally low and the default risk will be high. The project sponsors need to consider tax implications when assessing the debt and equity mix as it will impact the cost of capital and earnings.

Generally in PPPs, source of financing from private sector plays a major role since majority of the capital is brought by the private partner. The viability of the project depends on the ability to develop a financing package with a mix of various sources of finance suitable for the project. This mix varies from sector to sector. Telecommunications projects, which face relatively high market risks, may require a relatively low debt component, with debt to equity ratios close to 1:1. Power projects with assured power purchase arrangements may be financeable with debt to equity ratios of 2.5:1 or even 3:1. The maturity requirements of debt will also vary across sectors. Power and roads, which have longer pay-off periods, typically require long maturities, while telecommunications projects can manage with shorter maturities. Table 2.7 shows the various financing sources that can be tapped for devising financial packages.

Table 2.7

Financing Sources for PPP Projects

Domestic Sources	*External Sources*
Equity	
• Domestic developers (independently or in collaboration with international developers).	• International developers (independently or in collaboration with domestic developers).
• Public utilities (taking minority holdings).	• Equipment suppliers (in collaboration with domestic or international developers).
• Other institutional investors (likely to be very limited).	• Dedicated infrastructure funds.
	• Other international equity investors.
	• Multilateral agencies (IFC, ADB).
Debt	
• Domestic commercial banks (3-5 years).	• International commercial banks (7-10 years).
• Domestic term lending institutions. (7-10 years).	• Export credit agencies (7-10 years).
• Domestic bond markets (7-10 years).	• International bond markets (10-30 years).
• Specialised infrastructure. financing institutions.	• Multilateral agencies (15-20 years).
	• Bilateral aid agencies.

Source: Planning Commission, GoI

Domestic and Foreign Private Players Participation in PPP Projects

The central government is working with the state governments and all other stakeholders to expand the horizon of PPPs in infrastructure development in the country. It has created a favourable atmosphere, provided fiscal incentives and facilitated funding of PPP projects. The government now allows FDI in most infrastructure sectors to the extent of 100 per cent.

Foreign sponsors may often be keen to link up with domestic investors at this stage on the grounds that this will reduce political risk. Domestic investors tend to evaluate risk less conservatively than foreign investors, and their involvement often helps to improve the perceptions of foreign investors.

Well-structured projects can expect to mobilise equity from international infrastructure funds specialising in investment in infrastructure projects. The Global Power Fund, which has a target of $1 billion, is an example of an infrastructure fund aimed at financing power projects in emerging markets and the AIG Asian Infrastructure Fund, which will invest $1 billion in the Asia-Pacific region are examples of regional funds. The amounts available through these funds are very low when compared to the total requirement, but the pool of global capital they can tap is very large, and the flow of equity from this source could increase substantially if bankable projects become available and the track record of implementation improves.

An important aspect of these funds is that they allow international investors to pool risks by investing in a mix of projects. They also enable institutional investors, who are relatively risk averse, to invest in infrastructure projects after the construction stage, when project risks are much lower. This provides valuable opportunities for 'take-out' financing, enabling projects to be financed through the earlier and riskier stage by much larger involvement of equity from the sponsors or by high-cost debt, with a subsequent restructuring through attraction of equity from infrastructure funds through sale of sponsors' equity or refinancing of debt with equity.

A limited amount of equity support for private sector infrastructure is also available from multilateral organisations, such as the IFC and the private sector window of the ADB. Although these funds can provide only a small amount of capital, their participation in a project provides comfort to other investors.

The scope for raising equity from domestic capital markets is probably limited. Public utilities and domestic institutional investors may be willing to contribute part of the equity for project expansion, but significant domestic equity support may not be forthcoming for new infrastructure projects until there is a track record of performance. Once project implementation proceeds and revenues begin to be generated through partial commissioning, it may be possible to tap a wider range of equity investors. This can be a useful financing strategy in the case of power projects with more than one generating unit or in telecommunications projects, in which the build-up of line capacity occurs over time.

To ensure adequate financing for meeting financing and refinancing needs, India requires $500 billion of additional investments in infrastructure during 2007-2012, to sustain a GDP growth rate of 9 per cent per annum—of these, about 30 per cent ($150 billion) are expected to be through domestic private participation and foreign private participation.[1]

Major Financial Players for PPP Projects

i. Sponsors/Primary Investors
   a. Subcontractors
   b. Banks : IIFCL
   c. Public Provident Funds (PPF)
   d. Financial Facilitators

ii. Secondary Investors
   a. Contractors
   b. Secondary PPP Fund Investors
   c. Insurance Companies

Table 2.8

Overall Financing Gap in Infrastructure up to 2010-11

(Rs Billion)

Sectors	*Investment Needed*	*Financing Gap*
Roads	4670	1106
Ports	306	236
Aiports	191	72
Energy	10591	3500
Telecommunications	2143	478
Railways	1242	151
Total	19143	5542

Source: Planning Commission.

1. Ministry of Finance (2008). *Economic Survey 2007-08*. p.239.

Table 2.9

Private Domestic Investment in PPP Projects

Sector	*Investment in Crore*	*Per cent*
Roads	51398	38
Ports	43053	32
Aiports	19111	14
Energy	17802	13
Urban Development	1775	2
Railways	1007	1

Source: *www.pppindiadatabase.com*

Financial Appraisal

Financial appraisal means the cash flows and all those items which have an impact on the cash flows. A lot of importance is placed on the analysis of a project's cash flow, and the first step in a financial appraisal is development of financial cash flow model. The models are set up on case-to-case basis.

Developing a Financial Cash Flow Model

A financial cash flow model is developed to make the required calculations for the bid by the project sponsors. As there are three parties involved—public authority, the bidders and the lenders, there could be three parallel financial models, but this is rarely the case. It is usually public authority's financial advisors, and the lenders review the model prepared by the preferred bidder. Sometimes the public authority prepares a template financial model to be used to make the comparison of bids easier. There has to be transparency maintained on the model assumptions and calculations between both the parties. The model's initial purpose is to calculate the service fees based on the input assumptions. Capital investment, net cash flows, terminal cash flows, discount rate and assumptions are the critical components in developing a model.

i. *Capital Investment*: It is the total cost of developing project.

ii. *Net Cash Flow*: It is calculated as:

   Revenues Generated

   – Operating expenses

Earnings Before Interest Depreciation and Taxes (EBITD)

– Interest

– Depreciation

Earnings Before Taxes (EBT)

– Tax

Earnings After Tax (EAT)

+ Depreciation

Net Cash Flow

iii. *Terminal Cash Flow*: It is the cash flow which is generated from the sale and/or transfer of assets upon termination or completion of the project.

iv. *Discount Rate:* The weighted average cost of capital (WACC) calculated for the project is used as the discount rate to calculate the present value of the cash flows.

v. *Input Assumptions* to a typical PPP project financial model are

- Basic assumptions
  - o Start date of the project.
  - o Total period of concession agreement.
  - o Construction period.
  - o Operations period.
- Macroeconomic assumptions
  - o Average inflation rate.
  - o Revenue growth.
  - o Expense growth.
- Capital expenditure
  - o Bidding costs.
  - o Development costs.
  - o Reserve accounts.
  - o Contingency.

- Financing assumptions
  - Subsidies.
  - Equity.
  - Debt.
  - Drawdown period.
  - Moratorium.
  - Debt repayment period.
  - Interest rate.
  - Mode of repayment of loan.
  - Cash surplus and debt-service reserve account (DSRA)
  - Cash overdraft.
  - Grace period.
- Depreciation assumptions
- Tax assumptions
  - Corporate tax.
  - Minimum alternate tax.
  - Dividend distribution tax.
- Project assumptions
  - Land allocated.
  - Land market value.
  - Annual lease rental.
  - Increase in land value per year.
  - Lease deposit.
  - Expected rate of return.
- Construction assumptions
  - Basic infrastructure.
  - Water.

- Power backup.
- Land related costs.

- Revenue assumptions (will vary from project to project)
  - Service fees.
  - Other operating revenues.
  - Investor's returns.

Based on the input assumptions the output is generated which will give us project internal rate of return (IRR) and equity IRR which will tell us whether the project is viable or not.

Flexibility of the Model

The financial model needs to be sufficiently flexible to allow both the investors and lenders to calculate a series of 'sensitivities' showing the effects of variations in the key input assumptions. They are:

i. Construction cost over-run.
ii. Delay in completion.
iii. Deductions or penalties for failure to meet the service requirement.
iv. Reduced usage risk (where the project company takes the usage risk).
v. Higher operating expenditure.
vi. Changes in interest rates.
vii. Changes in inflation.

Once the financial structure model is finalised by the public party, sponsors and lenders, the final run of the model takes place just before the financial close. This is called as 'base case' or 'banking case'. The benefits of the model thus created continues to be used:

i. By the lenders to review the changing long term prospects in the project and their risk exposure.
ii. By the private party to check the price variations and compensation payments in PPP contract.
iii. By the public partner as a public sector comparator.

iv. To calculate the refinancing gain to be shared between both the parties.

v. A budgeting tool for the SPV created to run the PPP project.

Investment decision is taken after evaluation of cash flow analysis and financial parameters like WACC, net present value (NPV), IRR, debt service coverage ratio (DSCR), etc. All the financial parameters as well as cash flow analysis have been analysed and discussed in detail in chapter 7 under Financial Analysis.

Value For Money (VfM)

VfM according to the HM Treasury is defined as the optimum combination of whole-of-life costs and quality (or fitness for purpose) of the good or service to meet the user's requirement.

VfM is not the choice of goods and services based on the lowest cost bid. VfM assessment should ensure that the public sector focusses on the quality of work as well as the competencies of the private party and not on the lowest bid in the project statement.

The key factors that are considered as drivers of VfM in PPP projects are identified as:

Risk Transfer: The primary driver of VfM in PPP projects is the optimisation of the transfer of risk which is allocated to the party who can best manage it for the concession period. This implies that the risk should not only be allocated but optimally allocated. Optimal risk allocation depends upon the understanding of the project's risk identification, valuation, risk management plan, and making and execution of the risk management plan.

Performance Measurement and Incentives: These incentives are given to the private party to ensure that standards and specifications mentioned in the concession agreement are implemented. This is achieved through measures like enshrining the performance measures and continuously monitoring the performance of the private party.

Long-Term Nature of the Contract: Long-term contracts are regarded as the salient condition for delivering VfM, as the duration of the project should be long enough to allow the private party to recover the initial project outlay. This facilitates the private party to whole-life costing aspects so as to minimise the costs during the contract period.

Competition: Competition is very important in VfM analysis as it leads to improvement and quality among bidders and other alternative means of delivering VfM. Absence of competition or potential entry would lead to difficulties in attaining efficiency and VfM.

Private Party's Management Skills: The management skills and ability of the concessionaire to effectively manage the delivery and operation of the project is a very important VfM driver as it leads to reduced costs, increased efficiencies, improved standards of design, construction and operation of assets, and delivery of services.

Output Based Specifications: Service delivery to the end users is categorised as an output of a PPP project. An output specification will provide framework for the quality and timing of service delivery. By specifying the output, the public partner specifies the outputs they require from the contract instead of the inputs they need in order to meet the outputs. The output specification will measure the compliance of the private party through performance monitoring system and payment mechanism. The private party would use innovation and other new methods in delivering services which will achieve VfM.

There are other parameters also that have been identified as drivers for VfM like innovation, public sector project development skills, public sector comparator, quality of advice to public bidders, transparency process, cost of capital, public sector implementation, sufficient flexibility, financiers to the project, etc.

VfM Assessment

VfM in a PPP project has been assessed using different approaches in different countries. According to Grimsey and Lewis, there are four different approaches that could be used to assess VfM. They are:

1. *Full Cost: Benefit Analysis:* It is very difficult approach as it involves a lot of information and assumptions in terms of costs, risks and benefits. There is ambiguity created in determining the VfM created due to PPP. This method is mostly used in Germany.

2. *Public Sector Comparator (PSC):* It is the most widely used approach for VfM analysis. PSC is a hypothetical constructed benchmark to assess the VfM of conventionally financed procurement in comparison with

a privately financed scheme for delivering a publicly funded service. This can be essential for providing the quantitative justification for engaging in a PPP. Typically, VfM assessment of a PSC is a simple difference of total costs associated with a private bid compared to the PSC, adjusting for transferred and retained risk. VfM analysis is used at all stages of the project life cycle. It is conducted during the strategy formulation stage when the economic viability of the project is reviewed before it is open for bidding. It is widely used in Japan, Netherlands and South Africa. The key characteristics of PSC are:

i. It expresses the NPV of a projected cash flow based on the specified public sector discount rate for the entire contract period.

ii. It is based on the most current method of public sector delivery for similar infrastructure services.

iii. It includes a competitive neutrality adjustment so that there is no net financial advantage between public procurement and private ownership.

iv. It assesses the value of all material costs that are reasonably expected to be retained by government if the project is delivered under PPP mode.

v. It assesses the value of all material and quantifiable risks that would reasonably be expected to be transferred to bidders if the project is delivered in PPP mode.

3. *UK Style PSC- PPP VfM Test:* It is similar to PSC where comparison before bid and after bid is done of a PPP with traditional procurement so as to determine whether or not they represent VfM.

4. *Competitive Bidding:* This process is also called as 'restrictive bidding' and is divided into two phases—qualification phase (where interested participants qualify on the basis of pre-identified financial and technical qualifications) and the financial bid phase. In India, most of the PPP projects are allotted through a competitive bid process. This process promotes transparency and eliminates corruption and allows for better price discovery. The Planning Commission of India advocates competitive bidding as the only viable method for allocation of PPP projects in India. Another approach followed is the Swiss challenge approach.

Swiss Challenge Approach

Swiss challenge approach is used specifically when the government authority receives an unsolicited proposal for a project. The private entity submitting the unsolicited proposal is termed as the 'original project proponent' (OPP). The government evaluates the proposal submitted by the OPP and if it finds the proposal good then it invites other parties to submit competing proposals. The other parties are expected to match or better the terms of the OPP's proposal. To balance for the effort in bringing the original proposal, the OPP is given a chance to match or better any competing proposal at par with the original.

The Swiss challenge system enables the public sector to introduce some competitive pressure, thereby avoiding some of the non-competitive concerns raised by unsolicited proposals. The private sector is invited to match or better the OPP's proposal through innovation, quality and efficiency. Despite this, the system is not entirely competitive since it is difficult to avoid a bias in the evaluation towards the OPP and there could be some lack of enthusiasm by competitors to make their best effort since they would expect the OPP to have an advantage. This could be because the OPP has more information than its competitors. Swiss challenge might also not meet the conditions for procurement prescribed by relevant legislations. A major issue is that many unsolicited projects lack competition and transparency. Both the World Bank and the ADB do not allow such procedures under their published procurement guidelines.

In conclusion, financing PPPs and understanding its implications is the 'crux' for the success of PPP projects.

III

Risk Management in PPP Projects

'Risk' is the chance of an event occurring that would cause actual project circumstances to differ from those actually assumed when forecasting project benefits and costs. Risk is characterised by two main components: the probability of occurrence and its magnitude.

Risk in a PPP project:

i. Can never be eliminated.

ii. Can be allocated so it is borne in an agreed-upon fashion and in a given project it is allocated to the party 'who can best manage it'.

Risk is a fundamental feature of any PPP project and it substantially influences the total project cost. It is essential for the public and private partner to extensively evaluate all the potential risks throughout the whole life of the project to decide whether to take up the project or not and what type of PPP model would be most appropriate for the project. PPP projects carry several risks that are unique to this type of delivery system in addition to the risks associated with more traditional assignments. Once the bidder has been selected and the two parties are at the negotiation stage, both the parties need to determine the most suitable risk sharing arrangement that optimises the benefits and minimises the loss to both the parties.

Risk Management

Risk management is the process of identifying, analysing and addressing significant risks on an ongoing basis. The key aspect of a PPP project is that the risk is allocated to the party who can best manage it. There are three ways to allocate the risks in a PPP project:

i. Transferred Risks: Risks transferred to the concessionaire.

ii. Retained Risks: Risk retained by the public party.

iii. Shared Risks: Risks shared between the concessionaire and the public party.

Figure 2.3

Risk Factors/Matrix Provided with Tender Document

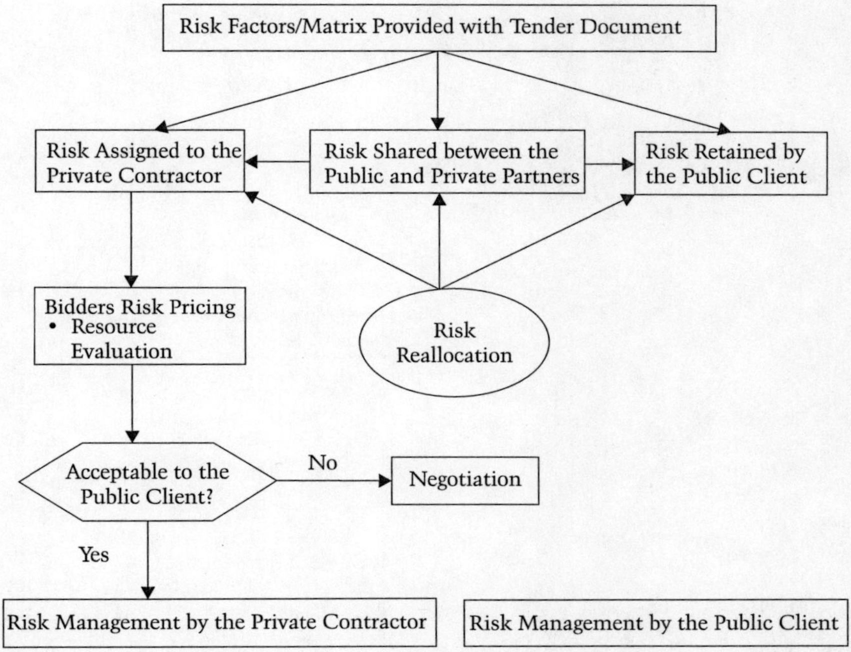

Source: Li Bing, A. Akintoye, P.J. Edwards (2005). *International Journal of Project Management* 23(1): 25-35. January 2005.

The risk management consists of the following phases subject to negotiations among the public and private partner.

i. *Risk Identification:* Set up the list of project risks and identify those with the most potentially adverse impact.

ii. *Risk Assessment:* Analyse the risk with different quantitative and qualitative tools.

iii. *Risk Allocation:* Distributing the various risks arising in the project to the party who can best manage it.

iv. *Risk Mitigation*: Both the parties can use different risk management strategies.

Risk Identification

Risks can be classified as:

i. *General Risk or External Risk*: Matters that arise outside of the confines of a project. External risk may be addressed in PPP contracts but are fundamentally outside the project itself and may be outside the control of the parties.

Figure 2.4

Taxonomy of Risks in BOT Projects

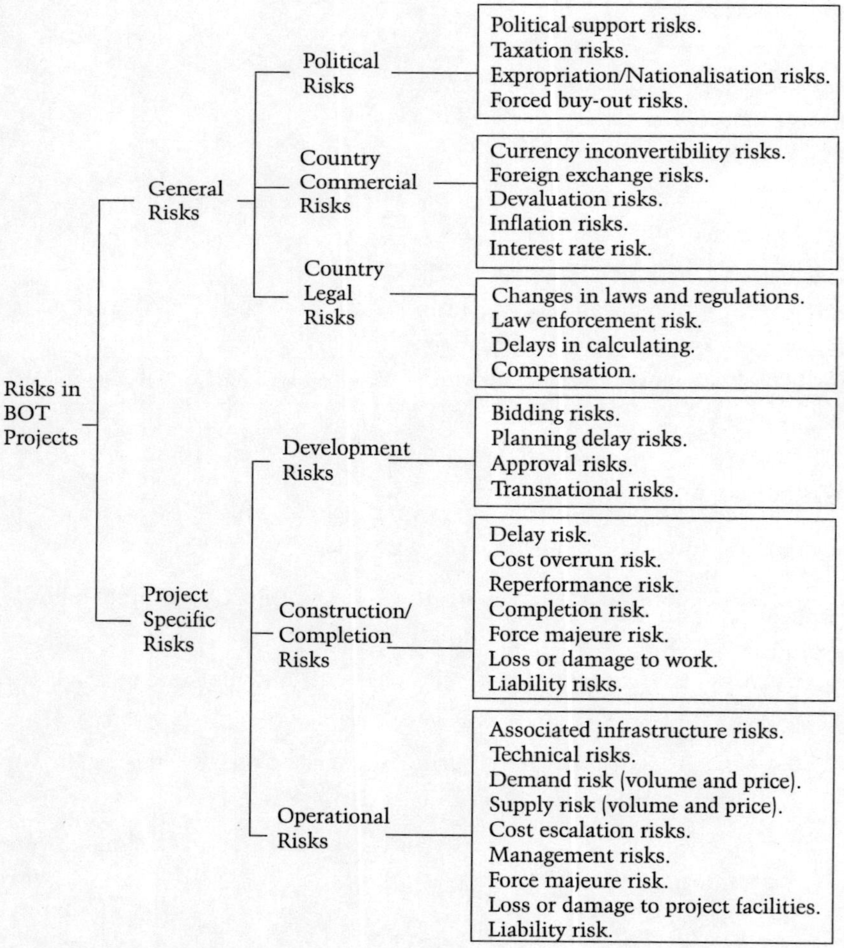

Source: UNIDO (1996).

ii. *Project-specific Risk or Internal Risk:* Particular to the project or the way it is constructed and operated. Generally subject to the control of the contracting parties. If internal risk matters are not subject to precise control by contract parties, they are agreed through negotiation to be allocated in a specified manner.

Types of Risks Associated with a PPP Project

Political Risk: Political risks have strong impact on opportunities in PPP projects. There is a risk of lack of consistency in the project awarding criteria, political support risks, restrictions on import and export, and failure to renew approvals. The project company and the lenders face the risks that the project execution may be negatively affected by the policies of the government like changes in taxes, development approvals, etc. If there is a change in the government, there is a chance that the new government may unilaterally change the rules.

Commercial Risks or Financial Risks: These would relate to financial risks due to changes in the cost of capital due to changes in exchange rates, inflation and prevailing lending rates in the country. Exchange rate risk relates to the possibility that changes in foreign exchange rates would alter the exchange value of cash flows from the project. Interest rate risks force the project to bear additional financing costs. The risk is significant because in PPP projects large sums are borrowed for long period of time. Commercial risks would also relate to revenue risks, and the greatest risk faced by the project is the revenue that a project would actually generate.

Legal Risks: These risks relate to the legal framework, dispute resolution, expropriation and nationalisation. Sometimes the concessionaire could face problems related to title or lease of property, insolvency of the parent company, changes in law and regulations, breach of financial documents, development approvals, etc.

Development Risk: These risks can be categorised as:

i. Project preparation risks.

ii. Bidding risk.

iii. Approval risks.

iv. Transnational risk.

Construction Risk: Refers to the risk that the construction of the assets required for the project will not be completed on time or to the specification. The time overrun may lead to additional construction costs like additional raw material, labour, overhead cost, etc. Sometimes the delay in the project is due to delay in obtaining approvals during the construction phase which will result in the delay as per the construction schedule leading to time and cost overruns. They include:

i. *Land expropriation.* These risks may flow to both the government and concessionaire. Available actions include claims under expropriation legislation or claims by the concession company of liquidated damages (LDs) from the contractor.

ii. *Cost overruns:* These risks affect the concession company directly. The available actions are to either claim LDs from the contractor or drawdown stand-by finance from the project lenders.

iii. *Cost and scope of unspecified work and variations after being identified:* These risks are assigned directly to the contractor and the concessionaire and represent a potential area of future disputes.

iv. *Increased financing costs.* This risk flows directly to the concession company, which may attempt to mitigate the risk either by a new injection of equity or subordinated debt from the sponsors. Alternatively, the concession company may drawdown stand-by finance from project lenders.

v. *Contractor default.* This is a risk to the concession company, which may claim LDs from the contractor or make a claim against the contractor's performance bond and bonding company.

vi. *Default by concession company.* This is the flip side of the prior risk. This risk is to the contractor, with the primary mitigating measure being claim of LDs from the concession company.

vii. *Environmental damage.* This risk accrues to the concession company primarily and may result in claims on insurers or the party causing the damage.

O&M Risk: These risks are borne by the concessionaire like cost overrun, time overrun, contractor default, etc. The operating risk has interrelated components: technical, management and costs. The ability to economically achieve the desired operating rate depends upon the engineering, experience and quality of staff applied to the project. Operating cost projection is the key element for assessing the project finance cost. Some of the risks and actions available to the concession company include:

i. *Performance risk:* The completed facility cannot be effectively operated or maintained to produce the expected capacity, output or efficiency.

ii. *Operation cost overrun:* The operating costs exceed the original estimates.

iii. *Operating contractor default:* The concession company may terminate the O&M contract and appoint a new O&M contractor.

iv. *Default:* The default may be caused by the actions of a third party, in which case the concession company could make claims of damages against that party.

v. *Demand risk or revenue risk:* One of the critical risks is demand risk—the risk that there will not be sufficient demand for the service to be provided under the PPP arrangement and the consequent likelihood that the project company will be unable to repay its financial obligations from project revenues. Reasons could be due to :

   a. *Inadequate revenue from fares :* In the case of a PPP project operating under a government concession, it would be expected that that the concession company would request a cash compensation from the government for a deficiency in income from fares or tolls, request authority to increase tolls or fares, or extend the concession period. Here it is necessary to identify its risks clearly with respect to cash flow or its returns, as they may be affected by an extended concession period.

   b. *Inadequate revenue from other operations.* In this case, similar opportunities exist for requesting the government to provide cash compensation for deficiencies and/or extending the concession period. The concession company would have opportunities to increase rents or pursue different business strategies, including alternate uses of major portions of the concession facility.

c. *Inadequate traffic*. It is essential for the PPP contractor to obtain a commitment from the government, to the extent possible, with respect to anticipated traffic levels and to negotiate a sufficient compensation arrangement for deficiencies. In the event that the government has not offered to provide such additional compensation, the contractor needs to review the role carefully as it relates to traffic and earnings forecasts for a PPP project.

Demand risk is very difficult to estimate, especially in developing economies where forecasting demand is a difficult exercise. The public partner commonly assumes that the private partner should take demand risk. Private partner, when it assumes demand risk, asks for more support from government in the form of subsidies, grants or guarantees in order to mitigate the effects of demand risk assumption.

vi. *Force majeure risk*: This risk reflects the occurrence of unexpected and uncontrollable natural and manmade conditions such as earthquakes, typhoons, flooding or war, which may negatively affect the construction or operations of the project. The defining of force majeure events include:

a. *Natural force majeure events*: Natural force majeure events comprise of all events that can be attributed to natural conditions or acts of God such as earthquakes, floods, cyclones and typhoons. These risks should be shared equally among the parties.

b. *Direct political force majeure events*: Direct political force majeure events are events attributable to political events that are specific to the project itself such as exploration, nationalisation, etc.

c. *Indirect political force majeure events:* Indirect political force majeure events are events that have their origins in political events but are not project specific such as war, riots, etc.

However, the mechanism of managing, allocating and mitigating such risks cannot be categorically stated as they vary with each project and the circumstances surrounding each project.

i. *Management risk:* Experienced personnel who can efficiently apply the given technology is crucial while considering the project operational performance. A management agreement may be needed to cover this risk component.

ii. *Design risk:* It is the risk of poor engineering and design flaws in a project which can have a crippling effect on the cash flow stream well after the capital has been spent. These risks can arise from poor professional advice or selection of an inexperienced personnel for technology or location decisions involved.

iii. *Cost escalation or cost overrun risk or completion risk*: Cost escalation due to delays is a common risk associated with a PPP project. The recently commissioned Bandra-Worli sea link project was planned at 300 cr to be completed by 2004 but has actually costed 1,600 cr in 2009. Logically, any delay in implementation causes increase in cost on account of inflation. This risk is usually not taken by the project lenders.The implication of a sponsor accepting the completion risk is that the cost overruns must be met by the company. Project finance completion test is usually undertaken to estimate this risk which is a very extensive process.

iv. *Supply risk:* It is the risk that the sponsors estimate about the throughput might be correct or not. If the supply is believed to be insufficient the financiers may ask for a warranty.

Figure 2.5

PPP: A Financiers Perspective

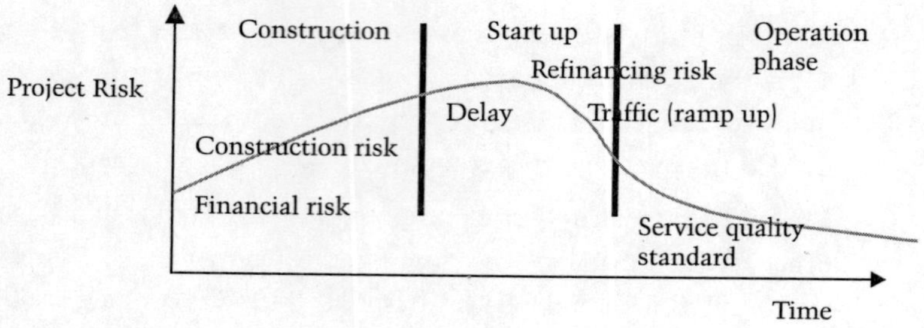

Source: UNESCAP

Table 2.10

Risk Allocation Trends

Type of Risk	*Allocation of Risk*	*Phase of Dominance*
Planning and conceptual design risk	Private partner	Project development
Land acquisition	Public/private partner	Project development
Construction risk	Private partner	Project development/ Construction period
Technology risk	Private partner	Construcution/operations period
Environmental risk	Public/private partner	Construction/operations period
Regulation risk	Private partner	Throughout the project lifecycle
Force majeure risk	Public/private partner	Throughout the project lifecycle
Financial risk		
• Exchange rate risk	Private partner	Construction/operations period
• Inflation risk		
• Interest rate risk		
• Tax policies risk		
Cost overrun risk	Private partner	Construction period
Demand risk/revenue risk	Private partner	Operations period

Risk Assessment

PPP projects require a sophisticated analysis of risk and their impact to adopt the strategies for risk management. There have been many analysis tools and procedures for mitigating the risky nature of construction projects. Historically, the probability theory is widely used as an uncertainty reasoning tool.

The techniques are generally categorised as:

Qualitative approach: It is intended to prioritise risks according to their potential effect on project objectives and is one way of determining the importance of addressing specific risks and guiding risk response measures. Such techniques are used for compiling a list of main risk sources and describing their likely consequences, without entering in detail about the quantification of the probability of their occurrence. Some of the commonly used qualitative techniques are:

i. Probability techniques.

ii. Cause and effect diagrams (CAEDS).

iii. Flow charts.

iv. Influence diagrams.

v. Event trees and fault trees.

Quantitative approach: The process aims to analyse numerically the probability of each risk and its impact on project objectives in terms of the usual planning measures, such as, time and money. The commonly used quantitative techniques are:

i. Decision trees.

ii. Sensitivity analysis.

iii. Monte Carlo simulation.

iv. Multi-criteria decision-making support methods (MDMSMs), such as, analytic hierarchy process (AHP), system dynamics and fuzzy logic.

Probability Techniques

Probability means how likely the risk event or condition is to occur. The probability of its occurring can range anywhere from just above 0 percent to just below 100 percent. (It can not be exactly 0 (impossible) or 100 per cent, because then it would be a certainty, not a risk.)

Impact describes the extent of what would happen if the risk is materialised.

Impact of risk = Risk intensity * Likely occurrence of risk

Risk intensity: The intensity of risk means its magnitude or impact, which is influenced by the effect and timing of risk on the project which may be expressed in number of ways. Effect of risk intensity will in turn have cost implications and impact on the estimated financial or economic result, e.g., 1 year delay in construction reduces traffic volume by 15 per cent. Different risks may effect at different times throughout the life of the project, e.g., design and construction risks may effect in an early period of the project.

'Probability' and 'impact' are used to describe the two dimensions—the uncertainty dimension and the effect dimension while assessing the risk in a project. Probability-Impact matrix is used for determining the riskiness of a PPP project.

Cause and Effect Diagram

The CAED organises and graphically represents the causes of a particular problem. It is also referred to as the Ishikawa diagram, or Fishbone diagram. This diagram-based technique combines brainstorming with a type of mind map and considers all possible causes of a problem, rather than just the ones that are most obvious.

Flow Charts

Flow charts are easy-to-understand diagrams showing how steps in a process fit together. This makes them useful tools for communicating how processes work and for clearly documenting how a particular job is done. A typical flow chart representing an analytical approach to assess risk is given in figure 2.6.

Influence Diagrams

Similar to a decision tree an influence diagram is a compact graphical and numerical framework, which identifies the critical variables and explicitly reveals any conditional independence between them.

Fault Trees Analysis

A fault tree is a logical diagram, which shows the relation between a specific undesirable event in the system and failures of the components of the system. It is a technique based on deductive logic. An undesirable event

Figure 2.6

Flow Chart of Analytical Approach

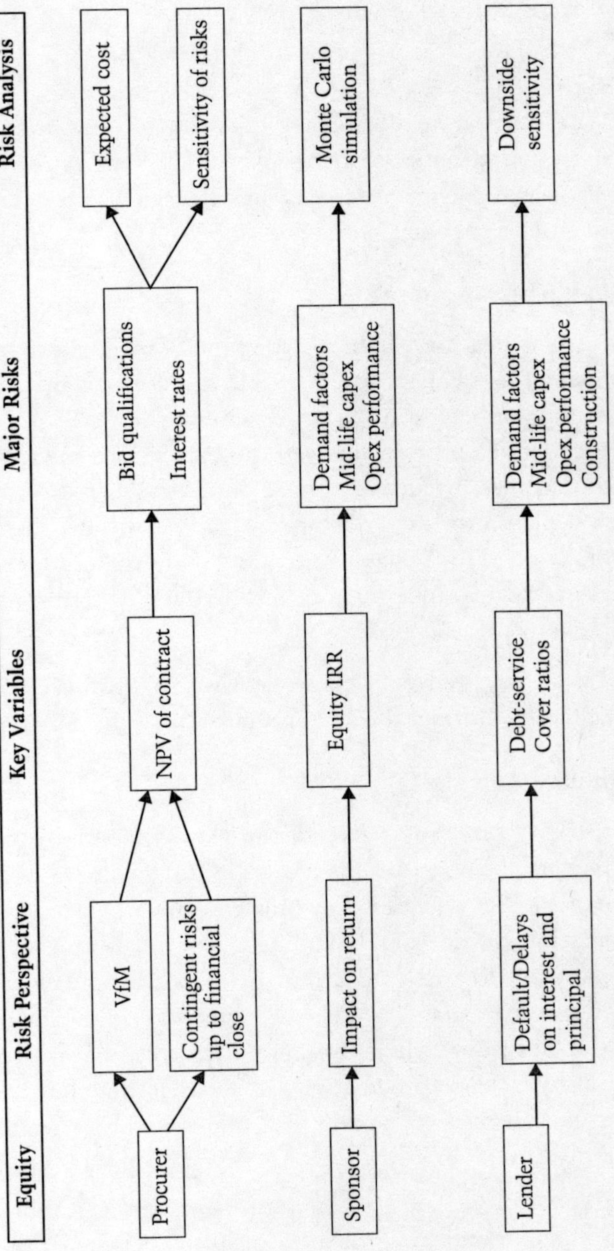

is first defined and causal relationships of the failures leading to that event are then identified.

Event Tree Analysis

It is a method for illustrating the sequence of outcomes, which may arise after the occurrence of a selected initial event. This technique, unlike fault tree, uses inductive logic. It is mainly used in consequence analysis for pre-incident and post-incident application.

Decision Tree Approach

Decision trees are graphical representations of alternative choices that can be made by a project, which enable the decision maker to identify the most suitable option in a particular circumstance.They provide a highly effective structure within which you can explore options and investigate the possible outcomes of choosing those options. They also help you to form a balanced picture of the risks and rewards associated with each possible course of action. This makes them particularly useful for choosing between different strategies and projects, particularly when your resources are limited.

Decision trees provide a convenient way to organise the calculations in a decision problem when the actions and state of the domain is finite.

Sensitivity Analysis

Sensitivity generally refers to the variation in outputs (construction costs, revenues, NPV, return on equity (ROE), etc.) of a model with respect to changes in the values of the model's input (concession life, interest rates, inflation rates, capital structure, cost of capital, capital subsidies, etc.). It is applied in risk management to understand how risk estimates are dependent on variability and uncertainty in the factors contributing to risk. It understands what is driving the risk estimates. The quantitative information provided by sensitivity analysis is important for guiding the complexity of analysis for project risk management. The common metrics of sensitivity are:

Pearson's correlation coefficient: A statistic r that measures the strength and direction of linear association between the values of two quantitative variables. The square of the coefficient (r^2) is the fraction of the variance of one variable that is explained by least squares regression on the variable, also called the coefficient of determination.

Sensitivity ratio: Ratio of the change in model output per unit in an input variable, also called elasticity.

Sensitivity score: A sensitivity ratio that is weighted by some characteristic of the input variable (e.g., variance, coefficient of variation, range, etc.).

Spearman rank order correlation coefficient—A 'distribution free' or non-parametric statistic *r* that measures the strength and direction of association between the ranks of the values of the quantitative variables.

Monte Carlo Simulation Method

It is a computerised mathematical technique that allows the project to account for risk in quantitative analysis and decision making. It performs risk analysis by building models of possible outcomes by substituting a range of values—a probability distribution—for any factor that has inherent uncertainty. It then calculates results over and over, each time using a different set of random values from the probability functions. Depending upon the number of uncertainties and the ranges specified for them, a Monte Carlo simulation involves thousands of recalculations before it is complete and produces distributions of possible outcome values. By using probability distributions, variables can have different probabilities of different outcomes occurring. Probability distributions are a much more realistic way of describing uncertainty in variables of a risk analysis. Common probability distributions include:

Normal or 'bell curve': The user simply defines the mean or expected value and a standard deviation to describe the variation about the mean. Values in the middle or near the mean are most likely to occur.

Lognormal: Values are positively skewed, not symmetric like a normal distribution. It is used to represent values that do not go below zero but have unlimited positive potential.

Uniform: All values have an equal chance of occurring, and the user simply defines the minimum and maximum. Examples of variables that could be uniformly distributed are future revenues for a new project

Triangular: The user defines the minimum, most likely, and maximum values. Values around the most likely are more likely to occur.

Project Evaluation and Review Technique (PERT): The user defines the minimum, most likely, and maximum values, just like the triangular distribution. Values around the most likely are more likely to occur. However, values between the most likely and extremes are more likely to occur than the triangular; that is, the extremes are not as emphasised. An example of the use of a PERT distribution is to describe the duration of a task in a project management model.

Discrete: The user defines specific values that may occur and the likelihood of each. An example might be the results of a lawsuit: 20 per cent chance of positive verdict, 30 per cent chance of negative verdict, 40 per cent chance of settlement and 10 per cent chance of mistrial.

During a Monte Carlo simulation, values are sampled at random from the input probability distributions. Each set of samples is called an iteration and the resulting outcome from that sample is recorded. Monte Carlo simulation does this hundreds or thousands of times, and the result is a probability distribution of possible outcomes. In this way, Monte Carlo simulation provides a much more comprehensive view of what may happen. It tells us not only what could happen, but how likely it is to happen.

Monte Carlo simulation provides a number of advantages over deterministic, or 'single-point estimate' analysis:

Probabilistic results: Results show not only what could happen, but how likely each outcome is.

Graphical results: Because of the data a Monte Carlo simulation generates, it is easy to create graphs of different outcomes and their chances of occurrence. This is important for communicating findings to other stakeholders.

Scenario analysis: In deterministic models, it is very difficult to model different combinations of values for different inputs to see the effects of truly different scenarios. Using Monte Carlo simulation, analysts can see exactly which inputs had which values together when certain outcomes occurred. This is invaluable for pursuing further analysis.

Correlation of inputs: In Monte Carlo simulation, it is possible to model interdependent relationships between input variables. It is important for accuracy to represent how, in reality, when some factors go up, others go up or down accordingly.

Risk allocation: Distributing the various risks arising in the project, to the party who can best manage it by creating a risk matrix. A risk matrix identifies project risks, consequences, probability of occurrence, costs and allocation that is used during risk assessment. This is a simple mechanism to increase visibility of risks and assist management decision making. Many standard risk matrices exist in different contexts, but individual projects and organisations may need to create their own or tailor an existing risk matrix.

Table 2.11

Risk Matrix

Category of Risk	*Description and Likely Effect*	*Mitigation Measures*	*Allocation*
Developmental risk	Insufficient preparatory tasks and project planning leading to delays in procurement and finance close.	- Good feasibility study (that includes comprehensive analysis of risks, possible effects and how to address them as well as derisking to the extent possible). - Institutional due diligence. - Competent transaction.	Government/ Implementing agency.
Sponsor risk	Finance strength (ability to participate with equity, can arrange third party equity, financially solvent and financial requirement does not exceed capacity, can provide limited recourse, if needed).	- Credit references and rating. - Minimum level of equity stake. - Bank guarantee and undertaking. - Bid bond from banker(s). - Track record. - Ensure adequacy of finance under loan facility. - Use of non-financial evaluation criteria and due diligence on private parties.	Government/ Implementing agency.

contd...

...contd...

Cost overrun risk	During the design and/or construction phase, the actual project costs exceed the estimated cost.	- Fixed price and fixed time engineering, procurement and construction (EPC) contract. - Review by lender's engineer. - Contingency provisions; stand by debt facilities/ additional equity commitments (commitments are needed upfront). - Equity stake of EPC contractor.	SPV/PP (can pass on to EPC contractor).
Time overrun risk	Takes longer time to complete the project.	- Technical competence and experience of EPC contractor and subcontractors. - Retaining, completion bond. - Penalty regime. - Full power for implementation to IA.	SPV/PP (can pass on to EPC contractors).
Input supply risk	Raw material and inputs not supplied in time or of less in quantity or of low quality, price escalation of inputs.	- Contractual framework (provisional for LDs. - Secured supply source. - Relief may be considered if failure or shortage not attributable to any private party.	SPV/PP (may pass on to input suppliers/EPC contractor).
Operating risk	Factors negatively impacting upon operation and available capacity such as, unreliable/ untested technology, increased cost of operation, lower capacity, and nature and cost of O&M inefficient operation.	- Proven technology, technology transfer. - clear output specification. - Independent/Lender's engineer report. - Guarantee by technology provider, EPC contract. - O&M contract. - Sinking fund, maintenance reserve. - Maintenance bond. - Contractual framework (penalty regime). - Substitution right.	SPV/PP/O&M contractor.

contd...

...contd...

Demand/Revenue risk	Insufficient demand and/or revenue (due to low demand, leakage, competing facilities, capacity, price setting, augmentation, etc.).	- Realistic demand studies, sensitivity analysis. - Regular monitoring. - Contractual framework. - Price indexation. - Long term off take contracts. - Take or pay.	SPV/PP; Government in case of PFI type or projects with off-take arguments with government.
Change in tax rates	Changes in tax law or policy that have negative effect on the private party, its asset, or the project.	- Sensitivity analysis to test the robustness of financial return. - Compensation if such effects are discriminatory.	SPV/PP if changes were foreseeable and not discriminatory, otherwise government.
Repatriation of capital and profit	Unable to repatriate capital or profit, currency convertibility and transfer.	- Partial risk guarantee provided by some development banks and (ECAs). - Insurance for political risks.	SPV/PP
Natural force majeure events	Flood, earthquake, cyclone, etc.; closure of operations and negative effects on assets and project.	- Robustness of cash flow. - Provision of reserves. - Contractual provisions to withstand effects of such periods. - Relief for short-term close down.	SPV/PP
Political force majeure events	Change in law, expropriation, revocation of licenses, permits, etc., civil disturbance, war, non-default termination of contract.	- Insurance for political risks. - Contractual framework. - Provision of compensation.	SPV/PP
Dispute between parties	Non-compliance of contract provisions, or difference in interpretation of provisions.	- Establishment of contract management framework and formalisation of management responsibilities. - Well–defined dispute resolution mechanism spelt out in the contract. - Appropriate regulatory mechanism. - Termination of contract.	Government/ SPV/PP

Source: *Public private partnerships – A Financiers Perspective*, UNESCAP

Risk Management Strategies

Risk mitigation is an action that is taken to:

i. Reduce the likelihood of materialisation of risk.

ii. Reduce the consequences if the risk materialises.

The strategies vary depending upon the risk and the party impacted by the risk. The various strategies are:

i. Portfolio management.

ii. Guarantees.

iii. Hedging using derivatives.

iv. Insurances.

v. Management of financial accounts by third parties.

Portfolio Management

Sponsors and financiers manage their risk exposure by having investment mandates and criteria that govern how much exposure to each investment they should have. These mandates dictate the type of projects, loan limits, and sectors that they are willing to invest in. The international FIs have also set country-specific lending based on the stability of the country. Financiers may also use syndication arrangements to spread the risk by involving other experienced FIs.

Guarantees

Guarantees are given by the government depending upon the nature of the project when the economic benefits are more than the financial benefits to the concessionaire. In such cases, the financiers to the project may ask for guarantees by the government to support the debt-service obligation depending on the risk assessment and financial viability of the project. This will add comfort to the investors as the project is supported by government guarantees. Guarantees could be financial in nature or could be in the form of assurance that there will be no change in the environment, regulatory or other policies that will have an adverse effect on the rights of the project sponsors or viability of the project. The international institutions that provides guarantees are:

i. *MIGA*: Multilateral Investment Guarantee Agency is a member of World Bank and promotes FDI by providing political risk insurance and guarantees to lenders against losses caused due to non-commercial risks to promote economic growth.

ii. *World Bank Guarantees:* World Bank guarantees promote private financing in member countries by providing guarantees and by covering the risks the private sector is not normally in a position to absorb or manage it. This helps mobilising private financing for infrastructure development and other projects of national importance.

iii. IFC guarantees, ADB political risk guarantees, African Development Bank guarantees, etc.

Hedging using Derivatives

Derivatives are financial instruments in the form of contracts under which the parties agree for payments between them based upon the value of an underlying asset or other data at a particular point in time. The main types of derivatives are futures, forwards, options, swaps, etc. They are based on different types of assets such as commodities, equities, bonds, interest rates, exchange rates, etc.

i. Forwards and Futures: These contracts are used to fix the price of commodities in future to mitigate fluctuations in price of materials used in construction and maintenance of the project.

ii. Swaps: Swaps are derivatives used by the project sponsors to protect themselves against fluctuations in interest rates and currency exchange. A swap is an agreement whereby two parties agree to exchange future cash flows at preset future dates to reduce losses as a result of future price movements. There are five generic types of swaps: interest rate swaps, currency swaps, credit swaps, commodity swaps and equity swaps. The most commonly used swaps by the project sponsor are interest rate swap and currency swap.

   a. Interest rate swaps: Interest rate swaps is a financial derivative instrument in which two parties agree to exchange interest rate cash flows based on a specified amount from fixed to floating rate and vice versa–are used to mitigate risks that can occur when an interest payment mismatch occurs. If a project is financed based on a floating rate, but the revenues are based on a fixed revenue stream, the SPV is exposed to interest rate volatility. The SPV can enter into an interest rate swap, where it pays a fixed payment rate to a FI and in exchange receives a payment based on a floating rate. The company's debt–service on its floating-rate loan is matched by the floating-rate cash flow received from FI under the swap, the company is left with a fixed-rate obligation. As a result, the interest rate swap has enabled the SPV to eliminate the risk caused by any interest rate volatility and effectively achieved fixed-rate funding for the project.

b. Currency swap: Currency swap is a foreign exchange agreement between two parties to exchange cash flows on future dates at predetermined rates in different currencies. A currency swap will enable the SPV to swap its local currency cash flow for foreign denominated cash flows, and the cash flows can be structured to exactly match the loan amounts. As a result, future volatility in income resulting from the currency mismatch on this particular loan is eliminated.

Insurance

It is form or risk mitigation technique used to hedge the risk of a contingent, uncertain loss in exchange of a periodic payment. The terms of the insurance policy will be specific to the project and will be outlined in the contract, and the claims from the insurance will enable the sponsors to use the funds for project completion. Usually the sponsors insure for force majeure risk and political risk, especially during the construction period.

Management of Financial Accounts by Third Parties

The revenues generated from a projects will be deposited in an escrow account which will be managed by a third party so that the bondholders are serviced first prior to any other disbursements. Some lenders to the project request for maintaining a DSRA carrying balance to service requirements for at least six months.

Enabling Framework for PPP Projects in India

To address various constraints in the PPP model, several initiatives have been taken by the GoI to create an enabling framework for PPPs by addressing issues relating to policy and regulatory environment. Progressively, more sectors have been opened to private and foreign investments, levy of user charges is being promoted, regulatory institutions are being set up and strengthened, and fiscal incentives are given to infrastructure projects. It has created an enabling environment for PPP's across the country through initiatives, guidelines, enabling funds and schemes, institutional structures and processes.

VGF Scheme

The VGF scheme of the GoI provides financial support in the form of grants to infrastructure projects undertaken on PPP mode—a capital grant at the stage of project construction.

Infrastructure Development Finance Corporation

IDFC was established in 1997 with the participation of the GoI the World Bank, KfW IPEX bank and several commercial banks in India, providing long-term loans and guarantees for public and private sector infrastructure projects. IDFC provided a total of US$ 1.3 billion in loans in 2005.

India Infrastructure Finance Company Limited

IIFCL has been set up with the specific mandate to play a catalytic role in the infrastructure sector by providing long-term financing to infrastructure projects in India. IIFCL raises funds both from the domestic as well as external markets on the strength of the government guarantees. IIFCL provides for funding viable infrastructure projects through long-term debt, or refinancing to banks and FIs for loans granted by them or with tenure exceeding 10 years, or any other mode, which may be from time to time, be approved by the government.

Indian Infrastructure Project Development Fund (IIPDF)

IIPDF is corpus fund set up for the purpose of providing financial support for quality project development activities to the states and the central ministries. IIPDF has been created in the Department of Economic Affairs (DEA), Ministry of Finance, and GoI for supporting the development of credible and bankable PPP projects that can be offered to the private sector. IIPDF is the scheme for funding to cover a portion of the PPP transaction costs, thereby reducing the impact of costs related to procurement on their budgets. Therefore, IIPDF is to assist projects that closely support the best practices in PPP project identification and preparation as set out in guidance to be issued by the DEA from time to time.

Public private partnership appraisal committee (PPPAC): This high-powered committee has been set up with an objective to reduce transaction costs, enhance coordination among ministries involved and ensure fast track approval of PPP projects. Secretary (Economic Affairs) is the Chairman and Secretary (Planning Commission), Secretary (Legal Affairs) and Secretary of the sponsoring department are the members of the committee. It appraises high central government cost projects; it has issued guidelines that are the reference point for NHAI.

The use of PPPs for the delivery of basic services by state and municipal governments would also be stimulated by the provision of central funds to support their payments under PPPs. Any additional funding of PPPs should be complemented by a more rapid development of capacities to monitor the fiscal costs of PPPs. The detailed design of such a PPP fund, including the type of support, project eligibility criteria, selection mechanism and how the quantum of support for a project is determined is beyond the scope of this report. A significant effort would have to go into this to ensure that it is well targeted and efficiently used. There is considerable experience internationally with the use of subsidy funds for the expansion of infrastructure services such as telecommunications and power, where government funds complement user fees. These are relatively straightforward, with a competition for funds typically being done on a minimum subsidy basis, for example, per new connection to be made. A fund that spans different sectors and also allows for different structures (for example, where governments are the sole purchasers of PPPs under contracts rather than government funds being used to supplement user fees) would be more challenging to implement.

Consultation with lenders, sponsors and state governments will be an important step in improving the design whilst at the same time ensuring that key central government concerns are met. It will be important to ensure that projects supported by the fund are priorities for the contracting governments. A substantial matching contribution from the state/municipal government contracting for the PPP would be important to provide commitment to the project and indicate that the project was a priority. It would, however, be important to clarify what, out of different possible forms of government support (e.g., land grants, tax breaks, risk bearing, cash subsidies), would represent a matching contribution.

It will be equally important to ensure that competition is used to reduce the demands for public funds. It would be far more difficult to size subsidies—and also less transparent—were projects first awarded by state governments on the basis of particular criteria and then subsequently developers approached the fund for support. Otherwise a promoter could 'low-ball' on the tariffs for a project to succeed in getting a project awarded, and then access monies from the PPP fund to make up the difference. Project design, risk allocation, affordability and VfM should also be assessed for these projects to ensure that the Centre is supporting well designed PPPs. This could be done by the central PPP unit—though there might be conflict of interest concerns if this unit received a success fee from working on transactions, in which case the involvement of others would be necessary in clearances.

Other Requirements

i. *Certain costs*: The government should ensure that the cost of construction, and O&M of the infrastructure facility are certain and can adequately balance the requirements of the private developer and those of the general users or consumers and the lenders.

ii. *Prevent unjust enrichment by developer:* The government should ensure that the private parties vested with the control and operation of a public service or a public facility should not abuse their position to unjustly profit from the venture at the expense of public money.

iii. *Prevent abuse of monopoly:* The government should ensure that the private developers do not abuse their natural monopoly position in respect of the provision of an infrastructure facility and that they exercise their rights specifically vested with a public character in the interests of the public, as a public utility.

iv. *Return of the facility to public*: The government should ensure that the facility is transferred for use to the public after the satisfaction of the terms on the basis of which private participation had been based.

v. *Environment*: The government should ensure that the facility is constructed, operated and maintained with the minimum possible impact on the environment or an acceptable level of impact on the environment.

vi. *Rehabilitation and social impact:* The government should ensure that the persons displaced by the implementation of a project are adequately rehabilitated and the social impact of the project is ascertained prior to its planning and implementation, as to provide for suitable mitigation measures.

vii. The government should support the development of infrastructure projects as it does not have the revenue or the technical resources to develop the required infrastructure in various sectors.

viii. The government should provide for a suitable legal framework and policies within which the specific concerns relating to the development of infrastructure projects through private participation and bankability of projects can be addressed.

ix. The private developer should not become the basket for storing all risks simply on the basis that it is obtaining a commercial return. It should be kept in mind that the commercial return would be derived over a long period of time and at the risk of a high degree of upfront investment. This also enables the government revenues from becoming free from the demands of providing such infrastructure facilities and at the same time allowing for the development of such facilities.

x. *Certainty of costs*: Each application, each risk and each uncertainty has an attached cost. The aim of the developer should be to ensure that project costs can be determined and controlled in a certain manner.

xi. *Return on investment:* The project and the documentation should be capable of providing an adequate return to investors in the project. This is a universal necessity in order to justify any private investment in any venture.

xii. *Bankability*: The project and the documentation should be bankable so as to enable the developer to arrange for the required debt facilities to implement the project.

xiii. *Distribution and management of risk:* The documentation in relation to the project should be such so as to enable passage of various risks that are not within the control of SPV but it has been allocated to it under the main concession or license. The developer should not be straddled between the various documents with risks it has no control over or is not capable of absorbing. Thus, the risks allotted under the concession or license should flow down to the various contractors under the relevant documentation with the contractors.

xiv. *Vesting of adequate rights*: The SPV should be vested with all the rights required for enabling it to develop the project. This includes the right to create adequate security in favour of the lenders.

xv. *Control over the revenue stream:* The SPV should have adequate control over the revenue stream to create security in favour of the lenders.

xvi. *Provision of level playing field:* In most infrastructure sectors, there is a great conflict of interest between the government as the service provider and government as the grantor of the concession. There should be specific arrangements provided for minimising the adverse impact of such a potential conflicts of interests.

Thus, risk management in executing PPPs plays a very important role.

3 Viability Gap Funding

Issues and Measures

Introduction

To remove the shortcomings arising out of non-availability of physical infrastructure, non-viability of the project because of long gestation periods and limited financial returns, and to bring in private sector resources and techno-managerial efficiencies, the government is promoting public private partnerships (PPPs) in infrastructure development through a special facility envisaging support to PPP projects through 'viability gap funding' (VGF). Primarily, this facility is meant to reduce capital cost of the projects by credit enhancement, and to make them viable and attractive for private investments through supplementary grant funding. Provisions for this facility are made on a year-to-year basis.

Government of India (GoI) has established a viability gap fund to aid the PPP infrastructure projects, which face the viability gap due to inherent nature of the project. The VGF scheme provides financial support in the form of grants, one time or deferred, to infrastructure projects undertaken through PPPs with a view to make them commercially viable. The scheme is administered by the Ministry of Finance.

Provision has been made to provide upto 20 per cent of total project cost as capital grant to meet the funding gap. Also in such projects, sponsoring agency/department/state can give additional 20 per cent of the project cost VGF support.

Under the VGF scheme, funds and concessions are provided to developers to make projects profitable for them. This funding could, at present, be up to 40 per cent of the total project cost.

Thus, VGF means a grant, one time or deferred, provided under the scheme as detailed, with the objective of making a project commercially viable.

VGF Scheme

VGF scheme aims toward addressing the following concerns:

i. The issue of 'affordability' of user fee.

ii. Leverage government grant to improve commercial viability of projects.

iii. Promote user pay principle.

iv. Ensure market based selection of promoter.

v. Promote the concept of developer (in place of contractor) and address project life cycle costs.

Applicability

i. These guidelines will apply to PPP projects posed by the central ministries, state governments and statutory authorities, as the case may be, which owns the underlying assets.

ii. Proposals to be made under this scheme shall be considered for providing VGF, one time or deferred, with the objective of making a PPP project commercially viable.

iii. This scheme will apply only if the contract/concession is awarded in favour of a private sector company in which 51 per cent or more of the subscribed and paid-up equity is owned and controlled by a private entity.

iv. A private sector company shall be eligible for VGF only if it is selected on the basis of open competitive bidding and is responsible for financing, construction, maintenance and operation of the project during the concession period.

v. The project should provide a service against payment of a predetermined tariff or user charge.

Criteria

The criteria for eligibility for funding are:

i. The project must be implemented, i.e., constructed, maintained and operated during the project term, by an entity with at least 40 per cent private equity.

ii. The project must belong to one of the following sectors:

   a. roads, railways, seaports, airports;

   b. power;

   c. water supply, sewerage and solid waste disposal in urban areas; and

   d. international convention centres.

iii. New sectors added under VGF: To attract private investment new sectors such as irrigation (including dams, channels and embankments), terminal markets, common infrastructure in agriculture markets, soil testing laboratories and capital investment in fertiliser, oil and gas/LNG storage facilities and oil and gas pipe lines fixed, network for telecommunication and telecommunication towers have been brought under VGF scheme.

iv. The projects should have been vetted/endorsed by the concerned line ministries in the GoI.

v. All central projects should have received requisite government approval at the appropriate level.

vi. The total government support required by the project, including support from the GoI under this facility, or any other sources of the GoI and its agencies, must not exceed 20 per cent of the total project cost as estimated in the preliminary project appraisal, or the actual project cost, whichever is lower.

vii. The implementing agency must be selected through a transparent and open competitive process. The main criterion for selection will be the extent of VGF required by the private partner to successfully implement the project. The extent of VGF shall be determined on the basis of the net present value of the actual

VGF required. For this purpose and for all calculations under these guidelines, the rate of discount shall be the rate of interest on 10-year gilts on the date of submission of the bid.

Funding

VGF can take various forms, including but not limited to capital grant, subordinated loans, operation and maintenance (O&M) support grants or interest subsidy. A mix of capital and revenue support may also be considered.

i. The funding is to be disbursed contingent on agreed milestones, preferably physical, and performance levels being achieved as detailed in funding agreements.

ii. The funding is to be provided in instalments, preferably in the form of annuities, and with at least 15 per cent of the funding to be disbursed only after the project is fully functional.

iii. In the first year of the facility, funding is to be allocated to projects on a first come, first served basis subject to meeting the eligibility criteria.

Appraisal and Approval Procedures and Monitoring by Lead Financial Institution

An empowered committee has been set up in the Department of Economic Affairs (DEA) under the Additional Secretary (EA) to consider and authorise sanction of funds up to Rs 50 crore, beyond which approval of the Finance Minster will be required. The projects may be posed by any: (a) public agency at the centre, state or urban local body, which owns the underlying assets; (b) private agency with sponsorship from the relevant central or state government agency. Project proposals must be accompanied by a preliminary project appraisal (covering: (a) techno-economic viability of the project, (b) financial appraisal and project financing arrangements, and (c) extent and nature of VGF proposed) and a commitment letter on behalf of the lending institutions. After approval of the project by the committee within 30 days of submission, the project will be put to bid by the public agency concerned through transparent and open competitive bidding indicating the extent of VGF that is actually required. The lead financial institution (FI) will present its detailed appraisal of the technical and economic viability of the project as proposed by the successful bidder, for the consideration of the committee. The transfer of viability gap funds and the schedule of such transfers will be approved by the committee. The lead FI will undertake regular monitoring and evaluation of project compliance with agreed milestones and performance levels.

The lead FI shall be responsible for regular monitoring and periodic evaluation of project compliance with agreed milestones and performance levels, particularly for the purpose of disbursement of VGF. It shall send quarterly progress report once every quarter for review by the empowered committee. In brief:

i. For speedy appraisal, empowered institution and empowered committee set up.

ii. VGF up to Rs 100 crore for each project will be sanctioned by the empowered institution.

iii. Proposals up to Rs 200 crore will be sanctioned by the empowered committee.

iv. Amounts exceeding Rs 200 crore will be sanctioned by the empowered committee with the approval of Finance Minister.

v. Limits likely to be revised upwards.

Disbursement of Grant

The empowered institution, the lead FI and the private sector company shall enter into a tripartite agreement for the purposes of this scheme.

The empowered institution will release the grant to the lead FI as and when due.

The grant will be disbursed only after the private sector company has subscribed and expended its equity contribution required for the project and will be released in proportion to debt disbursements remaining to be disbursed thereafter.

4 Financing Model and its Components

Introduction

Nature of financing to infrastructure projects primarily depends upon their composition and configuration. Hence, it is desirable to have the full view of the project. Once a project is conceived and conceptualised, and the broad contours drawn out, it has got its own highs and lows of expenditure dependent on the nature of the project and its operative stage. Funding is influenced by numerous variables, such as labour rates, material cost, services, facilities, inflation risk factors, contingencies, reserve and other variables. The amount and type of details supporting the funding requirement should be followed by the respective documents giving a clear and complete understanding of how the project cost is derived. Thus, the clarity and bankability of the project are crucial for developing the appropriate financial package.

In today's business environment, particularly when business and market conditions are continuously changing, it is necessary for banks/FIs to understand the project cost, capital cost, revenue, material and resource cost. It is also important to note that infrastructure projects require special kind of knowledge, skills, tools and techniques to understand the various traits and trends and also the mechanism flowing from the process of initiating/planning/executing/monitoring and controlling/closing. To ascertain the project debt requirement, it is therefore necessary to explore all sorts of information with papers/particulars to make the project's loan proposal more viable and acceptable.

Cost Baseline, Expenditures and Funding Requirements

The cost performance baseline is an authorised time phased budget used to determine funding requirements in terms of overall cost performance of the project. It is a developed as a summation of the approved budgets by time period and is typically displayed in Figure 4.1 in the form of curve. In the earned value management technique, the cost performance baseline is referred to as the performance measurement baseline.

Figure 4.1

Cost Performance Base Line

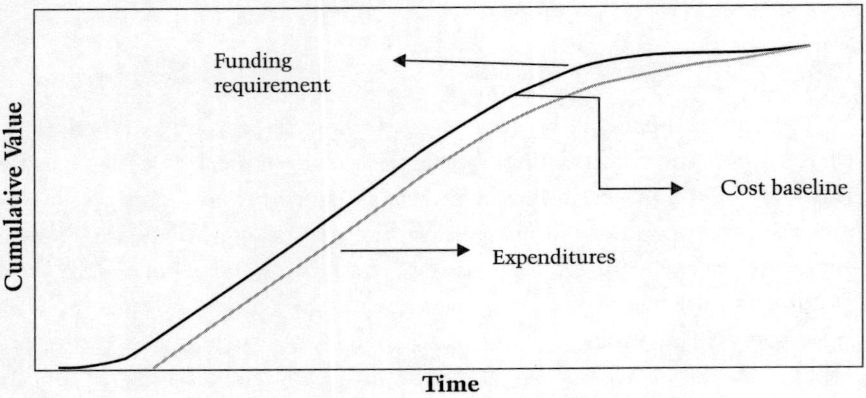

Figure 4.2

The Basic Elements of Project Financing

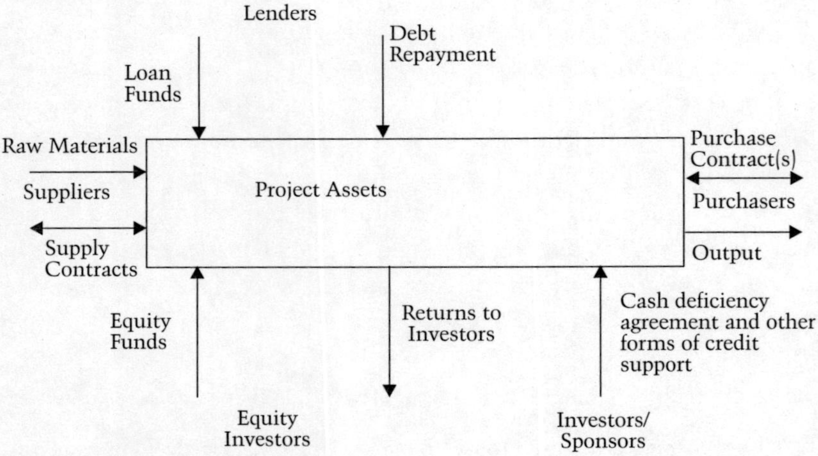

Parties Involved in Infrastructure Project

In infrastructure projects, several parties get involved from the development stages to financing and thereafter to construction and finally to operations. A brief description of each of the parties is given below:

i. *Project Sponsors:* Project Sponsors are responsible for converting a concept into a project and having a role in setting up a project vehicle, identifying and recruiting right managerial talent to implement and run the project and also subscribing a significant proportion of equity in the project vehicle.

ii. *Specifications of Project Vehicle:* The special purpose vehicle (SPV) is responsible for delivering a bankable project during the financing phase, implementing the project and thereafter operating it in a manner that is financially viable.

iii. *Project Lenders:* Project lenders provide the debt to finance the construction of the project.

iv. *Engineering, Procurement and Construction (EPC) Contractors:* The EPC contractor's role is to deliver a project as per the specifications, within a certain cost and time frame. It may choose to subcontract certain portions of the assignment to other contractors, but sub contracting does not relieve it from its sole responsibility of delivering a constructed project to the SPV.

v. *Operation and Maintenance (O&M) Contractors:* The O&M contractors are responsible for operating and maintaining the project in line with the industry's best practices.

vi. *Government:* The government is a key project party. It provides a concession to the SPV to set up the project and ensures that a proper legislative and a regulatory framework exists that allows the concerned SPV to complete on a level playing field along with existing, possibly government owned entities in the source field.

Sources of Finance

Part A

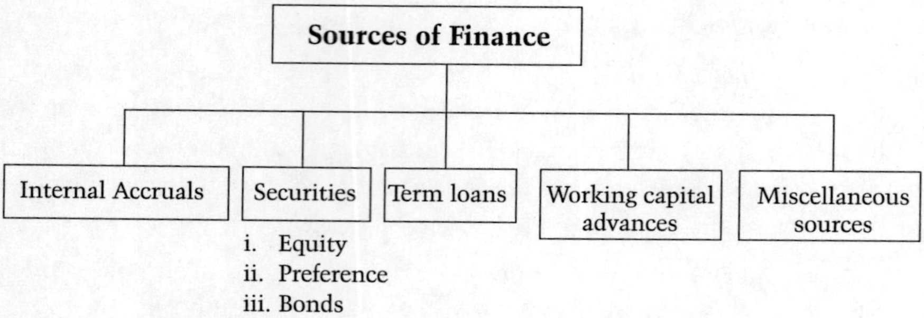

Part B

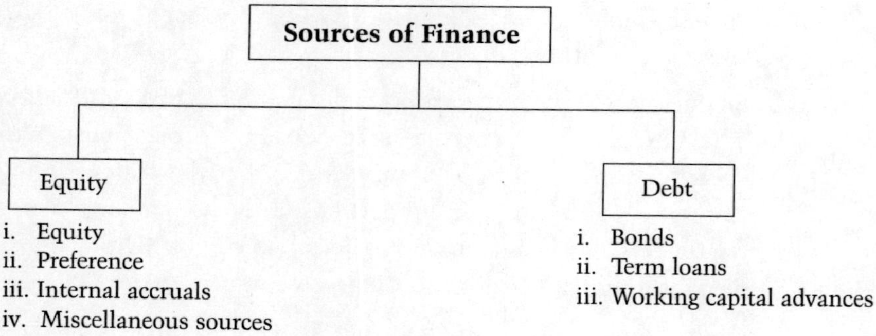

Information Required

To determine the basis of the loan requirement it is desirable to achieve the level of accuracy in terms of clarity and information related to various components of credit *vis-à-vis* project specific nature. It shall be based on highly detailed information in the structured format detailing the needs of the infrastructure project. Otherwise the total funding requirements and periodic funding requirements are difficult to determine. These are virtually derived from the cost baseline. The cost baseline will include projected expenditure plus anticipated liabilities. Funding often occurs in incremental amounts that are not continuous as shown in Figure 4.1.

The standard information to be furnished by the borrowing company is:

Particulars	Enclosures
a) Name of the company, constitution, registered office, list of the promoters, shareholding pattern, paid up capital, licensed and installed capacity, name of auditors, bankers, location and particulars of production facilities, number of employees, etc.	1. Memorandum and articles. 2. List of directors. 3. Income tax (IT) and wealth tax (WT) returns for the past three years of the company and promoters. 4. Bankers' references. 5. Board resolution. 6. Shareholder resolution under section 239(1) (d) of the Company Act.
b) Details of the present activities of the company, past financial performances, details of associated companies and their performances.	1. Past audited accounts for three years of the company and associated entities. 2. Details of existing term loans, unsecured loans and existing charge holders. 3. Group company details with annual reports. 4. Banker's report on the company and the main promoters. 5. Copies of IT returns filed by main promoters. 6. No objection certificate (NOC) for ceding exclusive/*pari passu* charge from the existing charge holders.
c) Promoters and management structure and profiles of whole time directors and key management personnel.	1. Details of shareholders agreement and copies thereof. 2. Details of board of directors, management and organisational setup. 3. Employment contracts with managing director (MD)/whole time directors. 4. Documents to substantiate the proposed promoter's contribution. 5. Names of the promoters, who would furnish personal guarantees and statement regarding net worth of promoters.
d) Particulars of the project i) Cost of break–up ii) Proposed financing pattern iii) Products and uses iv) Key raw materials and sourcing arrangements v) Location and justification	1. Copies of approvals such as Reserve Bank of India (RBI)/Foreign Investment Promotion Board (FIPB)/Ministry of Environment and Forests. 2. Other regulatory clearances from Central Electricity Authority (CEA)/ Telecom Regulatory Authority of India (TRAI)/ Electricity Regulatory Commissions (ERC) or other such authorities.

contd...

...contd...

	3. NOC from Pollution Control Board.
vi) Technology arrangements and equipment sourcing	4. Documents pertaining to title deeds of the land and location map.
vii) Manpower requirement and availability	5. Backup documents justifying the estimation of cost of the project such as civil work estimates, quotations for machinery, etc.
viii) Details of utilities and arrangements	6. Fuel supply/raw material sourcing agreement.
	7. Sources regarding market information.
ix) Statutory approvals	8. Details of effluents produced and measures for treatment and discharge.
e) Financial working for the project justifying the viability of the project.	1. Detailed bases of assumptions made for the workings and backup statements.

Special Purpose Vehicle (SPV)

i. A separate legal entity.

ii. It has a finite life since a project's life is finite.

iii. Project cash flows are distributed to lenders and equity investors.

iv. Equity investors make reinvestment decisions unlike in direct financing, where corporate managers may retain cash flows from profitable projects and/or reinvest in other projects of their own choice at the expense of lenders' and shareholders' interests.

An SPV is normally in the form of a limited company or joint venture, the ownership of which rests with a single or a consortium of private parties. The entity of such a company is independent of the entities of the participating companies. It is also now well established that creating a new and simple SPV with full empowerment and accountability is emerging as a more successful and preferable model for the development of infrastructure on PPP basis.

Government Subsidies and Assistance

i. Capital subsidy.

ii. Tax break/tax holiday.

iii. Exemption or reduction of import duty.

Figure 4.3

Infrastructure Project Finance Transaction Structure

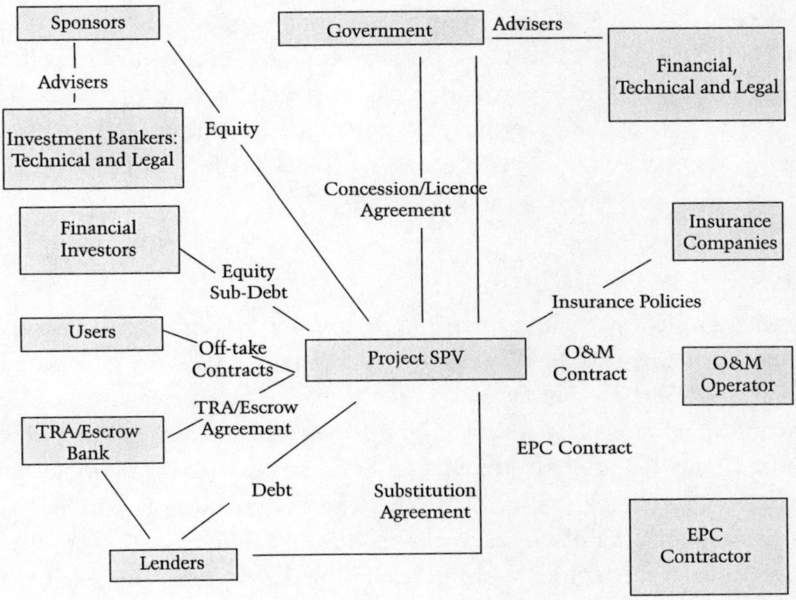

iv. Export credit financing—direct loan, loan guarantee and insurance.

v. Grant of land, free of cost or at a nominal price.

vi. Assurance of availability of raw materials, power, etc.

vii. Assurance of output off-take for a guaranteed price and duration.

viii. Infrastructural support at no or nominal cost.

ix. Arranging finance at concessional rates.

x. Accelerated depreciation for tax benefits.

Subsidy is a payment made by the government forming a wedge between the price consumers pay and the costs incurred by the producers such that the price is less than the margin cost. It should be out based and linked to the private operators' commitment to provide service of specific quality and price. It is also to be noted that a government may provide certain resources as free or at subsidised rates. This is done by giving land or right of ways at cost or at much lower than the market rates. Infrastructure projects are also eligible for tax breaks both direct and indirect taxes. Rebates can be provided in the levy of duties—custom, excise duties and VAT among others. In the determination of income tax, such projects can enjoy holiday as part of the government fiscal support. Section 80 IA of India's Income Tax Act 1961, provides credible tax holiday for a definite period in infrastructure projects.

Conclusion

Designing a particular financing pattern for a particular infrastructure project is a big task. All possible financing sources are evaluated to arrive at a solution which addresses the concerns of the project. Major contributions come from private companies whose initial investment is required both for pre-investment and development cost. Public authority also invest in the equity formulation to stake its claim as part owner of the project and maintain its socio-economic interest in the project. In recent times, international venture capital and private equity groups have also started investing in the equity of infrastructure projects. A number of bilateral and multilateral agencies are available to fund the infrastructure projects like ADB (Asian Development Bank), USAID (United States Agency for International Development), JAICA (Japan International Co-operation Agency). These agencies provide funds for a longer period against government guarantees in particular when the funds are being supplied on subsidised terms. IFC (International Financing Corporation) of the World Bank group also provides loan to the project where the private sector is substantially involved. However, these sources are often subjected to certain stringent measures and conditionalities. However, the Indian banking sector, these days, is providing infrastructure financing and 10-15 years loan facility in certain sectors of infrastructure projects has now been no uncommon to the Banks and FIs. To the fact that infrastructure project is typically a oneoff project for which SPV is formed. For such a company raising loan from capital market as bond in economical terms is very difficult. The task becomes more difficult because of the long duration of financing and security limited to future cash flows alone. Despite these constraints, these sources can be tapped by the creditworthy parties in the project participation. However, one should keep in mind that all such attempts of fine tuning can yield benefits to a limited extent only. The basic thing is the project's solid economic rationale which is the most critical point for developing a solid financial package which requires full familiarity with the facts/particulars and mode of financing.

5 Direct Lending through Consortium

Lending under Consortium

Credit in infrastructure sector has its own inherent risks, hence consortium arrangement is considered as the safest route to share the risks with the other banks.

Preparation of credit proposal is primarily based on detailed project report (DPR)/project information memorandum (PIM) by the syndicator or the appraising institutions. Hence, it is required to know about syndication.

Loan syndication provides substantial advantages to both the borrowers and lenders. Lending banks/appraising institutions use the syndication approach to improve the overall return by earning a higher amount of fee income. A brief nature of syndication is furnished as under:

1. What is syndication	Syndication is an arrangement where a group of banks/ financial institutions (FIs) participates for entire/part debt of the company/corporate.	
2. Why syndication		- Risk diversification. - Informative opinion by additional members. - Additional expertise after funding. - Involvement of various agencies i.e., lenders engineer, insurance advisor, etc., to have effective monitoring and control.
3. Benefits of loan syndication	To bankers/FIs	- Banks/FIs can compete effectively for corporate financing business. - Opportunity for cross selling its products to corporate/companies. - Risk diversification.

contd...

...contd...

		- Better administrative and operational control. - Cost effectiveness.
	To borrowers	- Borrowers do not have to look for different banks (loan requirement under single window system).
4. Types of syndication		- Underwritten deal. - Syndication of non-commitment basis: a) Best effort syndication. b) Club deal.

Banks/FIs will consider the proposal under syndication/underwriting (solely/jointly) from the companies within the single/group exposure prudential ceiling to the existing/new customers having internal credit rating as decided by their respective credit policies based on the latest financial statements of the company.

By way of underwriting, the bank/arranger guarantees the entire commitment/underwritten amount. In case of underwriting the debt, bank/arranger may have to disburse the entire underwritten amount before participation of the other banks/FIs. As such in underwritten deals, syndication of the debt may happen before disbursement of the loan and/or after disbursement (part/full) of the loan. Banks/FIs will downsell the balance (net of its hold position) within the prescribed period from the date of sanction of the underwritten amounts.

Furthermore, it is desirable for the credit personnel to be familiar with at least the bare features of the DPR/PIM, otherwise it will be difficult to analyse and appraise the details properly and logically and will lack the quality. To understand the DPR, whether it has properly and adequately captured all the features of the project or not, details of the required information in a few sectors in infrastructure, which are illustrative but not exhaustive, are given in Annexure A-5.1.

Factors Required to be Evaluated at the Time of Appraisal

In infrastructure sector, credit proposal is appraised by the lead bank/leading appraising institutions/the other lenders in the consortium to ascertain whether the project is sound—technically, economically, financially/commercially and managerially—and is finally found viable as a commercial proposition. The appraisal of a project broadly involves the evaluation of:

Technical Feasibility

i. It ensures that the project is technically feasible in the sense that all the inputs required to set up the project are available, and also facilitates the most optimal formulation of the project in terms of technology, size, location and so on.

ii. Technological superiority enables the company to finish the project timely and also to get excellent returns.

Box 5.1

Technical Feasibility

- Supply of raw materials, power, water, etc.
- Details of plant, machinery, equipment, etc.
- Transport and communication facilities
- Housing, education, health care, recreation, etc., if applicable
- Pollution control, effluent/waste disposal
- Requirement and availability of manpower
- Consultation with external specialists

Economic Feasibility

i. Break-even analysis
   - Break-even volume is given by Unit contribution x Break-even volume=Total fixed costs
   - Margin of safety=Installed capacity - Break–even volume

ii. NPV (Net Present Value) is called value additivity. It implies that the contribution of any project to a firm's value is simply the NPV of the project. The basic investment rule can be thus:
   - Accept a project if the NPV is greater than 0.
   - Reject a project if the NPV is less than 0.

iii. IRR (Internal Rate of Return): It provides a single number (that depends on the discount rate), summarising the merits of a project. It is internal or intrinsic to the project and does not depend upon anything except the cash flows of the project.

Commercial Feasibility

i. Projection of demand for project's output.
   - Market survey for project's output.
   - Demand forecasts of industry associations.

ii. Evaluation of the project firm's advertising, sales promotion, warehousing, distribution and other marketing aspects.

iii. Incorporation of forecast information into project time, cost and other parameters.

Managerial Competency

To ascertain that competent men are behind the project to ensure its successful implementation and efficient management after commencement of commercial production.

Box 5.2

Managerial Feasibility

- Experience and track record in previous similar projects
- Seriousness and financial soundness
- Technical background and competence
- Capabilities of key management personnel
- Review of staff assigned to the project
- Site visits and joint study with the project teams of FIs and experts
- FIs' nominees on board

Further, infrastructure projects are also evaluated in terms of environmental concerns and economic viability.

Environmental Concern

i. To ascertain whether the project is in compliance with the various environmental provisions in force.

ii. To carry out an examination of these aspects provided by the company from an acceptable consultant/project advisor/ merchant banker.

Economic Viability

i. To ascertain whether the project is in compliance with the various environmental provisions in force.

ii. To determine the conduciveness of economic parameters in setting up the project and their impact on the scale of operations.

Given the complex nature of the infrastructure projects—technical aspects, contractual arrangements and insurance requirements for risk mitigations—services of various consultants are required for detailed due diligence and advice during the appraisal and post-sanction credit processes.

The objective is to have the general understanding of the project in order to consider for providing debt facilities to the project.

Lender's Independent Engineer (LIE)

As a part of due diligence exercise, the lender usually appoints an LIE. An LIE is generally a reputed consultancy/engineering firm with relevant experience in evaluating large infrastructure projects. The LIE carries out an independent study of the project, examines the project cost and related aspects, project design and technical viability issues, financing model, etc., in the pre-financial closure stage, monitors the construction process and generates monitoring reports to enable the lenders to follow-up the project. The detailed scope of work of an LIE is given below:

Scope of Work

The activities of the LIE would be spread across three phases as described below:

i. Phase I: Project Review and Assessment (Phase I shall commence from the date of appointment of the LIE and continue till financial close.)

ii. Phase II: Construction Monitoring and Performance Testing. Phase II shall commence from financial close and shall continue till two months after COD (commercial operations date).

iii. Phase III: Annual Operational Review (Optional).

Scope of work under different phases is broadly described hereunder.

Phase I: From Commencement Date till Financial Close

Scope of work under this phase will broadly cover:

i. Review of the technical aspects of the project, including choice of technology, technical specifications and time schedule, and adequate provisions made for unknown or variable elements in the schedule, based on a review of the relevant project contracts, DPR and construction schedule as proposed by the company. The project shall be defined as a composite of on-site and off-site facilities for which financing is being sought. If any facilities necessary for commercial production and off-take are to be outsourced, review thereof will also form a part of the scope.

ii. Review and comment on the envisaged configuration and ability to produce the projected product output, given the inputs.

iii. Comment on the adherence of the technical and commercial aspects of the project contracts, including performance guarantees, warranties, liquidated damages (LD), performance bonuses with respect to the general industry practice and adequacy of these to mitigate project risks.

iv. Review the project cost including the engineering, procurement and construction (EPC) cost, all equipment procured under the bidding procedure, other contracts, adequacy of contingencies and comment on the appropriateness and reasonableness, and comparison of the cost estimate with other similar projects and base case business plan including operation and maintenance (O&M) costs (excluding financing costs).

v. Technical appraisal and review of the project's conceptual design, engineering, drawings, construction plans, material procurement schedule and operation plans. In doing so LIE shall also review the projected construction programme, expenditure schedule and adequacy of the arrangements made to achieve the projected construction schedule.

vi. Verification/support of financial model inputs and all technical inputs of the project proforma. How well the assumptions and projections are supported by contract guarantees, performance testing, quality of design/equipment, etc.

vii. Review of the environmental impact assessment (EIA) report prepared for the project with an assessment of outstanding/future risks and methods to mitigate the same.

viii. Advise the lenders on the steps proposed to be taken by the company for protection of the environment and avoid damage to persons and property. Also comment on any material environmental issues that may have an impact to proceed or complete the project.

ix. Determine a limited number of downside scenarios, which address possible failure in meeting project milestones.

x. Preparation of a detailed initial project assessment report, including an assessment of the construction and maintenance risks and the adequacy of the risk mitigation measures.

xi. Apprise the lenders of resettlement and rehabilitation issues, if any.

xii. Review the status of obtaining necessary approvals, permits, licenses, project completion certificates, etc., as may be required by the company for implementation of the project.

xiii. Comment on the adequacy of approval/clearances for starting construction.

xiv. Review of proposed performance testing criteria.

xv. Review of the proposed drawdown schedule.

xvi. Attending meetings with the lenders as may be required.

xvii. Coordinate with the lender's insurance advisor (LIA) for providing inputs for designing/ analysing adequacy of insurance package.

xviii. Review of performance shortfalls compared to LDs.

xix. Review the consistency of individual equipment/contracts warranties with the overall plant performance guarantees by the project management consultants (PMC) and their level of support.

For the scope of services related to Phase I, the LIE shall submit a draft due diligence report followed by a final due diligence report, taking into account observations from the lenders/company.

Phase II: From Financial Close till Two Months after COD

Scope of work under this phase will broadly cover:

- *Construction Monitoring*

  i. Review the bid procedure/selection of bidders and the progress of issue of bids/procurement contracts for conformity with the project schedule.

  ii. Review and comment on the cost of the equipment under bidding process and its design/technical specifications, to be in line as originally envisaged. Any adverse variations should be brought to the notice of the lenders.

  iii. Review the projected construction programme, expenditure schedule and adequacy of the arrangements made at the site to achieve the projected construction schedule at the specified periodicity (monthly, bi-monthly, etc.).

  iv. Review, assist and advise about the progress of work at the specified periodicity (monthly, bi-monthly, etc.) *vis-à-vis* programme of construction and milestone dates as per the relevant project documents.

  v. Review of contractor's invoices and supporting documents at the specified periodicity (monthly, bi-monthly, etc.), and certification of the capital cost incurred and approval of disbursements during construction.

  vi. Spot verification of the quality of the construction work *vis-à-vis* approved specifications and periodic progress reports to lenders in this regard.

  vii. Review and monitor quality control tests carried out. Assessment of variation orders. Monitor adherence to environmental regulations and report on any present/future risks that arise during project implementation.

viii. Review the status of obtaining necessary approvals, permits, licenses, project completion certificates, etc., as may be required by the company for commencing commercial operations.

ix. Provide necessary assistance to lenders in case of any disputes.

x. Attending meetings with the lenders, as may be required.

xi. Advising lenders of any delays/major problems that may arise in future and conflict between the borrower and various contractors/equipment suppliers, etc., and adverse development that would affect the lenders.

xii. Any other aspects on which the lenders/company may like comments of the LIE.

- *Performance Testing:* During start-up and performance testing, the independent engineer will:

  i. Monitor on-site overall plant performance tests, including data collection procedures, testing instrumentation, and plant operating and testing personnel throughout the plant performance test.

  ii. Review

   a. The test reports prepared by contractor or contractor's testing consultant, and verify data reduction procedures and correction calculations to the various contracts' guarantee conditions.

   b. Facility design versus actual installation.

   c. Compliance with health, safety and other regulatory requirements.

   d. Confirmation that required governmental permits and licenses obtained for operation.

   e. Certification of performance test results.

Phase III: Annual Operational Review

During this phase, the LIE will:

i. Advise lenders if the O&M are being carried out as per stipulated requirements.

ii. Review the O&M manuals and comment on their completeness and compatibility to those of similar facilities. In particular, the scheduled maintenance, preventive maintenance programmes and maintenance dredging programmes shall be reviewed.

iii. Review the actual performance in respect of performance parameters specified for the project and in the O&M agreement.

iv. Review and evaluate conformance with scheduled maintenance, preventive maintenance and spare parts programmes.

v. Conduct periodic site visits to assess overall operations. Any planned modifications for the period since the last visit would be reviewed.

vi. Monitoring and reporting of statutory compliance including environmental requirements.

vii. Provide recommendations regarding remedial measures for identified deficiencies, which are appropriate to meet the lenders' requirement.

viii. Attend meetings, etc., and brief the lenders as needed.

ix. Prepare and submit a report addressing all the issues mentioned above to the lenders every quarter.

In addition to the aforesaid, the scope of services of the LIE, in all the phases, would include advising lenders on all technical matters in order to protect the lenders' interest under the financing documents and all other project documents.

Lenders' Insurance Advisor (LIA)

LIA is required to advise on the insurance requirements for the project during construction as well as operations phases. A broad scope of work/ services for LIA is as follows:

Financial Closure

i. Prior to financial closure, LIA will prepare a report (a draft of which is to be provided to the lenders within an acceptable time period for all parties to review and comment on), which will cover, *inter alia* the following:

a. Review all project agreements/documents and comment on the insurance requirements.

b. Identify risks and interrelationship of risks associated with the project, including contractual risks, financial risks (relating to delay or termination), political risks, risk associated with third parties, technical risks, or the risk of business interruption and insurance implications for the lenders and project as a whole.

c. Overview of the insurance market conditions (both international and local) with regard to capacity within the insurance market and cost in terms of likely future premium payable to maintain an adequate level of cover.

d. Research of Indian insurance legislation with assistance of the lenders' legal counsel and advise the lenders and legal/technical advisors of any implications to the proposed construction and operational cover, as well as any implications to the perfection of the lenders' security interest in the insurance policies and proceeds.

e. Based upon the main risks defined in (a) above, provide an opinion on the structure and adequacy of the proposed insurance cover for the construction and operational phases, and detailed policies, as available.

f. Discuss the exclusions, deductibles and excesses applicable to the proposed insurances and comment on any potential risks to the lenders and what is considered normally available.

g. Confirm the market availability of the proposed insurance package and provide an opinion as can be reasonably made, on the continued availability of this coverage in the market; and

h. Provide a recommendation on the minimum financial rating standard of the insurers (and reinsurers, as applicable).

ii. Liaise with the legal counsel and the lenders with respect to the drafting of all elements of the insurance requirements in the loan documentation and the perfection of the lenders' security interest in the insurance proceeds. Draft the schedule of minimum insurance requirements.

iii. Liaise with the lenders' engineer and the lenders with regard to the cost in terms of likely future premium payable to maintain an adequate level of insurance cover as allocated within the financial proforma.

iv. Immediately, prior to the financial close, the LIA will certify (in a form acceptable to the lenders or advice of any changes) that the required insurances are in place and conform to the requirements of the loan documentation.

Construction Phase

i. Undertake a risk review of the project, identify the major exposures and advise as to how they can be mitigated by insurance cover/arrangements in line with good industry practice including, but not limited to the following:

   a. Physical damage risks to the project facilities during the construction phase.

   b. Advance loss of profits and/or business interruption risks.

   c. Employer/workman's compensation, third party liability insurance with cross liability and/or common law liability exposures.

   d. Liability risks (including employers liability, marine, cargo and goods in transit).

   e. Environmental liability risks including risk to tile surrounding property.

   f. Physical damage risks to other assets such as offices, vehicles, plant, machinery and equipment, etc..

   g. Sub-contractors insurances, if applicable; and

   h. Any other risks.

ii. Indicate the minimum schedule of insurance.

iii. Review and comment upon the proposed insurance package, including:

a. Suitability of sums insured.

b. Adequacy of the insurance policy wordings.

c. Adequacy of sums insured and limits (taking probable maximum loss estimates into account).

d. Premium costs and projections.

e. Deductible levels.

f. Warranties and exclusions.

g. Identification of significant residual risks that are uninsured and comment on their insurability, e.g., those that are generally insurable, or have limited insurability and/or difficult and/or expensive to insure.

h. Insurance and alternative project insurance structures having regard to cost and availability.

i. Identification of additional insurance protection for lenders, including the availability of non-vitiation, assignments and loss payee clauses; and

j. Ensure compliance with all applicable legislation/laws.

iv. Review and comment on the insurance related provisions in the loan documentation/security documents (including assisting legal counsel in the drafting of the minimum schedule of insurance). Ensuring proper insurance related documentation and also inclusion of insurance related relevant clauses in the lenders' loan documentation/security documents.

v. Review and comment on secondary insurance affected by the borrower and/or other project participants.

vi. Review local insurance law and its implications for the project.

vii. Comment on the financial integrity of the selected insurance companies.

vii. Reinsurance.

ix. Issue insurance report highlighting the critical issues raised for carrying out the scope of work.

Operational Phase

i. Undertake a risk review of the project, identify the major exposures and advise as to how they can be mitigated by insurance cover/arrangements in line with good industry practice including, but not limited to the following:

   a. All risks to the project facilities during the operational phase.

   b. Loss of profits and/or business interruption risks.

   c. Employer/workman's compensation, third party liability insurance with cross liability and/or common law liability exposures.

   d. Liability risks (including employers liability, marine, cargo goods in transit).

   e. Environmental liability risks including loss of risk to the surrounding property; and

   f. Physical damage risks to other assets such as offices, vehicles, plant, machinery and equipment, etc.

ii. Advise the administrative agent in monitoring insurance package during operational phase.

iii. Prior to the project completion, audit and report that the operational insurance package is in accordance with the good industry practice.

iv. Audit and report on the annual renewal of operational insurance package in general, and with respect to the following in particular:

   a. Availability of insurance and whether they are properly affected.

   b. Security of insurers.

   c. Compliance with schedule of minimum insurance requirements for operational phase.

   d. Incorporation of the agreed lenders' interest provisions in the insurance package.

   e. Continuity of cover throughout operational phase.

   f. Market availability of insurance; and

g. Inflation and capital additions, which need to be reflected in the sums insured.

v. Advise lenders of any material changes in circumstances, which may necessitate an immediate review in whole or in part, of the insurance package.

vi. Advise and assist in the negotiation of any changing requirements for the insurance package.

vii. Provide ongoing advice, assistance and services on risk and insurance related aspects of the project, as required by company and the lenders from time to time.

viii. Identify and comment on residual risks.

ix. Reinsurance

Advise the lender on adequacy etc., of various insurance arrangements, packages, the contractors' all risks (CAR), escalations, extended maintenance, design drafts, etc.

Advise the lender on issues relating to renewals, reinsurance, assignment of the policies, settlement of claims, etc., on continuing basis.

Any other matters relevant to the project in the considered view of the LIA. The scope of services provided above is not exhaustive, but only indicative and it shall be the sole responsibility of the LIA to render all consultancy and advisory services required to fulfill the obligations broadly envisaged herein.

Lenders' Legal Counsel (LLC)

Project financing depends to a large extent for risk mitigation on the various contracts/agreements that are entered into between various stakeholders in the project. Further, given the size of funding requirements, there would normally be more than one lender involved. Foreign suppliers, contractors and lenders also participate. Services of reputed legal counsel are, therefore, required for legal due diligence on the contracts etc., as well as for drafting of the project specific loan documents.

Scope of Work

Project Documentation

i. Carry out legal due diligence of the project contracts/agreements and advise the lenders on the risk sharing and comprehensiveness of the project contracts and provide specific legal advice, as requested by lenders, on all the project contracts, *inter alia*, including the following:

   a. Joint venture/special purpose vehicle (SPV) agreement by the promoters.

   b. Memorandum/articles of association.

   c. Shareholders agreement.

   d. Revenue shortfall agreement.

   e. Board resolutions.

   f. Concession agreement.

   g. State support agreement.

   h. EPC contracts.

   i. Title documents pertaining to the properties of the company (if any).

ii. Review and comment on project contracts executed or to be executed.

iii. Review and comment on the compliance of the obligations of the company in terms of the agreements and on the guarantees obtained under the project contracts.

iv. Provide a legal opinion on, *inter alia,* the statutory and regulatory approvals and consents required for the project and the validity of the project documentation.

v. Review and comment on any applicable laws, regulations, code of conduct or similar requirements, any rules of general law or any requirements of any regulatory body with jurisdiction over the project.

vi. Submit legal due diligence report covering all the aspects mentioned above.

vii. Any other matters at the discretion of lenders.

Financing and Security Documents

i. Formulate and finalise drafts of documents as set forth below, including preparation of any other documents, which might be considered necessary by the lenders (including all type and category of lenders) and the company in connection with financing the project, and discuss, negotiate and finalise such documents with the lenders and the company and provide specific local law advice, as requested by the lenders and their counsel, on all finance documentation and security documentation required or produced in connection with the project, including *inter alia*—

   a. Common terms agreement.
   b. Rupee term loan agreement.
   c. Foreign currency loan agreement.
   d. Inter-creditor agreement amongst the lenders.
   e. Lender's agent agreement.
   f. Security agency trustee agreement.
   g. Indenture of mortgage.
   h. Deed of hypothecation.
   i. Trust and retention account agreement/escrow agreement.
   j. Undertakings for cost overrun/shortfall, creation of debt service reserve account (DSRA), temporary infusion of funds for delay in receipt of grant from National Highways Authority of India (NHAI).
   k. Share pledge agreement.
   l. Undertakings for non-disposal of shareholdings.
   m. Declarations and undertakings as per sanctions.
   n. Consents and agreements.
   o. Trust deed.
   p. Power of attorneys.
   q. Such other documents as the lenders/LLC may feel necessary.
   r. Review of letter of credits (LCs) to be issued in favour of the project company.

ii. Drafting of any additional local loan documents, as the lenders may require.

iii. Advise on appropriate transaction mechanism to have minimum cost with efficiency.

iv. Liasioning, as required throughout the matter, with the counsel of the project company, counsel of the sponsors and providing such other advice and assistance and undertaking of such other work or services as may be required by the lenders from time to time in the course of the matter.

v. Submit closing opinion confirming that the financing documents and securities created or to be created are valid in law and enforceable.

vi. Advise and assist on all legal and documentary arrangements required for the purpose of financial closure up to and including the first drawl of the lenders' loan by the project company and issue necessary certificates conforming fulfillment of conditions precedent to first disbursement by the lenders.

vii. O&M agreement/toll agreement will be finalised by the consultant as and when required. The scope of services provided above is not exhaustive and it shall be the sole responsibility of the legal counsel to render all services required to fulfill the obligations broadly envisaged herein.

Terms and Conditions

Sanction advice for infrastructure project contain a clear and categorical terms and conditions detailing nature of loan with gestation and payment period of infusion of equity/funds by promoters in such a way that the stipulated DER is maintained at all times. Fixation of rate of interest linked with base rate of interest and also the reset clause as well as panel interest are also incorporated. In cases where reset clause is to be exercised, the matter for resetting rate of interest to be taken up with the company is also to be categorically stipulated. Panel rate of interest is recorded with clarity elaborating the broad areas where banks/FIs shall charge—like default in the payment of loans, or default in borrowing covenants/terms of sanctions. Even the amount of the term loan shall be within the prudential exposure norms prescribed by RBI from time to time and followed by respective banks and FIs accordingly. The release of term loan is also related to phases depending upon the progress of the construction and submission of the certificate by the LIE and compliance of the terms and conditions related to that disbursement.

Illustrative list of main terms and conditions is detailed below:

Name of the company:

i. Credit facilities
ii. Security
iii. Rate of interest
iv. Upfront charges
v. Tenor including repayment programme
vi. Insurance
vii. Commitment charges
viii. Penal rate of interest/prepayment penalty
ix. Any other conditions as deemed fit by banks/FIs after analysing the project will be added before execution of the document.

Pre-Commitment Conditions

These are the conditions that need to be satisfied before documentation. These are critical basic requirements for a sector/project to be satisfied before the bank will even commit itself to the project (by way of documentation). In general such conditions include:

i. Signing of a valid principal agreement enabling the promoters to develop the project, e.g., concession agreement, power purchase agreement (PPA), etc.
ii. All project documents would be reviewed by the LIE/LLC and all issues raised by them would be settled to the satisfaction of lenders.
iii. The insurance arrangements would be made to the satisfaction of the lenders after incorporating the suggestions made by the LIA and with suitable bank clause.

iv. Equity contribution: A letter of comfort undertaking/equity support guarantee from the promoters towards their equity contribution would be submitted to the lenders/lead bank.

v. Management control: Any conditions regarding the promoters to collectively hold adequate percentage of share capital during the currency (tenure) of the loan like pledge of majority shares in project company etc. (Normally the core promoters should continue to have management control during the loan period.)

vi. Furnish a guarantee/undertaking to bring in funds in a manner acceptable to the lenders to cover cost overrun, if any (say 10%—negotiable) of the project cost. The amount and nature of the cost overrun would be determined based on the certificate given by the promoter's auditor and LIE.

vii. Assignment of benefits under various project related contracts like LDs under PPA etc., in favour of lenders.

viii. Company should have possession and title of entire land, which should be assignable to the lenders.

ix. The shareholders' agreement for the equity of the formed SPV would be finalised and signed to the satisfaction of lenders.

x. Conditions precedent for validity of the state government guarantee/Government of India (GoI) counter.

xi. Modifications to/termination of the shareholders' agreement to be in consultation with and prior written approval of lenders.

xii. In the event of delay in completion of the interconnection (in respect of telecom, power, etc.) facilities, the project company would not request for rescheduling of the repayment of project debt.

xiii. Any amendments to the EPC or other contract will be carried out to LIE/lender's satisfaction.

xiv. Agree to the effect that changes, if any, in the project related agreements like PPA etc., would be subject to the approval of lenders.

xv. Undertake that in the event of any cost savings on account of custom duties/other taxes and duties, a prorata reduction in debt as well equity in the ratio of the project debt-equity ratio (DER) would take place.

xvi. Obtain necessary approvals from the GoI and Reserve Bank of India (RBI) for the proposed foreign investment in the equity share capital of the company, if any.

xvii. The company should agree to maintain various stipulated reserves, e.g., DSRA, reserves for general operating expenses, fuel, major maintenance, etc.

xviii. Repatriation of profits/declaration of dividends would be permitted only if the project company meets the dividend tests (to be defined in consultation with other lenders), reserves are full and there is no default by the project company to lenders.

xix. The company to increase the authorised and paid-up capital of the project company to the required levels.

xx. Obtain all statutory/non-statutory clearances for the project as certified by the LIE.

xxi. Agree that the LIE will review all contracts to be awarded to the satisfaction of lenders.

xxii. Any other conditions deemed fit, depending upon case to case basis.

Pre-Disbursement Conditions

i. Modify the memorandum and articles of association of the project company to enhance the authorised share capital and borrowing powers as per the envisaged means of financing.

ii. The sponsors to the project to bring specified proportion of their equity contribution up front (say 25%—negotiable) and the balance in proportion to the debt draw down as per the agreed upon DER.

iii. The project company would open and maintain a trust and retention account (TRA) and shall deposit all the cash inflows of the company in the said account and the proceeds should be utilised in a manner and priority to be decided by the lenders. There would be a specific provision in the TRA that any monies coming from LDs payment made to the project company from the EPC contractor/fuel supplier/any other contractor would be first deposited in this account on which lenders will have the first charge.

iv. Take possession of entire envisaged land for the plant satisfactory to lenders, with a provision to mortgage leasehold rights in favour of lenders and obtain all the necessary approvals for the use of land for the purpose of the proposed project.

v. Agree for a review of the cost of project by lenders with inputs from the lenders' engineer prior to financial closure, and to tie up additional means of financing for any increase in the estimated cost of project.

vi. Agree and undertake to furnish to lenders such information and data as may be required by lenders to ensure that the physical progress as well as expenditure incurred on the project are as per the schedule.

vii. Agree that lenders have the right to review the cost of the project at any time during the implementation of the project as also before the final disbursement of the loan amount. Pending completion of the review, the project company to obtain prior approval of lenders for utilising the amount of the loans equivalent to the contingency provision in the cost of project.

viii. Agree that the preliminary and preoperative expenses would be allowed as a part of the project cost only to the extent they are found to be reasonable, as examined by lenders' engineer, and to the extent that they are certified by auditors of repute that they have been actually incurred and relate to the proposed project only.

ix. Obtain all the remaining statutory/non-statutory clearances for the project to be obtained before and after construction as certified by the LIE.

x. The company to obtain clarification from the respective Pollution Control Board .

Other Conditions

The project company would:

i. Finalise/strengthen its organisation and management set-up to ensure good corporate governance.

ii. Make satisfactory arrangements with its bankers for meeting its working capital requirements and would furnish a letter from its bankers in this regard.

iii. Agree that lenders may, at their discretion, withhold disbursement of the amount of loan equivalent to the provision against margin money for working capital in the cost of the project till such time as the project is completed and the build-up of working capital commences.

iv. Maintain conditions stipulated for financial assistance by other FIs/banks/foreign lenders.

v. Ensure that the equipment for the plant is adequate and appropriate to meet the pollution control norms.

vi. Maintain retention reserves, as per lenders' requirements, at all times during the currency of the loan.

vii. Satisfy the lenders of the adequacy of its organisational set-up for smooth operation of the project.

viii. Agree that any prepayment of loans by the company, will be on such terms as may be agreed to by lenders and no premium shall be payable if the prepayment is effected at the instance of lenders.

ix. Satisfy lenders that the physical progress as well as expenditure incurred on the project is as per the original schedule.

x. Agree and undertake to furnish to lenders such information and data as may be required by lenders.

xi. Agree not to reduce its paid-up share capital during the (period of rupee/foreign currency term) loan and/or guarantees (without the approval of lenders).

Environmental and Social Safeguards Assessment

In infrastructure projects environmental/social safeguards and project factors are incorporated into the project strategy and controls which give longer time scale benefit to the society. The pros and the cons of the environmental and social factors are to be assessed properly to move as per the plan and to obtain necessary permits and approvals from the competent authority. Whereever project affects resettlement plan or the tribal development plan it should move as per the plan decided and follow it in orderly manner and keep the record in the structured way.

In order to set up an infrastructure project, the project company should carry out a detailed environmental and social safeguards assessment.

i. EIA report.

ii. Environmental management plan (EMP).

iii. Other relevant environmental permits.

iv. Resettlement action plan (RAP), social impact assessment report.

v. Tribal development plan, if applicable.

Procurement Assessment

Procurement assessment involves the contract management and changed control processes required to develop and administer contracts or purchase order issued by authorised project team members. It involves contract that are legal documents mutually binding both the parties. A procurement contract includes terms and conditions laying down what the company is to perform or provide. It meets the specific needs of the project while adhering to procurement policies. It relates to project requirements that are considered during planning for procurement. Common terms are in use for different types of procurement documents, for example RFP and RFQ etc. These documents include a description of the desired form of the response, the relevant procurement statement of works (SOW) and any required contractual provisions.

The following documents may be obtained from the company for evaluating procurement process:

i. Request for proposal (RFP).

ii. Request for quotation (RFQ)

ii. Any subsequent changes/amendments

Conclusion

Financing to infrastructure projects through consortium route is an appropriate and accepted method followed invariably by banks and FIs keeping two factors in view—collective efforts and collective risk sharing. Consortium provides clarity over the issues pertaining to the project, understanding of long and detailed documents, papers and particulars, evaluation of the mode of financing in terms of project requirement and assessment of various strengths and weaknesses of the company. Maintaining ongoing contact with the company and co-lenders and development in the company's execution to the project and business environment have thoroughly been assessed and understood. Even the control over the project account is of quality. Inspection is carried out by the lead bank and one or two members jointly in such a manner that by rotations all the member banks get involved. The inspection note is circulated to all member banks for their review and suggestions. During the subsequent inspections it is verified as to whether the issues raised during the previous inspection are receiving the attention of the company and corrective measures have been initiated. The focus of the consortium meeting is to evaluate the projected levels of operations and profitability as projected and also to ensure that lenders interest is protected.

Annexure A-5.1

DPR for a Coal Based Project

Section - 1 Introduction and Executive Summary

1.1 Foreword

1.2 Executive summary

Section - 2 Need for the Project

2.1 Introduction

2.2 Power scenario in a region

2.3 Power position in the state

2.4 Justification of the project

2.5 Fuel availability scenario

Section - 3 Basic Requirements

3.1 Introduction

3.2 Land area requirement

3.3 Water requirement, source and availability

3.4 Fuel—requirement, availability and transportation

3.5 Power evacuation

3.6 Other infrastructural facilities

Section - 4 Site Features

4.1 Introduction

4.2 Study of the existing station

4.3 Additional land requirement for ash disposal

4.4 Access

4.5 Meteorological data

Section - 5 Technical Features

5.1 Introduction

5.2 Thermodynamic cycle

5.3 Main plant and equipment

5.4 Auxiliary systems

5.5 Miscellaneous auxiliaries

5.6 Electrical system

5.7 Instrumentation and control

5.8 Plant layout

5.9 Main plant and equipment layout

5.10 Civil engineering aspects

Section - 6 Environmental Aspects

6.1 Introduction

6.2 Environmental factors

6.3 Commercial utilisation of fly ash

Section - 7 Construction Facilities

7.1 Introduction

7.2 Construction equipment

7.3 Construction materials

7.4 Organisational set-up for plant construction

Section - 8 Project Implementation and Monitoring

8.1 Introduction

8.2 Project organisation of the owner

8.3 Project execution

8.4 Project monitoring, coordination and control

8.5 Project implementation schedule

Section - 9 Organisation Structure and Employee Facilities

9.1 Introduction

9.2 Organisation set-up for plant operation

9.3 Training

9.4 Employee facilities

Section - 10 Project Cost Estimate and Financial Aspects

10.1 Basis of estimates

10.2 Project cost estimate

10.3 Estimation of cost of generation of power

10.4 Major assumptions like:

- The project would be implemented.
- The project would be financed by an overall interest rate of the total investment.
- Interest during construction to be capitalised.
- Price of coal including transportation.
- O&M (operation and maintenance).
- Cost of generation has been calculated as per the norms of the state.

DPR For Solar Power Plant

1. Introduction
    - 1.1 Background of promoter/developer
    - 1.2 Introduction to solar energy
    - 1.3 Introduction of proposed project
2. Economic Outlook of Solar Energy
    - 2.1 World solar energy market
    - 2.2 Renewable industry in India
    - 2.3 Solar energy in India
    - 2.4 Central and state government policies and incentives/Jawaharlal Nehru National Solar Mission (JNNSM)
3. Project Details
    - 3.1 Proposed location and site analysis
    - 3.2 Technical specifications for proposed project
    - 3.3 Operator capability and project experience
    - 3.4 Supplier/operator scope and responsibilites
        - 3.4.1 Site development
        - 3.4.2 Foundation/installation
        - 3.4.3 Mechanical and electrical connectivity
        - 3.4.4 Project completion

4. Project Financials and Analysis

4.1 Project cost and means of finance

A. Solar:

S. No.	*Particulars*	*Cost per MW*	*Total for ------ MW*
a.	Land		
b.	Machinery including installation		
c.	Preoperative expenses		
d.	Contingencies		

Total Project Cost

↓

Equity (30%) | Term Loan from Lenders/FIs (70%)

B. Revenue Assumptions

1. Installed Capacity		
a. Total installed capacity	MW	
b. Per hour unit generation per MW	KW	
c. Annual unit generation per MW	KWH	
d. Total unit generation per annum	KWH	
2. Operating capacity per year		
3. Production at operating capacity		
Year-1 KWH		
Year-2 KWH		
4. Selling price		
Selling price per KWH		

C. Project Revenues → Operating Cost and Expenses → Projected Profit and Loss (P&L) → Projected Cash Flow → Debt Schedule → Debt Service Coverage Ratio (DSCR) → Analysis of Internal Rate of Return (IRR) and Net Present Value (NPV)

4.2 Project implementation schedule

4.3 Revenue assumptions

4.4 Project cash flows

5. Benefits Available to the Solar Projects

   5.1 20% capital subsidy under special incentive package scheme (SIPS)

   5.2 Exemption of central sales tax (CST)/Service tax

   5.3 Exemption of state taxes and levies

   5.4 No duties on imported equipment and raw materials

   5.5 Value added tax (VAT) exemptions

DPR for Road Project

Section - 1 Introduction

   1.1 Award of the project

   1.2 Project location

   1.3 Extent of land available

   1.4 Connectivity

Section - 2 Sponsor Analysis

   2.1 Concession agreement (CA)/Concession period (CP)

   2.2 Sponsor analysis with business activities and consolidated P&L for 3 years

Section - 3 Cash Flow Projection

Section - 4 Project Details and Project Cost

   4.1 Engineering, procurement and construction (EPC) cost

   4.2 Premium payable during construction

   4.3 Interest during construction (including upfront fees paid)

   4.4 Preliminary and preoperative expenses

   4.5 DSRA (debt service reserve account)

   4.6 Contingencies

Section - 5 Key Timelines/Milestones

   5.1 CA signing date

   5.2 Appointed date

   5.3 Commercial operation date

   5.4 Debt drawn date

5.5 Repayment start and repayment end date

Section - 6 Revenue Analysis

6.1 Traffic study in terms of average daily traffic (ADT), hourly variation and peak hour share, traffic composition and annual ADT. (Toll rate and willingness to pay toll surveys and axle load surveys, including demand forecasting and assessment of vehicle damage factor and also capacity assessment.)

6.2 Toll rate assumed

6.3 Expenses assumptions

6.4 Annual routine maintenance

6.5 Periodic maintenance

6.6 Interest rate on debt

Section - 7 Profitability Projections, Sensitivity Analysis and Risk Analysis

Some key narrative features are also given hereunder to make the credit personnel to understand whether features have been captured in the way required:

DPR for Port Sector

Chapter 1 – Introduction

Chapter 2 – Project Site Environment

a. Project location

b. Extent of land available

c. Connectivity and existing facilities

Chapter 3 – Field Surveys and Investigation

Chapter 4 – Traffic Projection

Chapter 5 – Vessel Size Analysis and Facility Requirements

Chapter 6 – Analysis of Alternatives

Chapter 7 – Development Plan and Preliminary Engineering

Chapter 8 – Cost Estimate

An estimate of the capital cost and annual O&M cost for the various facilities identified in terms of unit/quantity/rate has been prepared for the project. The assumptions for arriving at the annual O&M cost of facilities that would be incurred annually is also presented.

Chapter 9 – Project Implementation Schedule

It involves pre-development as well as development activities.

Pre-development activities:

a. Technical closure

b. Financial closure

c. Tendering process

Chapter 10 – Traffic Analysis

Chapter 11 – Financial Analysis

The overall approach to evaluate financial feasibility of the project involves determination of IRR for the project and comparing it with the weighted average cost of capital (WACC). This approach is preferred for infrastructure projects in which tariff can be levied and recovered with a reasonable certainty. The emphasis is on checking the adequacy of projected revenue streams to recover the capital investment and desire returns. The steps followed under the approach are:

1. Project phasing and estimation of capital expenditure
2. Means of finance
3. Identifying revenue sources and estimating the project revenues
4. Estimation of operating expenses and financing costs over the period horizon
5. Drawing up of P&L a/c, cash flow statement and balance sheet for the project
6. Estimation of net operating cash flows for the project
7. Calculation of IRR and average DSCR

Chapter 12 – Traffic Risk Study *vis-à-vis* Financing Structure

The financing structure reflects the risk of the project, the security requirement of the lenders and financing requirement of the sponsors. The financing structure of the project also depends on the stage in life cycle of the project. Infrastructure projects have three distinct phases with different risk. Both equity investors and lenders can be expected to seek different rewards and expect different guarantees depending upon which phase they are investing in.

Different Phases of Port Sector

	Phase	*Risk*	*Financing*
1.	Development phase	Very high risk	Only equity, mainly from sponsors
2.	Construction and start up phase	High risk	Large volume of finance required. Mixture of equity, senior debt and performance guarantees used. An additional subordinate debt shall be required where subsequent phases to be developed and the entire development cannot be funded through internal accruals.
3.	Public utility/ operation phase	Lower risk	Refinancing with bonds or equity. Possibilities for high debt-equity ratio could be explored.

DPR : Airport

1.0 Introduction

- 1.1 Background
- 1.2 Role of state government
- 1.3 Award of the project
- 1.4 Development partners

2.0 State Government Vision for Airport

- 2.1 Need for greenfield airport

3.0 Overview of Aviation in India

- 3.1 General
- 3.2 Sector organisation
- 3.3 Civil aviation infrastructure in the country
- 3.4 Air traffic growth in the country
- 3.5 Airline scenario
- 3.6 Air cargo market
- 3.7 Tariff structure
- 3.8 New initiatives of the government

4.0 Challenges and Opportunities of Regional Airports

6.4.B Industrial activity as an economy base

6.5 Acquisition of land for the airport

7.0 Traffic Forecast for Greenfield Airport

7.1 Greenfield airport

7.2 Traffic forecast methodology

7.3 Demographic profile of the city

7.4 Passenger traffic forecast for airport

7.5 Passenger traffic demand for airport

7.6 Cargo forecast

7.7 Conclusion

8.0 Airport Component – Planning and Design

8.1 Standard and codes followed

8.2 Runway design

8.3 Taxiway

8.4 Apron

8.5 Terminal

8.6 Ancillary developments

9.0 Obstacle Limitation Surfaces

9.1 Definition

9.2 Configuration of obstacle limitation surfaces

9.3 Obstacle survey and analysis

10.0 Landside Opportunities of Assessment

10.1 Location analysis

10.2 Site connectivity

10.3 Perception of the market

10.4 Market value realisable

11.0 City Side Infrastructure Development

11.1 Area for development

11.2 Permissible land uses

11.3 Framework for development

11.4 Proposed land uses

11.5 Integration of airside and landside

11.6 Provision for infrastructure

11.6.A Roads

11.6.B Water supply and sewerage

11.6.C Power

11.6.D Telecom

12.0 Environmental Impact Analysis

12.1 Description of the environment

12.2 Anticipated environmental impacts and mitigation measures

12.3 Environment monitoring programme

12.3.A Budgetary allocation for environmental protection

12.4 Project benefits

12.5 Conclusions

13.0 Capital Cost Estimates

13.1 General

13.2 Methodology adopted

13.2.A Inputs

13.2.B Estimation of quantities

13.2.C Rates

13.3 Detailed bills and cost estimates

13.4 Summary cost estimates

13.4.A Airport component

13.4.B Aircraft procurement

13.4.C Landside infrastructure development

13.4.D Total development cost

13.4.E Cost comparison with similar developments

14.0 Project Development Schedule

14.1 Development phasing

14.2 Activities in the initial phase

14.2.A Schedule of development

14.2.B Schedule of project cost

15.0 Financial Analysis

15.1 Introduction

15.2 Assumptions and inputs

15.3 Revenue streams

15.3.A Aeronautical revenues

15.3.B Non-aeronautical revenues

15.4 O&M expenses

15.5 Conclusions

16.0 Status of Approvals

16.1 Ministry of Civil Aviation (MoCA) and Government of India (GoI) cabinet approval

16.2 Directorate General Civil Aviation (DGCA) approvals

16.2.A Final site approval

16.2.B Aerodrome license

16.3 Ministry of Defence clearance

16.4 Ministry of Environment and Forests

16.5 Summary

17.0 Conclusions

6 Pre-Sanction Credit Process

Introduction

The credit process has been broadly divided under two heads, *viz.*, pre-sanction process and post-sanction process. The pre and post-sanction processes are further subdivided into three stages as given below.

Pre-Sanction Process

i. Appraisal and recommendation.

ii. Assessment.

iii. Sanction.

Post-Sanction Process

i. Follow up.

ii. Supervision.

iii. Monitoring and control.

Pre-Sanction Process

Assistance for projects should be considered on the basis of viability assessment. The appraisal process includes a site visit of the project, discussions with the promoters, analysis of the past performance of borrower/other concerns in the group and evaluation of the technical, commercial, financial and economic viability. A site visit is necessary to assess the suitability of the project location, availability of essential utilities/logistics like power and water supply, labour, transportation, infrastructure, etc., besides assessing the environment impact.

The deficiencies, if any, relating to the company's accounts as brought out on different report *viz.*, internal audit, site visit, statutory audit, etc., and ratification thereof should also be covered. Further, position of receipt of quarterly progress reports/balance sheets/other returns and analysis thereof, and major observations made at officers level meeting(s)/senior executive meeting(s) should also be included in such appraisal notes.

Banks and FIs follow the credit process in the structured manner determining eligibility for credit, quantum of credit, credit delivery and terms and conditions of credit. Before approving a credit they ensure sufficient information to make proper credit decisions at the back of the credit rating of the company. They have to identify group of obligors or connected counter parties who are identical based on financial interdependence under common ownership or control or with strong connecting links. They collect and collate all the information on the basis of detailed project report under different required heads to understand the mechanism of the project and its execution followed with the financial strengths of the company. The company's business expertise and the status of company's economic sector and its position within that sector are also assessed. Assessment of the risk and reward relationship of the credit as well as overall profitability of the account relationship is also looked into. Assessment also requires the source of repayment and current risk profile including the nature and aggregate amount of risk of the company and collateral and its sensitivity to economic and market developments. Proposal is prepared after careful analysis of technical feasibility, managerial efficiency, financial strengths/performances and bankability i.e., assessment of risk and corresponding mitigating factors. The sanction advice is prepared in the most structured format based on all the details relevant to the project as incorporated in project information memorandum (PIM) to the competent authority.

Post-Sanction Process

The post-sanction credit process ensures an efficient and effective credit management maintaining high levels of standard assets. As a term loan is repayable out of cash accruals generated over a period of time, it is essential that a project is monitored, supervised and followed up on an ongoing basis through-out the tenure of the term loan. The post-sanction follow up, in case of term loans, can be divided into two categories i.e., follow up during implementation stage and follow up after commercial production (COD).

Follow up during implementation stage: It begins soon after sanction of the term loan is communicated to the borrower. Here, periodic progress report, site visit, obtention of an audited annual financial statements, progress in mobilisation in the means of financing, etc are done.

Follow up post commercial production: At the end of the every year the performance of the company is determined in terms of benchmark levels of current ratio, TOL/TNW and interest coverage ratio, default in payment of interest or installments and default in covenants of the sanction advice. Lastly, compliance of all internal and external reporting requirements.

Supervision function: To ensure that effective follow up of advances is in place and asset quality of good order is maintained. In monitoring and control, to supervise the project by tracking changes from time to time and to ensure that the project execution and movement is as per the projected level.

Lending to Public Private Partnership (PPP) Projects

A project awarded to a private sector company for development, financing, construction, maintenance and operation through PPP shall be accorded priority for lending.

In case of PPP projects, the private sector company shall be selected through a transparent and open competitive bidding process.

According to the Government of India (GoI) a PPP project is a project based on a contract or concession agreement between a government or statutory entity and a private sector company for delivering an infrastructure service on payment of user charges. A private sector company is a company in which 51 per cent or more of equity is owned or controlled by a private entity.

Hence, the project stems from a government led planning and prioritisation process and there is a genuine sharing of risks between the government and the private sector. This means that the government accepts some risks and does not transfer the entire risk to the private sector and vice versa.

PPP projects based on standardised/model documents duly approved by the respective government would be preferred.

Viability of Project

The viability of the project has to be studied as under:

a. Management.

b. Commercial.

c. Technical.

d. Financial.

e. Economic.

The viability of the project equally depends upon the factors like commercial, technical, financial and economic as mentioned above. If any factors slips or changes differently, at least one other factor is likely to be affected. Hence to make the project viable, it is imperative to have all these factors scanned adequately. An infrastructure project is viewed in terms of economic viability determining the conduciveness of economic parameter for its setting up and their impact on the scale of operations. To determine commercial viability, the extent of profitability of the project and its sufficiency in relation to repayment, obligations is properly assessed and understood. The project passes through a series of engineering processes of high degrees and high dimensions; technology plays a key role in relation to time, cost, productivity, reliability and finally execution. Thus the suitability of the project selected and the adequacy of the technical investigation and design are necessary to make the project viable for finance. Accuracy of cost estimates, suitability of the envisaged pattern of financing and capital structure also need to be assessed and analysed.

Management

In predicting performance of a project, assessment of management quality is a critical factor. One of the major reasons for project failures/delays/cost overrun/time overrun can be attributed to inefficient management. Management inefficiency can stem from lack of integrity and commitment to lack of necessary expertise and inability to raise resources in time of need. Assessment of management is also difficult as quite a few of the attributes of efficient management need qualitative assessment.

Management efficiency reflects the way it maintains its accounts with banks/financial institutions (FIs), its ability to raise resources in time and the accounting practices that are followed and reported. In predicting management success in managing projects, these factors have been found to be relevant:

i. Management experience.

ii. Management qualification and knowledge.

iii. Past track record/creditworthiness.

iv. International scale operations/global presence.

v. Order book size.

vi. Geographic location.

vii. Third party contracts (outsourced).

Management Experience

Management experience is one of the most important factors that have a direct impact on the outcome of the project. Some of the features of a project it may affect would be like technological feasibility, timely completion of the project, foreseeing the possible hindrances in the project implementation and their ability to make suitable arrangement for same, their ability to address issues relating to concerns raised by lenders and other parties to the project, management experience in the projects of similar nature, better utilisation of resources, better financial management etc.

Management Qualification and Knowledge

The ability to understand, analyse, assess and make arrangements for contractual obligations, logistics, designs, technology and placement of foreseeable contracts (operation & management (O&M), insurance etc.) give the project a natural advantage for timely completion.

The strengths/weaknesses of the promoter/management are critical for any project during construction and operations phase.

Past Track Record

Past track record mainly reflects the performance of the company in past in various projects, in relation to defaults in payments, managing contractual obligations covering power purchase agreements (PPAs), fuel supply agreements (FSAs), fuel transport agreement (FTAs), ability to handle adverse situations, track record in dealing with banks/FIs, ability to fund cost overruns, timely completion of project, capability to handle similar scale/size/technology/vendor arrangements, project management services (PMS) and trained manpower availability.

International Scale Operations

Where the promoters developing the project have experience of carrying out the projects on international scale would reflect the ability of the developers to make use of latest technology in the project, draw on inputs from experts in various sectors/geographies, procure coal linkages, sources of cheaper funds, etc.

Order Book Size

It reflects the marketing ability of the company to bring the order as per the schedule and shows the good marketing skill.

Geographic Location of the Project

This would have a direct impact on the ability of the management to carry out the work as per schedule. Management experience with projects in similar or nearby geographic location would be an advantage for the developers—providing faster access to economies of scale, using the same labour, easier execution with government, faster clearances and similarly, having experience in carrying out projects in locations with difficult terrain or areas, which are politically disturbed, would again be an advantage.

Third Party Contracts (Outsourced Contracts)

This would affect the ability of the management to deal with the major contractors for the project, specially negotiating with them at the time of entering into the contracts. Apart from this, if the contractors in the project are the companies of the promoters itself, then this will be a direct reflection on the engineering capabilities of the promoter group and their experience in handling the project through engineering, procurement and construction (EPC) contractors, O&M contracts, traffic and toll management, etc.

Management Appraisal

The background, creditworthiness, track record and managerial/financial resourcefulness of the promoters and their past dealings with institutions/banks should be ascertained. A proper evaluation of management is key part of the overall appraisal of a project. Applications for assistance may be received either from first generation/new promoters for setting up a new project or from existing promoters for new project or for expansion/diversification/modernisation. In case of first generation/new promoters, the size of the project *vis-à-vis* resourcefulness of the promoters and other sources of funds should be thoroughly examined. An indicative checklist to facilitate management appraisal is given below:

Borrower and the Technical Feasibility

The technical feasibility study would include the following:

a. Process technology.

b. Technical know–how consultancy.

c. Size of the plant.

d. Plant and machinery.

e. Location.

f. Layout.

g. Raw material and other inputs.

h. Utilities.

i. Labour.

j. Effluent disposal/pollution control.

k. Project scheduling and monitoring.

l. Cost of project.

m. Cost of production.

Feasibility of Projections/Estimates in Terms of Cost, Sales and Profit

i. Profitability estimates, projected cash flow and balance sheet should be prepared both for the specific project(s) and for the concern as a whole. The projections should cover the entire duration of the loan. These financial projections should be scrutinised with reference to cost of project, means of financing thereof, and the underlying assumption relating to schedule of implantation, capacity utilisation, cost of production, administrative expenses, sales realisation, specific tax benefits, etc. If the assumptions are unrealistic, the projections should be suitably modified. Based on the projections, various ratios such as debt-equity ratio (DER), current ratio, fixed asset coverage ratio, gross profit, operating profit and net profit ratios, and debt service coverage ratio (DSCR) should be worked out and analysed to ensure whether they are satisfactory and conform to norms. The underlying assumptions for arriving at the projected profitability estimates should be examined carefully to avoid overstating or understating of the position.

ii. Company will participate in infrastructure financing for the purposes/activities of genuine commercial purpose. However, bank's participation in such type of long term financing will be on selective basis based on the viability of the project and considering the company's asset-liability position available with Risk Management Department and other parameters as under:

   a. Exposure as per company's internal prudential norms.

   b. The minimum DSCR and average DSCR for infrastructure project should not be less than 1.10:1 and 1.30:1 respectively, computed after the commercially operation date.

   c. The DER shall not exceed.

   d. The loan shall be sanctioned after proper risk mitigation evaluation process by way of appraisal with regard to technical feasibility and economic viability.

   e. The credential of foreign participants in the projects should be obtained from accredited agencies.

   f. The financial closure/funds tie up should be ensured before release of funds.

g. The moratorium period should not generally exceed three years.

h. In respect of projects that are undertaken by public sector units (PSUs), term loans may be sanctioned only for corporate entities (i.e. public sector undertakings registered under Companies Act or a corporation established under the relevant statute). Further, such term loans should not be in lieu of or to substitute budgetary resources envisaged for the project. The term loan could supplement the budgetary resources if such supplementing was contemplated in the project design. While such PSUs may include special purpose vehicles (SPVs) registered under the Companies Act particularly set up for financing infrastructure projects, it should be ensured that these loans/investments are not used for financing the budget support of the state governments. Whether such financing is done by way of extending loans or investing in bonds, the bank should undertake due diligence on the viability and bankability of such projects to ensure that revenue stream from the project is sufficient to take care of the debt servicing obligations and that the repayment/servicing of debt is not out of budgetary resources.

i. Banks/FIs may also lend to SPVs in the private sector, registered under Companies Act, for directly undertaking infrastructure projects, which are financially viable and not for acting as mere financial intermediaries.

j. A due diligence on the viability/bankability of such projects should be ensured to the effect that revenue stream from the project is sufficient to take care of the debt servicing obligations.

k. Projects undertaken by public sector entities, which are not corporate bodies (i.e. public sector undertakings that are not registered under Companies Act or that are not corporations established under the relevant statute) may not be financed by banks/FIs.

Cost of Project

The reasonableness of the cost of the project as submitted by the borrower should be thoroughly examined. Realistic estimates based on the industry trends and past similar projects comparisons should be used so as to conserve scare resources and prevent cost overruns.

The main components as well as the issues of the project cost are:

Land and Site Development

The cost of land must include conveyance charges and should be based on actual, as per the agreement with the vendors. Other costs to be examined are premium on leasehold, development charges, etc. The copy of sale/lease deed should be obtained and examined for ascertaining the sale consideration. The prevailing prices in nearby area could be obtained. Land Registration Department of the *panchayat*/village officer/corporations development expenses must include cost of leveling of land and laying of roads and gates etc. Assessment of land cost should include costs involved viz., roads, railway sidings, etc. For large projects there are other costs involved in selection of certain sites in terms of resettlement of displaced inhabitants. This should be accounted for in the project cost. Depending on the characteristics of the site in terms of soil quality, meteorological conditions, etc., there may be additional costs in terms of development expenditure.

Building and Civil Works

The cost of proposed building should include the cost of factory, administrative building, housing, civil work for effluent treatment plant, godowns, railway siding, boundary walls, garages, sewers, water tanks, drainage, architect/consultant fees, etc. The cost should be based on the architect's estimates. The rate (per sq m) of construction should be compared with the cost of like structures in case of similar projects. This may, however, vary depending on site conditions and other meteorological and geological factors.

While assessing the cost of civil works in respect of projects with a relatively shorter implementation period of up to one year, the current estimates with regard to various building materials as also construction charges could be used. In the case of projects with implementation schedules exceeding one year, the current cost estimates should be suitably adjusted for escalation during the period of implementation.

While assessing the cost of civil works, the following aspects might also be kept in view:

i. Adequacy/reasonableness of built-up area of various sections.

ii. Obtaining competitive bids for civil contracts with arms length relationship between parties concerned.

iii. Discouraging departmental execution of civil work.

iv. Adequate provision for housing in respect of projects located in remote/rural areas should be made in the project cost estimates.

Plant & Machinery

Estimates of plant & machinery should be based on quotations/purchase contracts entered into between the applicant and the suppliers. These contracts should have been finalised after obtaining competitive quotations from alternate suppliers and selection should be done not merely on the basis of price alone, but also technical evaluation, reputation of suppliers, delivery period, terms of payment, etc. For large sized projects, international competitive bidding procedure or limited competitive bidding procedure should be followed. The cost estimates should be scrutinised to ensure that erection and commissioning charges, taxes and duties, insurance, freight charges, etc., are included, and detailed break up thereof should be given. Provision should be made for foundation, installation, spares, electrical, piping, insulation needs, etc. Some of the main points to be noted in this regard are:

i. Wherever latest quotations with firm prices are available, the same (after due scrutiny) may be relied upon in the case of equipment and no further escalation in cost be provided.

ii. Where the quotation is not firm but escalation clause is provided in supply contracts, the cost of equipment might be worked out taking into account the impact of escalation clause.

iii. Where the quotations/prices are only indicative/budgetary, suitable escalation on account of inflation should be provided.

Technical Know-how and Engineering Fees

The reasonableness of technical know-how fees should be examined and the contract terms with the consultants/supplies of know-how should be scrutinised. Besides the main fees, the expenses for visiting technicians should be provided for, based on the agreement entered into between the company and the consultant/supplier of know-how.

Miscellaneous Fixed Assets

This would normally include furniture, office equipment, tools, vehicles, equipment for distribution of water, steam, power and lighting, laboratory and workshop equipment, effluent disposal plant, firefighting equipment, etc. It is necessary to ensure that all necessary items are reckoned in the cost estimation.

Preliminary and Preoperative Expenses

In the case of new concerns, preliminary expenses incurred by the promoters in connection with incorporation/formation of the concern and other related legal expenses may be reckoned in the cost estimates. The concern would need to incur certain essential expenses during the implementation period, *viz.*, capital issue expenses, expenses for raising equity, finance charges on borrowings during construction period, establishment expenses, guarantee commission, commitment charges/ front end fees, start-up expenses, security deposit with Electricity Boards for power connection, margin for bank guarantee, where applicable, under the Export Promotion Capital Goods Scheme, etc. Proper estimation and provision for such expenses should be ensured.

Contingencies

This is intended to provide for unforeseen expenses over and above the project cost estimates due to additions or increase in duties, taxes, transportation charges, minor project scope/design changes, etc. While there can be no hard and fast rule regarding the quantum to be provided, normally it should be 5 per cent of the firm costs and 10 per cent of the non-firm costs. The extent of provision will vary depending upon the extent of cost heads that remain untied and the period of project implementation.

Cost Comparison

In addition to the micro assessment of various aspects of the costs discussed above, it is necessary to compare the cost of the proposed project with costs of similar projects appraised in banks and FIs in the recent past to ensure the reasonableness of the cost estimates. However, it should be borne in mind that variations in scope of the project, implementation schedule, means of financing, etc., will have a bearing on the total cost of the project and suitable adjustments should be made while comparing with similar assisted projects.

Means of Financing

The proposed means of financing of a project proposal, as regard its reasonableness must similarly be examined. The means of financing should conform to a financially sound capital structuring of the company.

To meet the cost of project, the following means of finance are available.

i. Share capital.

ii. Term loans.

iii. Debenture capital.

iv. Deferred credit.

v. Incentive sources.

vi. Miscellaneous sources.

vii. Others

Share Capital

It is necessary to strike a proper mix between share capital (which is essentially the risk capital) and debt. The share capital envisaged should be reasonable and a realistic assessment should be made whether the same can be mobilised in the given economic/capital market environment during the implementation period within a reasonable period of time. The right mix of share capital to debt is a prudent.

The equity by the promoters is assessed and ensured that it is infused into the project by the following funds flow, observing the project before the commercial operation date (COD):

i. Equity from internal accruals

ii. Quasi-equity through structured products like sub-debt, partly convertible debentures (PCD), etc.

iii. Resource raising by private equity and strategic investors

iv. Initial public offering (IPOs) etc.

Term Loans

When the term loan is proposed to be sourced from different lenders, it should be ensured that the other expected sources of loans are properly tied up, since any gap in the means of financing will adversely affect the project. There are two broad types of term loans available in India—rupee term loans and foreign currency term loans. While the former are given for financing land, building, civil works, indigenous plant and machinery and so on, the latter are provided for meeting the foreign currency expenditure towards the import of equipment and technical know-how.

Debenture Capital

Debenture capital is convertible wholly or partly into equity shares. The conversion period and price is determined in advance. Whereas non-convertible debenture carries a fixed rate of interest and has a maturity period of 5-9 years.

Deferred Credit

Many times a supplier of the plant and machinery offer a deferred credit facility under which payment of purchase of the plant and machinery can be made over a period of time.

Incentive Sources

The government and its agencies may provide financial support as a capital subsidy or seed capital assistance at a nominal rate of interest to enable the company to meets its contribution to the projects.

Miscellaneous Sources

A small portion of the project finance may come from miscellaneous sources like unsecure loan, public deposit and leasing an hire purchase finance.

Others

At times government subsidy/grants are available for certain projects, the same will not be part of total project cost.

Conclusion

Pre-sanctioned credit process shall be done in accordance with the schemes designed and followed by the respective banks/FIs. It would follow due diligence on promoters and line of business and should be in accordance with the prudential guidelines. All proposals will be cleared by NBC (New Business Committee) as followed by banks/FIs giving in-principle approval for a detailed appraisal. At the time of appraising, asset classification of the group company, credit rating and management rating are to be looked into. The proposal shall be assessed on the basis of financial indicators, managerial efficiency and the group to which it belongs. In addition to obtaining market reports, obtaining search reports from CIBIL database regarding credit liability of the company/promoters has been made mandatory, forming an integral part of memorandum to be put up before the competent authority for consideration. While processing a credit proposal it is necessary that the credit risks involved be identified and incorporated in the appraisal note with possible mitigating factors. Thus pre-sanction exercise as suggested is to be carried out meticulously.

7 Financial Analysis

Financial Ratio Analysis

Analysis of financial data in terms of comparison of key financial ratios, movement of funds, structural ratios, etc., should be done to bring out a reasonably clear picture of the parent company's financial history and present position, indicating at the same time the likely future prospects. The debt-equity ratio (DER) will disclose if the company's capital structure is balanced or whether there is a any imbalance in the debt-equity gearing requiring correction/rectification.

In the infrastructure project lending, the financial ratio analysis is the commonly used tool for the financial analysis. Financial ratios assess and analyse the strengths and weaknesses of a given project with regard to such measures as liquidity, performance, profitability, leverage, and growth on an absolute basis and by comparison to other companies/projects in its industry or to an industry standard.

Financial Ratios

In case of an infrastructure project, following ratios are usually considered.

Profitability Ratios

Profitability ratios measure the ability of a company to generate returns for its shareholders. Profitability ratios also measure financial performance and management strength.

Profitability ratios can be calculated on three bases:

Profitability Ratio

On Sales:	On Assets:	On Net Worth:
– Operating profit margin	– Return on total assets	– Return on net worth
– Net profit margin	– Return on capital employed	– Dividend yield
		– Earnings per share

In infrastructure lending, asset based profitability ratio is counted. Here return on capital employed (ROCE) shows the profitability on assets (or capital) employed within the business that is financed from the long term sources. Capital employed does not include the investments made outside the business in shares and other securities.

Rate of Return Ratios

Since the capital structure of most companies includes both debt capital and equity capital, it is important to measure the return to each of the capital providers.

i. Return on net worth = Net income/Average (common stockholder's equity + reserves and surplus)

   This ratio measures the after-tax return on investment to the equity capital providers of the company.

ii. Return on capital employed = [Net income + Interest (1-tax rate)]/Average (stockholder's equity + long-term debt)

   This ratio measures the return to all capital providers of the company. Interest (net of tax) is added back since it also involves a return to debt capital providers.

iii. Return on total assets = [Net income + Interest (1-tax rate)]/ Average total assets

   This ratio measures the return on the assets employed in the business. In effect, it measures management's performance in the utilisation of the company's asset base.

Solvency Ratio

This ratio provides a measure of a company's ability to service debts, expressed as a percentage. A high solvency ratio indicates a healthy company, while a low ratio indicates the opposite. A low solvency ratio further indicates likelihood of default. Different industries have different standards as to what qualifies as an acceptable solvency ratio, but in general, a ratio of 20 per cent or higher is considered healthy.

It provides a measurement of how likely a company can continue to meet its debt obligations. The measure is calculated as shown here:

DER = Long-term debt/Shareholders' equity

DER is the ratio that remains after liability divided by equity from all the shareholders. Another way to understand DER is—it's the amount that is owed divided by what is owned. The lower the number, the more attractive the investment.

Annual Coverage Tests

Three financial ratios are widely used to measure a project's ability to service its debt:

Interest Coverage Ratio

The interest coverage ratio, expressed as:

$$\text{Interest coverage} = \frac{\text{Profit before tax (PBT)} + \text{Depreciation} + \text{Interest}}{\text{Interest}}$$

It measures the project's ability to cover interest charges. It equals earnings before interest and taxes (EBIT), or the amount of funds available to pay interest, divided by interest charges. Interest charges represent interest that must be paid in cash, whether or not it is capitalised for accounting purposes. An interest coverage ratio below one would indicate that a project cannot cover its interest charges fully out of operating income. An interest coverage ratio below one for the first few years of project operations would indicate that the project will be incapable of supporting the level of borrowings planned for it. Because of uncertainty regarding future income and cash flow, lenders typically set a threshold greater than one.

Debt Service Coverage Ratio (DSCR)

The DSCR accounts for all debt service payment obligations. It is expressed as:

$$\text{DSCR} = \frac{\text{Profit after tax (PAT)} + \text{Depreciation and amortisation} + \text{Interest on term loan}}{\text{Repayment of term loan} + \text{Interest of term loan}}$$

The average DSCR is computed by taking the total of all values of the numerator and denominator for the entire period of the proposed term loans, commencing from the year in which commercial production starts and not by taking the DSCR for each year. When debt service coverage falls below one, the project cannot fully service its debt out of project cash flow and will have to borrow funds or seek equity contributions to obtain funds to cover the shortfall. The DSCR is particularly useful in designing the amortization schedule for project debt.

Cash Flow Available for Debt Service

This ratio, expressed as:

$$\frac{\text{Cash flow from operations}}{\dfrac{\text{Interest} + \text{Principal repayments}}{(1-\text{ Tax rate})}}$$

indicates the project's ability to cover debt obligations along with interest charges. It equals cash flow from operations available to pay interest and debt repayment, divided by interest charges along with principal repayments. The method for calculation along with the interpretation of the ratio is similar to that of DSCR.

Estimating the Borrowing Capacity of a Project

The borrowing capacity of a project is defined as the amount of debt the project can fully service during the loan repayment period. This period is determined by such factors as the bank lenders' general lending policies, the risk characteristics of the project, and the state of the market for bank loans as well as other considerations.

Banks/financial institutions (FIs) to a project typically estimate the borrowing capacity of a project by testing the ability of the project entity to meet its debt service payment obligations year by year. In particular, project lenders are generally willing to lend an amount that does not exceed some specified fraction of the stream of cash flow expected to be available for debt service during the loan repayment period. They also establish certain coverage benchmarks that must be satisfied.

Loan Repayment Parameters

Bank lenders to discrete, stand-alone projects are seldom willing to lend for periods that exceed 10 years from the date the project is completed. Exceptions to this policy do exist, for example, lenders to infrastructure projects, which are typically long-lived, will lend for longer periods. Sponsors of infrastructure projects have been able at times to arrange bank loan facilities that provide for a scheduled final loan repayment of 12 years from completion of construction. As a general rule, project financings are structured so that the project borrowing entity's leverage is consistent with BBB credit quality.

Financial Appraisal of the Project: NPV and IRR Calculations

Projects typically involve the purchase of capital assets—long-lived tangible assets such as land, plant and machinery. When considering a proposed project that would involve investing in capital assets, the sponsors should evaluate the expected future cash flows in relation to the amount of the initial investment.

Discounted cash flow techniques are available to facilitate the evaluation process. The objective is to find projects that are worth more to the sponsors than they cost—projects that have a positive net present value (NPV). A sponsor's evaluation of a proposed project is not unlike an individual's investment decision. The steps are the same:

i. Estimate the expected future cash flows from the project. This is like estimating the coupon payments for a bond or the dividend stream for a stock, and a maturity value or terminal sale price.

ii. Assess the risk and determine a required rate of return (cost of capital) for discounting the expected future cash flows.

iii. Compute the present value of the expected future cash flows.

iv. Determine the cost of the project and compare it to what the project is worth. If the project is worth more than it costs—if it has a positive NPV—it is worth undertaking.

Weighted Average Cost of Capital (WACC)

It is the most important input to present value analysis as it is used as the 'discount rate' or the 'required rate of return' while calculating the financial viability of the project. WACC is used as the discounting rate in calculating the NPV of the project.

$$WACC = \left[\frac{E}{E+D} * Re\right] + \left[\frac{D}{E+D} * Rd * (1-T)\right]$$

Where:

E = Market value of equity

D = Company's debt

Re = Required rate of return on equity

Rd = Required rate of return on equity on debt

T = Effective tax rate (as debt interest is tax deductible)

NPV Analysis

The NPV of a project is the difference between what the project costs and what it is worth. The best we can do in advance is to estimate a project's NPV. We will not know its true market value or what it is really worth, until the project is completed and the returns are collected.

The Procedure

The NPV of a capital investment project is the present value of all of the after-tax cash flows (CF) connected with the project—all its costs and revenues, now and in the future:

$$NPV = CF_0 + CF_1/(1+r) + CF_2/(1+r)^2 + \ldots + CF_n/(1+r)^n$$

Where

CF_0 = cash out flow at inception

CF_1 = cash flow at end of year 1, and so on

r = cost of capital

The decision rule to follow when applying NPV is: undertake the capital investment project if the NPV is positive.

We estimate the value of a project by using discounted cash flow (DCF) analysis and computing the present value of all the cash flows connected with ownership. This procedure is similar to discounting the interest payments on a bond or dividends on a stock, and it is the essence of the NPV method.

Internal Rate of Return Analysis (IRR)

IRR of a project is a discount rate, which makes its NPV equal to zero. It is the discount rate that equates the present values of future cash flows with the initial investment.

$$NPV = CF_0 + CF_1/(1+r) + CF_2/(1+r)^2 + \ldots + CF_n/(1+r)^n$$

IRR is the cost of capital, i.e., value of r, at which NPV = 0

A project is viable if IRR for the project exceeds the cost of the capital.

Cash Flows

The estimates of cash flows are a key element in infrastructure projects involving numerous variables. They should be based on a set of consistent economy assumptions. Generally in capital budgeting we look at the cash flows to all investors (equity share holders as well as lenders) and apply the weighted average cost of the company. A project can, of course, be viewed from other points of view like the equity point of view, long term funds point of view and total funds point of view. Obviously the project cash flow structure will vary with the point of view adopted. Banks/FIs look at the project from the point of view of all investors. The Planning Commission suggests that a project may be viewed from the point of view of equity capital or long-term funds.

Statement of Cash Flows Reports

Cash inflows and outflows based on the company's operating activities, investing activities and financing activities is discussed herewith.

Cash Flow from Operating Activities

It shows impact of transactions not defined as investing or financing activities. These cash flows are generally the cash effects of transactions that enter into the determination of the net income.

Cash Inflows

i. From sales of goods and services.

ii. From interest and dividend income.

Cash Outflows

i. To pay suppliers for inventory.

ii. To pay employees for services.

iii. To pay lenders (interests).

iv. To pay government for taxes.

v. To pay other suppliers for other operating expenses..

Cash Flow from Investing Activities

Cash Inflows

i. From sale of fixed assets (property, plant, equipment).

ii. From intangible assets.

iii. From sale of debt or equity securities.(Other than common equity) of others entities.

Cash Flow from Financing Activities

Cash Inflows

i. From borrowing.

ii. From the sale of the company's own equity securities.

Cash Outflows

i. To repay amounts borrowed.

ii. To repurchase the company's own equity securities.

iii. To pay shareholders dividends.

Computation of Cash Flow Adequacy

Indirect Method: Statement of Cash Flows

i. Cash flows from operating activities:

   a. Net income/depreciation/decrease, accounts receivable/ increase, inventories/increase accumulated/tax prepay.

   b. Net cash provided (used) by operating activities.

ii. Cash flow from investing activities:

   a. Additions to fixed assets.

   b. Net cash provided (used) by investing activities.

iii. Cash flow from financing activities:

   a. Increase in notes payable/increase, long term debt/dividends paid.

   b. Net cash provided (used) by financing activities.

Direct Method: Statement of Cash Flows

i. Cash flows from operating activities:

   a. Cash received from customers/cash paid to suppliers and employees/interest paid/taxes paid.

   b. Net cash provided (used) by operating activities

ii. Cash flow from investing activities:

   a. Additions to fixed assets.

   b. Net cash provided (used) by investing activities.

iii. Cash flow from financing activities:

   a. Decrease, notes payable/increase, long terms debt/dividends paid.

   b. Net cash provided (used)by financing activities.

Thus, cash flow adequacy is computed as:

$$\frac{\text{Cash flows from operations}}{\text{Fixed asset purchased + Long term debt paid + Cash dividends distributed}}$$

Sensitivity Analysis

While appraising a project the critical parameters of risks shall be identified and expressed in terms of quantifiable variables such as price, cost, capacity utilisation, etc. Thereafter, the financial projections should be subjected to sensitivity analysis and the projects viability in such adverse scenarios should be assessed. Thus, sensitivity analysis indicates the sensitivity of the criterion of the merit (NPV, IRR or any other) to variations in basic factors. Banks/FIs carry out this analysis to assess the impact of adverse changes in the operating conditions of the project on its viability. The standard sensitivity involves assessing the impact of 10 per cent adverse variation in selling price, quantity and operating costs on IRR, DSCR and BEP (break-even point).

Examples of Financial Viability

Some examples of financial viability are discussed below:

Project cost = 100; Debt-equity ratio = 3:1; For a private limited company with no capital subsidy, Promoter's contribution (equity) = 25% and Debt = 75%.

Example 1:

– If capital subsidy is 10%, promoter's equity is 15%.

• Equity	
– Promoter's contribution	15
– Capital subsidy	10
Total	25
• Debt	75
Project cost	100

Example 2:

- Promoter's contribution drops to 15%.
- If DER falls or capital subsidy is reduced, promoter's contribution increases, which may necessitate public issues.
- Public issue = 60%, Promoter's equity = 40%

• Equity	
– Promoter's contribution	10
– Public issue	15
Total equity	25
• Debt	75
Project cost	100

Example 3:

- Promoter's contribution drops to 10%.
- Minimum promoter's contribution = 15%

• Equity	
– Promoter's contribution	10
– Public issue	15
Total equity	25
• Debt	
– Unsecured loan arranged by promoter	5
– Term loan	70
Total debt	75
Project cost	100

Example 4:

- Promoter's contribution = Promoter's equity + Unsecured loan arranged by promoter = 10 + 5 =15; Promoter's contribution = 15%
- DER = 70:30=2.33:1<3:1

– Public issue = 40%, Promoter's equity = 60%

• Equity	
– Promoter's contribution	10
– FI's contribution	5
– Public issue	10
Total equity	25
• Debt	75
Project cost	100

Example of Economic Feasibility

Investment = 100, DER = 60:40

Useful life = 2 years, $C_1=C_2=34.48$

$CF_1=48$, $CF_2=74$, Tax rate = 0.30

Risk free rate of return $(r_f) = 0.08$, market rate of return $(r_m) = 0.2$, sensitivity to market risk $(\beta) = 1$

Cost of debt:

$$60 = \frac{34.48}{(1+r_d)} + \frac{34.48}{(1+r_d)^2} \Rightarrow r_d = 0.1 \text{ or } 10\%$$

Cost of equity:

$$r_e = 0.08 + 1(0.2-0.08) = 0.2 \text{ or } 20\%$$

Weighted average cost of capital (WACC) = 0.6 x (1-0.3) x 0.1+0.4 x 0.2 = 0.122

or 12.2%

Therefore

$$\text{NPV at } 12.2\% = \frac{48}{(1+0.122)} + \frac{74}{(1+0.122)^2} - 100$$

$$= 101.56-100 = 1.56>0$$

Since NPV>0, the project is economically viable.

Internal Rate of Return (IRR)

Considering the previous example, IRR can be obtained by solving the following equation:

$$\sum_{t=1}^{n} \frac{CF_t}{(1+IRR)^t} - I = 0$$

Thus, IRR = 13.3%

Since IRR>WACC, the project is viable.

- NPV and IRR may lead to contradictory decisions depending on the size and cash flows of projects.
- Considering the previous example, if CF_1=113.5 and CF_2=0 for an alternative way of operation, NPV=1.16 and IRR=13.5%.
- For size differential, NPV is a better rule since it adds more wealth.
- For cash flow differential also, NPV makes more realistic reinvestment assumptions.

Social Rate of Discount and Economic Rate of Return (ERR)

ERR is the rate of return when the present value (PV) of all social benefits equals the PV of all social costs. Discrepancies between social valuations and market valuations occur due to:

i. Price distortions.
ii. Administered/regulated pricing.
iii. Taxes and duties.
iv. Foreign exchange regulations.
v. Monopolistic status of the company, etc.

Social valuations should reflect opportunity costs of resources, i.e., the valuations of foregone economic outputs. Taxes and duties are passed on to the government. Since they do not consume resources, they cost nothing to the society. Hence, their inclusions give rise to price aberrations.

Based on the previous example of economic feasibility:

	Year		
	0	1	2
Capital cost			
Land	8	-	-
Plant and machinery	80	10	-
Duties/taxes	6	4	-
Others	6	6	-
Total	100	20	-
Operating cost	-	82	126
Total cost	100	102	126
Revenue	-	150	200
Cash flow	-100	48	74

Considering social valuations

- Agricultural land. The PV of the agricultural outputs during the project's useful life is, say, 5.
- Plant and machinery are imported. Say about 20 per cent of their costs is accounted for by import duties, which must be deducted.
- Duties/taxes should be removed.

The following table shows social costs, social benefits and resultant cash flows.

	Year		
	0	1	2
Capital cost			
Land	5	-	-
Plant and machinery	64	8	-
Duties/taxes	-	-	-
Others	6	6	-
Total	75	14	-
Operating cost	-	82	126
Total cost	75	96	126
Revenue	-	150	200
Cash flow	-75	54	74

Considering a social rate of discount, 12%

- NPV at 12%$=54/1.12+74/(1.12)^2-75=32.2$
- ERR = 40.5%

Since NPV>0 and ERR>Social rate of discount, the project is socially desirable.

- If it is an import substitution project and the imported output would have cost more to the society, the project would be more socially desirable.
- Suppose now that the project company is a monopolist, charging 15% more than the economic worth of the output.
- Then social benefits in year 1 and year 2 should be 150/1.15 and 200/1.15 or 130 and 174, respectively.
- Also cash flows in year 1 and year 2 would become 34 and 48, respectively.
- Therefore, NPV at 12% = $34/1.12+48/(1.12)^2-75 = -6.4$
- ERR = 5.8%

Since NPV<0 and ERR<Social rate of discount, the project is not socially viable. Hence, a project which is otherwise viable may not be desirable from the social point of view.

8 Credit Rating

Introduction

All accounts with the banks/financial institutions (FIs) under infrastructure lending need to be rated in terms of guidelines of Reserve Bank of India (RBI).

Banks/FI's virtually originate loans on the basis of credit rating, if not done externally by the accredited credit rating agencies than internally by their own risk departments. They charge an interest rate over a base rate/ bench mark rate that primarily depends upon credit rating plus other related factors. They use credit rating to measure the quality of loan that they sell on to other institutions and to monitor the portion they retain. Credit ratings are indeed highly correlated with yields/returns, therefore they are done in an orderly way to insure that no element is overlooked.

The credit module adopted by banks/FIs for infrastructure accounts takes into consideration following relevant factors grouped under three heads:

Management

Following relevant factors would be taken into consideration:

i. Integrity/commitment.

ii. Financial strength.

iii. Technical/finance knowledge.

iv. Organisational structure/succession plan.

v. Selling and distribution network.

vi. Experience of directors and promoters.

vii. Pending litigations.

viii. Market reputation and past track record.

Project Financial Evolution

i. Project debt equity ratio (DER).

ii. Timing of capital infusion.

iii. Cash flow from other sources.

Project Rating Index (PRI)

Assessment on management should be based on market and banker's report, willingness to offer securities to secure banks/FIs loan, commitment of the management towards project and management's track record in honouring its commitment in the past. A qualitative view on the management should be taken on the attributes mentioned above and the management can be categorised as good, average or excellent.

Banks/FIs' comfort in project finance comes from the promoter's stakes in the project. Where the stake of the promoter is higher, the comfort level is also higher. Secondly, timing of owners' capital infusion also adds to the comforts of banks/FIs. Where promoters bring in their share in the project upfront, banks/FIs' comfort is more as compared to the situation where the promoter brings in funds in equitable proportion. It is also observed—where a project is not entirely on stand alone basis, repayment of interest and principal would also come, in addition to the cash flow generated by the project undertaken, from the cash flow generated by the existing installation. To this stand, a project on a stand alone basis is more risky as compared to a project that is an expansion of an existing project.

Business units may have different strengths *vis-à-vis* industry specific attributes. In view of this, in case of project finance, repayable over a longer period, PRI is estimated and factored into in lieu of simply incorporating industry rating agency. Based on the environment and industry analysis, 7 to 10 factors may be identified that are most likely to impact the success probability of the project under evaluation. These are called critical success factors (CSFs) or indicators for industry attractiveness. An illustrative list of such factors is given below:

i Market size.

ii. Market growth rate.

iii. Cyclicality.

iii. Competitive structure.
iv. Barriers to entry.
v. Industry profitability.
vi. Technology.
vii. Inflation.
viii. Regulation.
ix. Work force availability.
x. Social issues.
xi. Environmental issues.
xii. Political issues.
xiii. Legal issues.

Strategic group and borrower analysis have also been taken into consideration, indicating the strengths and weaknesses, and the core competencies of the borrower group in relation to CSFs identified for the project. The capacity of the borrower group to respond to changes in the environmental and industry characteristics would be a critical input. The PRI may change as the external factor changes. It may also change as a group's strengths or weaknesses undergo changes due to proactive approaches by them or due to lack of it. The above analysis, it may be noted, is an approach to objective measurement, which is akin to strengths, weaknesses, opportunities and threats (SWOT) analysis that are carried out. Strengths and weaknesses are internal to the organisation whereas threats and opportunities are external to the organisation and are captured under the environmental and industry analysis. Accordingly, the PRI would be factored in the PRI model.

Credit Rating Followed

Assessment of a project is done by an analyst in the developmental, construction or operational stage. Selection of stage to be scored is based on the status of the project. Figure 8.1 explains the concept of obtaining three levels of ratings.

Figure 8.1

Rating Methodology

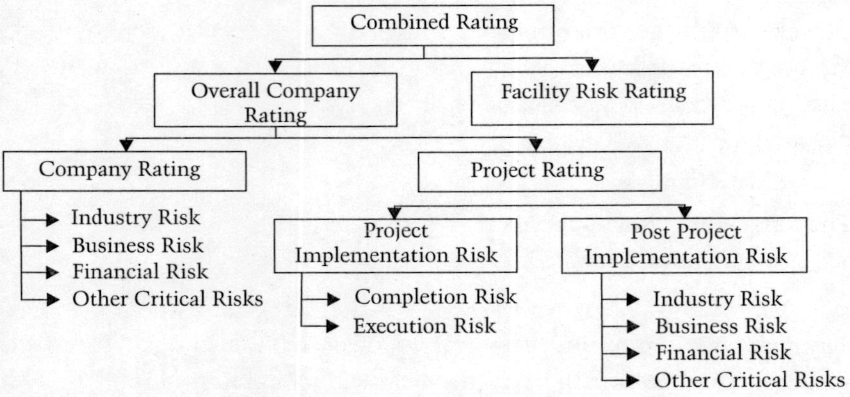

i. Overall company rating (interim rating) reflects the probability of default (PD) of the borrower.

ii. Facility risk rating reflects the loss given default (LGD) of the transaction (secured as well as unsecured portion).

iii. The combination of PD and LGDs gives the expected loss (EL), which is eventually reflected in the combined rating grade.

Rating Analysis

The proposal 'credit risk rating analysis' is done broadly on objectivity and subjectivity based on the various parameters, judgements, and industry trends and movements in the following:

i. Sector policies on a continuous basis

ii. Sector latest regulation on a continuous basis

iii. Banking regulations and norms

iv. Project financial and capital structuring

v. Project assumptions, reasonability and sensitivity

vi. Project location and demography

vii. Execution capabilities and overall financial and operational ratios and indices

Facility Risk Rating (FRR)

The obligor rating (interim rating) for all the projects in build phase is obtained by making use of the risk assessment management (RAM) model. However, the other important step involves providing the FRR based on the project's security and valuation in the final loan agreement to all the existing proposals to finalise the entire interim rated portfolio and arrive at the combined final rating.

FIs and banks will also undertake the FRR of all the interim proposals. The implementation of above step helps to arrive at not only PD estimates, but also LGD and EL analysis.

Banks/FIs (non-banking financial institutions (NBFC)-Infrastructure Finance Corporation (IFC)) shall follow prudential guidelines of RBI applicable to NBFC-IFC and shall confirm to the risk weighted as per the ratings assigned by the rating agency registered with the Securities and Exchange Board of India (SEBI) and accredited by RBI. The following table indicates the applicable risk weights:

Domestic rating agencies	AAA	AA	A	BBB	BB and Below	Unrated
Risk Weight (per cent)	20	30	50	100	150	100

The comparative chart in terms on internal and external rating is given below:

Internal rating grade	*Description*	*Equivalent external rating***
Grade 1	Investment grade – Highest safety	AAA
Grade 2 and 3	Investment grade – High safety	AA
Grade 4	Investment grade –Adequate safety	A
Grade 5	Investment grade – Moderate safety	BBB
Grade 6 and 7	Investment grade – Minimum safety	BB
Grade 8, 9 and 10	Do not Lend	Below BB

Note: ** The application of '+' (plus) or '-'(minus) signs associated with the rating category would have the same risk weights as prescribed by the norms.

The banks/FIs shall follow the lower credit rating in case of a conflict between the external rating agency and internal rating. Further to note that once the account is rated by the external rating agency, its tenor will, as per RBI guidelines, be 15 months. Banks and FIs will follow the RBI guidelines, which stipulate that the rating agency should have reviewed the rating at least once during the previous 15 months.

Revision of Credit Rating

The external rating agency follows a very structured system to review the rating of the existing account. For example, the rating revision of the road toll project takes into account the constraint liquidity position on account of lower than the projected toll collection (if happened so), given lower than anticipated traffic on the project stretch. Consequently, timely debt servicing has been maintained by funding support received from the promoter. Further, the rating continues to factor in the sensitivity of the project to growth rates in traffic levels, adverse movement in interest rates and wholesale price index (WPI). However, the rating is supported by commencement of commercial operations (following declaration of provisional commercial operation albeit with a delay), which eliminates the execution risk, attractiveness of the project given the high traffic density on the route and low threat from alternate/competing routes. Going forward actual toll collection and timely debt servicing by the company would remain key sensitivity factors.

External Rating of Borrower Accounts with Exposures

As per the existing guidelines of RBI on implementation of the new capital adequacy framework dated July 1, 2008, all the corporate borrowal accounts with aggregate exposures (Fund based (FB) + Non-fund based (NFB)) exceeding Rs 50 crore are to be assigned risk weights as per their external rating by approved credit rating agencies (ICRA, CARE, CRISIL, FITCH) for FY 2008-09. In case these corporate borrowals remain unrated, it will attract risk weights of 150 per cent. However, with effect from 1st April, 2009 all fresh sanctions or renewals with exposure (FB+NFB) exceeding Rs 10 crore have to be externally rated. As a temporary measure, the risk weight on unrated claims has been reduced from 150 per cent to 100 per cent by RBI due to recession and slowdown in the economy, but it may be increased to 150 per cent later on. Accordingly the exposure will have to be priced for factoring in the higher risk weight as well as higher capital requirement.

9 Risk and Pricing

Infrastructure lending involves a number of risks. Hence, banks/financial institutions (FIs) should have comprehensive risks scoring/rating systems that serve as a single point indicator of diverse risk factors and for taking credit decisions in a consistent manner. To facilitate this, a substantial degree of standardisation is required in rating across the companies. The risk rating system should be drawn up in a structured manner incorporating *inter alia* financial analysis, projections, sensitivity, industrial and management risks. The overall score for risk is to be placed between 1-6, 1-8, etc., on the basis of credit quality. For each numerical category, a quantitative definition of the borrower, the loans underlying quality and an analytical representation of the underlying financials of the company should be presented. Further, as a prudent risk management policy, each lender should prescribe the minimum rating below which no exposure would be undertaken. Any flexibility in the minimum standards and conditions for relaxation and authority therefore should be clearly articulated in the credit policies of their respective lenders.

The credit risk assessment exercise should be repeated as per periodicity fixed by the banks/FIs. It involves setting risk limits based on economic risk measures of risk and simultaneously ensuring best risk adjusted return keeping in view capital constraint. It is a question of banks/FIs' policy in balancing risks, return and capital. Variations in the rating of the company overtime indicate changes in credit quality and expected loan losses from the credit portfolios. Banks/FIs should undertake comprehensive study on migration (upward-lower to higher and downward-higher to lower) of borrowers in the rating to add accuracy in expected loan loss calculations.

Identification of various risks in the project in a more granular basis shall form a part of score approach for assessing risk which shall be undertaken by the banks/FIs. This calls for establishment of necessary and accurate management information system (MIS) that is needed to assess and manage banks/FIs' risk which is shared with market also. This exercise has a direct bearing on goals of credit quality, earnings and growth.

Risk Management Steps

- Identification of risks.
- Assessment of risks.
- Management of risks.

Identification of Risks

- Sources of risks:
  - Internal.
  - External.
- Identification techniques:
  - Documentation.
  - Process flowcharts.
  - Brainstorming.
  - Cause and effect/Fishbone diagram.

Cause and Effect Diagram

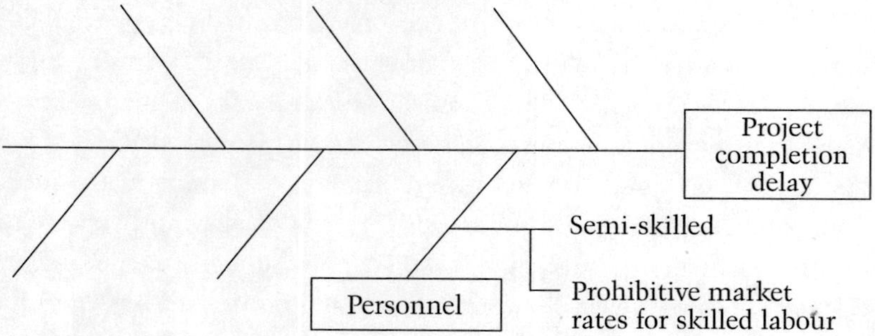

Assessment of Risks

- Probability/chance of occurrence:
  - Objective/subjective.

- Expected time of occurrence.
- Detection difficulty.
- Impact on project time, cost and performance:
  - Affected activities/other projects.
  - Outcomes and magnitude/severity.
- Objective and subjective.

Case Study

Project: Conversion of MS Office 97 into MS Office 2000 XP

Risk Event	*Likelihood*	*Impact*	*Detection Difficulty*	*When*
Interface problems	4	4	4	Conversion
System freezing	2	5	5	Start-up
User backlash	4	3	3	Post-installation
Hardware malfunction	1	5	5	Installation

Risk Severity Matrix

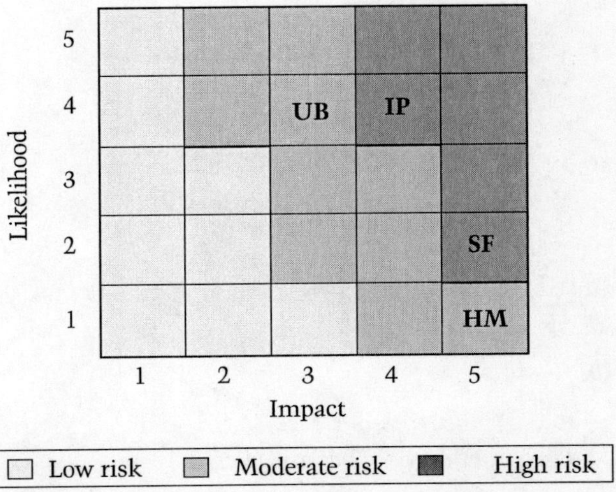

Note: Ratings on a scale of 1-5, where '1' is 'very low' and '5' is 'very high'

Risk value = Likelihood x Impact x Detection difficulty

Management of Risks

- Avoid risks.
- Reduce risks.
- Transfer risks.
- Contingency planning.
- Accept risks.

Case Study

Investment: \$100 m, Risk impact: \$10 m

Option 1: Do nothing ⇒ \$100 m — 0.6 → \$10 m; 0.4 → Expected cost: \$106 m

Option 2: Invest \$1 m ⇒ \$101 m — 0.4 → \$10 m; 0.6 → Expected cost: \$105 m

Option 3: Invest \$2 m ⇒ \$102 m — 0.2 → \$10 m; 0.8 → Expected cost: \$104 m

Choose Option 3: Invest \$2 m

Risk Profile

Each project has different risk profile, and magnitude of risks differs from project to project. Risk normally taken into consideration by banks/FIs are:

i. Construction risk: This is referred to as completion, development and cost overrun.

   Mitigants

   - Fixed price-fixed time Engineering, Procurement and Construction (EPC) contract.
   - Performance bonds, defects liability period.
   - Lenders' engineer study.
   - Equity stake of contractor.

- Sponsor support.
- Insurance.

ii. Sponsor risk: Sponsors risk is closely associated with construction risk/completion risk. It may be broken down into two elements:

a. Equity commitment.

b. Corporate strength.

Mitigants

- Balance sheet analysis.
- Track record.
- Credit references, market feedback.
- Minimum level of equity stake, upfront equity.
- Bank guarantees/Undertaking for equity contribution.
- Step-in rights, pledge of shares.

iii. Operating risk: It consists of three components:

a. Technical.

b. Management.

c. Cost.

Mitigants

- Known and proven technology preferred.
- Quality/Quantity assurances through warranties.
- Annual maintenance contract (AMCs) from equipment suppliers.
- Lenders' engineer report.
- Operation and maintenance (O&M) contracts.
- Maintenance reserve creation, debt service coverage ratio (DSCR) post reserve.
- Sensitivity analysis.

The ability to achieve the desired level of affordable infrastructure service depends on the optimum utilisation of technology to be used, management quality, project execution and cost of production by minimising the following risks:

   i. Technology risk.
   ii. Management risk.
   iii. Cost risk component.
   iv. Supply risk.
   v. Environmental risk.
   vi. Force majeure (FM) risk.
   vii. Interest rate risk.
   viii. Legal risk.

iv. Promoter risk: Depends upon:
   a. Experience of the lead sponsor of the project, its financial capabilities, project management skills, etc.
   b. Promoter commitment (capital to be infused) in the project. More the commitment, lower the risk.
   c. Syndicated cost as a proportion of approved cost (less the better). In case of private projects, general trend in the market like cost base projects etc., should be considered.

v. Regulatory and policy risk: Depends upon:
   a. The government policy applicable for an industry during each stage of the project.
   b. Relationship between the Centre and the state, availability of state support agreements, favourable public private partnership (PPP) laws and presence of a PPP cell (for effective monitoring and control).

vi. Financial risk: Depends upon:
   a. Project debt-equity ratio (DER) as well as total outside liability (TOL)/tangible net worth (TNW).

b. Reasonability of project assumptions, project ratios (like DSCR, DER, Project internal rate of return (IRR), fixed asset coverage ratio, etc.).

c. Sensitivity to project revenue and project cost (lower the sensitivity, lower the risk), break-even period and the remaining concession period after the break-even.

d. Degree of exposure to interest rate and exchange rate risk.

e. Terms of payments in years.

vii. Completion/execution/maintenance/operation risk: Depends upon:

a. Financial closure/tying up of funds, flexibility of the promoters to raise additional resources.

b. The number of clearances obtained by the projects, the relevance of those clearances and the expected hurdles in obtaining the remaining clearances, if any.

c. Construction period (more the construction period, greater the risk).

d. Land acquisition: This is the single most critical factor that could delay any project. However, due importance should be given to sponsor who could aid the speedy process of land acquisition.

e. Transparency in the bidding process—both tariff based and bidding process—leads to better pricing of the project.

f. Reputation of the design consultant to have an idea of the quality of the design done.

g. Technology proposed to be used for the project. Additionally, the technology risk can also be assessed by identifying the strengths/ weaknesses/reputation of the consultant/sponsor engaged for the design of the project.

h. Contractors' (EPC and O&M) creditworthiness (as construction involves high risk and possibility of losses to the contractors, slippage from commitments, etc.) and its experience in the projects of similar nature.

i. Safeguards in the contracts available for the lenders.

j. The reputation, capability, past track record and credibility of the O&M contractor.

k. Operating efficiency: Various factors like efficiency in toll collections in roads; plant load factors (PLF), fuel risk, etc., for power sector; pricing ability impacting aeronautical revenue for airports; and labor productivity, average ship turnaround, berth throughput, etc., for ports; etc.

l. External risk: Presence of any competitive/alternate routes/ports etc. In case of roads, the feeder roads or connection roads that may have to be linked to the project road so as to enable commercial operation of the road form a key external risk to the project. This risk can be mitigated if the control over construction of such roads is with the project sponsors.

viii. Business risk: For various sectors, depends upon:

a. Demand and supply risk, counterparty risk (creditworthiness), pricing ability, appropriateness of pricing and general willingness of the users to pay, competition, demand and supply position, location of the project, potential for supplemental revenue, offtake risk, environmental/social impact, etc.

b. In respect of loans and advances to borrowers, who are not covered by the credit risk assessment (CRA) system, changes in rates of interest will be advised periodically.

Various Risk Factors and Mitigants

Power Projects

Type of Risk	*Allocated to*	*Mitigation Measures*
Pre-construction Delay Risk		
Finalisation of key contracts	Project company	Signing of all key contracts to be made a condition precedent.
Approvals and permits	Project company/ Promoters	Obtaining all approvals and clearances to be made a condition precedent.
Construction Risk		
Land availability	Project company	Signing of land lease agreement to be made a pre-commitment condition.
Cost overrun	Project company/EPC contractor/Promoters	Fixed price turnkey contracts on a completed cost basis, risk on non-EPC cost to be borne by project company/Promoters.
Time overrun	Project company/EPC contractor/Promoters	Liquidated damages (LDs) for non-completion of EPC contracts.
Delay in transmission agreements	Project company/ Offtaker	Entering into suitable contract made as pre-disbursement condition.
Damage/Construction	Project company/ EPC contractor/ Insurance company	Commercial insurance coverage sought for all associated risks.
Operational Risk		
Equipment underperformance	EPC contractor/ Equipment supplier/ Project company	Reputed EPC contractor, equipment vendor, experienced power plant sponsor.
Environmental requirements	EPC contractor/ Equipment supplier/ Project company	Clearance from Ministry of Environment and Forest (MoEF) required.
Fuel supply risk	Fuel supplier/ Project company	Fuel supply agreement for committed supply of fuel, LDs in case of short supply of fuel.
Fuel price risk	Fuel supplier/ Project company	Fuel supply agreement for longer tenor with renewal option. Price fixed during initial agreement period with provision for price increase linked to reputed price benchmark.

contd...

...contd...

		In case of imported fuel, proper arrangement to cover currency exchange risk.
Fuel transportation risk	Fuel supplier/transporter/ Project company	Fuel transportation agreement with predetermined freight rate with provisions for periodical increases. In case of imported fuel, arrangement for port facility should be tied up.
Evacuation risk	Offtaker	Payment of deemed generation charges by the offtaker in case it is unable to evacuate power.
Payment risk	Power offtaker/ Project company	Credit enhancement mechanism like letter of credit (LC), Escrow, etc.
FM risk	EPC contractor/ Project company/Insurer	Covered by suitable insurance arrangements.
Equity infusion risk	Promoters	Higher upfront equity infusion by the promoters before debt drawdown. Tie-up of entire equity required for the project and set timeframe for bringing the same. Balance to be brought in proportion to the debt drawdown.
Termination risk	Promoters/ Project company	The project will be bought out by other promoters at a buyout price covering outstanding dues of existing lenders.

Road Projects

Risk Factor	*Responsibility*	*Mitigation*
Project Development Phase		
Land acquisition	Licensor	Land to be in possession. If any balance land remains to be acquired, follow-up with National Highways Authority of India (NHAI) and remedial steps of action to be taken.
Project Construction Phase		
Project completion risk	Promoters, company and EPC contractor	Good track record of EPC contractor and transparent bidding Fixed time contract with adequate LDs and fixed price with cap on the escalation.

contd...

...contd...

Cost increase risk	Project company/ Promoters	Construction and O&M contract on a fixed price basis and with limited escalation clause. Adequate contingency provision and insurance cost for unforeseen circumstances to be built into the project. Strict monitoring by the project company through appointment of independent engineer.
Inflation risk	Project company	EPC contract to be fixed-price and provide sufficient contingency.
Operation Phase		
Price risk	Project company/ Licensor	Toll rates should be linked to inflation as per concession agreement.
Shortfall in traffic	Project company/ Licensor	Traffic studies done by reputed traffic consultants for bank/ NHAI/company. A cushion of 4-5 years (gap between ending of repayment period and concession period) is desirable. Otherwise credit enhancements need to be put in place. Credit enhancements in the form of debt service reserve account (DSRA) etc., may be explored.
Leakage of toll revenue	Licensor	Licensor (generally the government) to provide legal support to penalize the non-payers. Existing alternative routes and possibilities for traffic diversion need to be investigated before sanction.
O&M risk	Project company	O&M cost to be frozen.
FM risk	Project company/Insurer	Comprehensive insurance coverage. Provision in concession agreement to increase the concession period equal to the period of the event.

Figures 9.1 and 9.2 depict the risk cycles and their mitigating factors:

Figure 9.1

Risk Groups

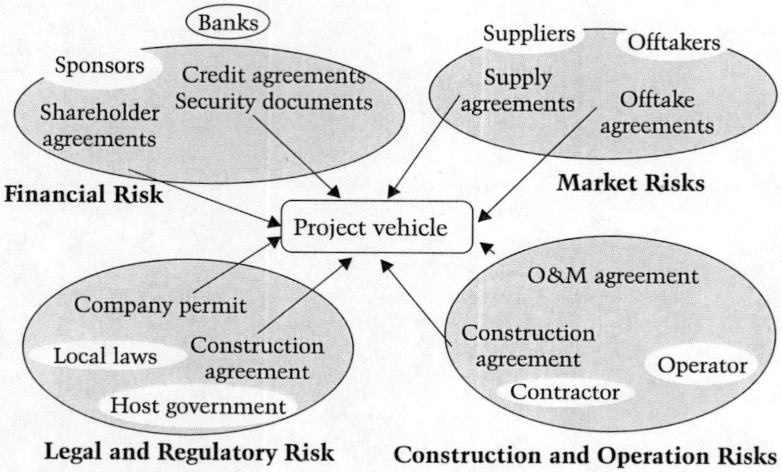

Figure 9.2

Risk Mitigation for Project

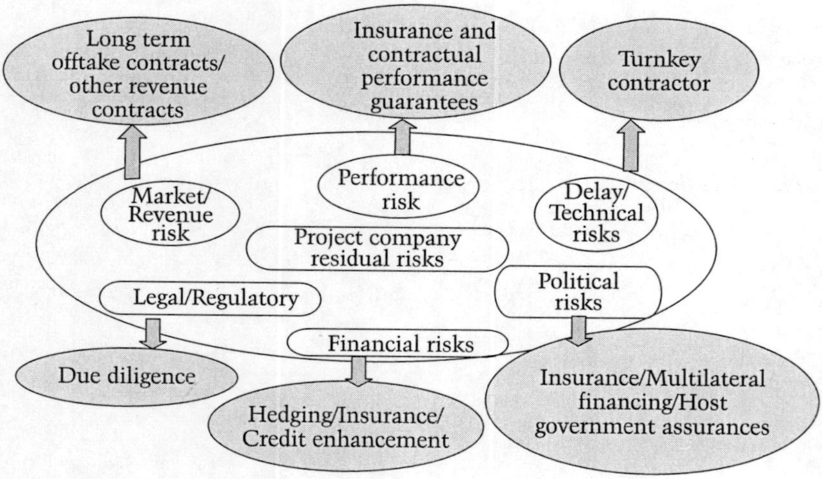

Power Sector: Risk Assessment

In order to have the clarity, risk factors analysed under three stages in power sector (in relation to a particular project) have been given below, enabling the credit personnel in capturing them at the time of preparing the memorandum for sanction:

Risk	*Risk Bearing*	*Mitigation Measure*
Development Risk		
Land acquisition	Major part of land for main power plant has been acquired and no problem is anticipated since there are no forests in the area and issue of resettlement etc., do not arise.	Not applicable
Approvals/Clearances	Company is confident of obtaining these well in time.	In view of completion of public hearing and environmental studies and final stage of clearance from Government of India (GoI).
Financial Risk		
	The financial closure is yet to be completed.	We will stipulate that the release is after the financial closure only. The financial position of the offtakers like the company (as mentioned in the proposal) is satisfactory. Further, payments from the offtakers to corporations (as given in the proposal) shall be backed by a LC/security deposit. As such the risk of a payment default is considered to be minimal.
Construction Risk		
Project management risk	Delay on account of large size of project and lack of prior experience of promoters in implementing such project earlier.	The project is being implemented by the M/s KSK Mahanadi Power Company Ltd. who have sufficient experience in this field. Also project is being implemented on EPC basis by EPC contractor, one of the leading names in power projects with good experience in projects of large size.
Cost and time overrun	Cost	The project will be implemented through a fixed price-fixed time, turnkey EPC contract with an internationally reputed EPC contractor. Majority of the non-EPC costs will be entrusted to reputed contractor via fixed price lump sum contracts.

contd...

...contd...

	Time	As mentioned earlier, the project would be implemented by an EPC contractor with an established track record, through a date-certain EPC contract. The EPC contract provides for penalties/LDs in case of a delay in completion of the project and the same are adequate to cover penalties and debt servicing costs. Further, based on the recommendation of the lenders' insurance consultant (LIC), suitable insurance may also be obtained to cover for delays in the project implementation. Appointment of an LIC has been stipulated as a pre-commitment condition.
Procurement of machinery	On EPC	Not applicable
Operating Risk		
O&M		The EPC contract provides for performance guarantees on key operational parameters such as heat rate and net energy output, along with LDs for shortfall in performance. The details have been given earlier in the note. Further, the O&M contract will consist of a guaranteed target plant load factor (PLF) and incentives to achieve target availability. Liability to pay penalties to consumers will rest with the O&M contractor on account of misdeclaration of available output. Further, the EPC contractors provide warranties for at least 12 months from the takeover of the plant. In addition, the contract also provides remedy against latent defects due to contractor's fault. Further, warranty period of 10 years commencing on the expiry of the warranty period is provided for latent defects. Appropriate insurance cover is to be taken for consequential losses, to take into account loss of profit due to reduced generation and disincentive payments.
Raw material risk		The company has already entered fuel supply agreement with the company (as shown in detailed project report (DPR)/ project information memorandum (PIM)) for the supply of coal from coal blocks. Tapering linkage is also available from the EPC contractor.
Power availability		Not Applicable

contd...

...contd...

Risk Factor	Allocated to	Mitigation Measures
FM		The pre-development agreement (PDAs) proposed to be signed by Wardha Power Company Ltd. (WPCL) with the offtakers, shall provide for reschedulement of the commercial operations date of the project in case of FM events. Suitable insurance covers are proposed to be obtained to cover for FM events based on the recommendations of the LIC. Appointment of LIC has been stipulated as a pre-commitment condition.
Interest Risk		
Revenue Risk		Revenue risks reflect uncertainties in income generation. It is a product of volume/demand risk and price risk. It commands considerable importance in infrastructure and weighs heavily on the minds of private investors before they decide to participate in the project. The revenue generation of sensitive services like power and water pose another kind of risk—the risk of equitable tariff. There are many ramifications in the determination of their price structure. The risk of political interference and resistance from the influential quarter is very high in such services in view of their large consumer base compelling the operator to charge lower prices.
Demand shortfall	Already committed to supply to the company	
Competition		Not applicable
Pricing pressures		Nil
Technology risk		The power station is based on pulverised fuel fired single boiler and single steam turbine of 600 MW module size, which is a proven technology thereby reducing the scope for technical complications during the assembly of the plant components, and minimising risks of technical failure during the commissioning and operating phases. Hence, this risk is minimal.
Risk Factor	*Allocated to*	*Mitigation Measures*
Management Risk		
Promoter/ Sponsor risk	Group companies	Though the particular group companies have no existing generation capacity, it has strong network with vendors and

contd...

...contd...

		suppliers worldwide. The group companies have considerable track record of project execution capabilities of their existing and ongoing projects. Further, special purpose vehicles (SPV) has already appointed reputed consultants as owner's consultant for assisting in design and engineering, selection of boiler turbine generator (BTG) and balance of plant (BOP) contractors, etc. The company is in negotiation with reputed suppliers for award of the BTG contract and reputed contractors for award of the BOP contract. The project is proposed to be executed on a fixed price-fixed time BTG contract and the proposed suppliers have vast credentials and large reputation in the field. EPC contractor already has in place a team of highly experienced and qualified persons to execute this power project, and employees at various levels are in the process of being appointed. With a market capitalisation of around Rs 15,500 cr (US $3.2 bn), net assets in excess of Rs 7,600 cr (US $1.58 bn), and net worth to the tune of Rs 7,060 cr (US $1.47 bn), the group is among the India's top private sector business house.
Withdrawl of promoters	Group companies	The lenders may stipulate that promoters shall undertake that the management and control of the borrower shall not change and promoters/sponsor shall continue to hold a minimum 51 per cent equity stake in the company throughout during the currency of the loans for the project. The group is committed to the project and would continue to hold majority stake in the project.
Pre-Completion Risk		
Environment and forest clearance	Company	Environment clearance from MoEF for the project has been obtained on March 4, 2009. However, lenders would suitably stipulate a condition that the company would obtain necessary environmental clearance from MoEF/ other statutory bodies, as may be required for the project at least six months prior to commercial operation date (COD) of the 1st unit.

contd...

...contd...

		Further, lender independent engineer (LIE)/lender's legal counsel (LLC) shall also review the approvals and clearances required by the company for complying with the requirements of Coastal Regulation Zone, if any, and shall take all necessary steps to obtain such approvals/clearances as may be required for smooth implementation of the project at least six months prior to the COD of the 1st unit of the project. Hence, the risk related to environmental and forest clearance is suitably mitigated.
Land acquisition	Company	Land of 1,123 acres, which is adequate for the main plant and auxiliary systems of the proposed 1040 MW power project, is already in possession of company. 325 acres of land required for railway siding is to be acquired within the necessary timeframe for smooth implementation of the project, to the satisfaction of lenders. Hence, the risk is substantially mitigated
Water allocation approval	Company	For sweet water requirement (mainly for Demineralisation (DM) plant, heating, ventilation and air conditioning (HVAC) make up, coal dust suppression and portable water) during construction and operations, water allocation has been committed by Andhra Pradesh Industrial Infrastructure Corporation (APIIC), Government of Andhra Pradesh (GoAP) for seven cusec of sweet water from Yellaru canal. For sea water drawl (to be used for condensate cooling purposes), a new water line would be laid from sea water intake point at coast of Bay of Bengal. Company would obtain the necessary approval as may be required in this regard. Given the above arrangements, no difficulty is envisaged for availability of water for the proposed project; hence, the risk is substantially mitigated.
Financial risk—Equity	Group companies	The promoters/sponsor have adequate resources to fund the necessary promoter's contribution.

contd...

...contd...

		Equity requirement of the project is estimated to be Rs 1,386 cr, which would be brought in by group companies. The group may raise part of the equity from strategic investors or by way of private placement of equity. As on March, 2009, the promoter group companies had cash and cash equivalent investments of around Rs 1,000 cr (approx) and they would be able to generate around Rs 500 cr of cash each year after meeting their repayment and other obligations. Company would avail proposed term loans only after promoter's contribution to the extent of 50 per cent has been infused. Lenders may stipulate a suitable condition that the sponsors shall bring in 50 per cent of the equity required for the project upfront and sponsors shall provide suitable undertaking in the form and manner acceptable to the lenders to bring in the balance 50 per cent of the equity as per the requirements of the project.
Financial risk – Debt	Company/Sponsor	The group has satisfactory credit track record and strong financial position and is highly acceptable by banks and institutions. The company has already received in-principle approval for much higher loan amount than required for the project. Hence, no difficulty is envisaged in raising funds through various sources of debt finance as envisaged. Company would seek disbursement of funds only after securing full tie-up of entire debt requirement for the project.
Technology risk	BTG and BOP contractor/Company	Company is in advanced stage of negotiation with reputed suppliers for award of BTG contract. Further, sub-critical technology proposed to be used by the company is proven and would have minimal technology risk. BOP would be from vendors with proven quality and experience selected from an agreed list of reputed vendors, and stringent technical specification would be stipulated.

contd...

...contd...

		Considering the proposed procurement of BTG and BOP from reputed companies with adoption of proven and timely tested technology, the technology risk is substantially mitigated.
Cost risk/ Cost overrun risk/Delay in commissioning/ Performance shortfall	BTG contractor/ The group companies/Sponsor/ Company	Company would be implementing the project through fixed price-fixed time BTG contract which substantially mitigate the risk of cost and time overrun. For any other reasons for cost overrun, the contingency provisions in the cost of project would be adequate to meet such cost overrun. Company would also procure insurance cover during construction period, which would cover cost overruns and construction delay due to any FM events. The project construction progress would be monitored by company, owner's engineer and lender's engineer. In addition to this and to take care of the cost overruns, the lenders may stipulate that sponsor shall finance any cost overrun by way of additional equity/unsecured loans from its own resources or loans arranged by sponsor without recourse to the project assets, to the satisfaction of the lenders. Further, lenders may stipulate that the BTG contract shall stipulate adequate LDs for delay in commissioning of plant and shortfall in performance guarantees, which would be reviewed by LIE.
Evacuation facilities	Andhra Pradesh Central Power Distribution Corporation Limited (APDISCOM)/Pass through certificates (PTC)	For evacuation of power to be supplied to PTC and on merchant sale basis (around 75 per cent of its net capacity), proposed interconnection point would be the nearest sub-station/pooling station (400 kV at Ukkunagaram) of Power Grid Corporation of India Limited (PGCIL), which is about 11 kms from the plant site. PTC on behalf of the company will obtain long term open access (LTOA) from central transmission utility (CTU), i.e., PGCIL for evacuation of power to other states/consumers. Company will develop a dedicated transmission line of around 11 km upto nearest sub-station/ pooling station of PGCIL for connectivity through open access.

contd...

...contd...

		PTC will also assist company in getting the power evacuation study for onward evacuation of power to be done by PGCIL. It would be the responsibility of PTC to offtake the power from company at the interconnection point and use associated transmission system (ATS) for onward transmission of power up to delivery point at the procuring state periphery. The company may enter into a long term power purchase agreement (PPA) with government of state for sale of the balance 25 per cent of net generated power at Andhra Pradesh Electricity Regulatory Commission (APERC) based tariff, which would be supplied to various state distribution companies at the plant bus bar. Hence, the risk is substantially mitigated.
Post-completion Risk		
Performance shortfall	Company/BTG contractor/O&M contractor	Shortfall in performance parameters, *viz.,* rated capacity and other associated parameters (such as station heat rate, auxiliary power consumption and PLF) would result in a reduction in cash accruals. The BTG supplier likely to be selected would be internationally renowned with extensive experience in supply to coal based thermal power plant equipments. Contract for BTG package would have necessary provisions for guaranteed parameters along with provisions for LDs for any underperformance of the plant in terms of increase in heat rate and auxiliary consumption. The BTG contractor would also be obliged to provide free repair/ replacement during warranty period. The company proposes to develop a good internal team with qualified professionals having requisite experience for O&M of the project. The company is also exploring the option to outsource O&M of the plant to a reputed agency having requisite experience and credentials. Further, lenders may stipulate that the BTG contract shall stipulate adequate LDs for shortfall in performance guarantees, which would be reviewed by LIE.

contd...

...contd...

Fuel supply	Company/ The group companies	The company has received letter of assurance (LoA) for supply of 4.63 mtpa of coal from the coal blocks of Mahanadi Coalfields Limited (MCL), which would be adequate to meet the 100 per cent of the normative coal requirement. The company would enter into fuel supply agreement with MCL as per the terms of LoA prior to COD of unit 1 of the project. Hence, the risk of fuel supply tie-up is substantially mitigated.
Fuel transportation	Company	Fuel transportation agreement would be signed with Indian Railways for supply of coal from delivery point of MCL to the nearest railway station to the plant. For unloading, handling and inland transportation of coal, the company proposes to implement transportation services from railway siding at Jaggyapalem to the coal stock yard at plant site. Coal will be transported on rail through the wagon tippler system at the plant site and the locos would be owned by company. The company would also create other necessary facilities for handling, receipt and dispatch of coal. The cost for establishing the wagon tippler system/ other related infrastructure is also included in the project cost. The company has already received in-principle approval of Railway Transport Clearance (RTC) dated May 22, 2009 for transportation of coal, secondary oil and proposed railway siding at Jagyyapalem. Based on the study/route survey being conducted by Rail India Technical and Economic Services (RITES), existing railway network on Howrah-Chennai route will be used for transportation of coal. Hence, the risk is substantially mitigated.
Payment security	Company	PPA for the power which may be supplied to distribution company (DISCOM) and on long term sale with PTC would have provision of revolving LC, of value equivalent to average revenue of 11 months, valid for a term not less than 12 months.

contd...

...contd...

		Company could draw upon the LCs in case of non-payment of monthly invoice by procurers. As per the proposed PPA with PTC, company shall have a lien on the amount due and received by PTC in its revenue collection account during the term of agreement, which would provide additional security to lenders apart from revolving LC for 11 times of monthly sales. Merchant sale would be made to the credible parties either directly/through trading companies/through the power exchanges. The payment terms of such merchant sale would be as per the market practice and would adequately take care of the associated payment risk. Company would also agree to create a DSRA equivalent to succeeding two quarter debt service to mitigate any risk of delay on receipt of receivable from procurers. In case of payment default by the procurers/PTC, company would also have the option of selling the power to third parties. Considering the proposed tie-up with reputed companies like PTC and the proposed payment security structure, the payment risk is substantially mitigated. Further, DISCOMs and PTC have considerable reputation of timely payment.
Market Risk		
Offtake risk	Company	25 per cent of the power generated from the project is proposed to be sold to DISCOM. Further, 60 per cent of the power will be sold on long term basis to PTC and the balance 15 per cent would be sold on merchant basis. In case of non offtake of power, company also has an option to sell power to third parties; however, considering the tariff at which the power is made available to these procurers, chances of their not considering offtake is remote. On the other hand, with an opportunity to sell to third parties, company would be in a position to sell the power at higher tariff which would improve its cash accruals.

contd...

...contd...

		As per the negotiated PPA with PTC, PTC has agreed to buy power at a minimum levellised tariff of Rs 3.25 per kWh, including trading margin. Further, balance 15 per cent of the net power generated would be sold on merchant basis. For financial projections purpose, Rs 3.50 per unit has been considered for merchant sale with increase of 25 paisa after every 11 years. Looking at the demand-supply scenario, the price considered for supply of power is conservative. Hence, no difficulty is envisaged for offtake of power.
		Lenders may stipulate a suitable condition that borrower shall enter into a firm PPA on long term basis for sale of power generated from the project so as to achieve a minimum DSCR of 1:1 to the satisfaction of the lenders. In case of PPA entered by the borrower with a power trading company, which is acceptable to the lenders, does not have a firm offtake commitment from the power trading company, the company shall ensure that such power trading company shall enter into a firm back to back PPA on long term basis with state utilities/other consumers within 12 months from the date of first disbursement to the satisfaction of the lenders.
Foreign exchange risk	Company/ Procurers	For estimation of project cost, the exchange rate has been considered at Rs 48 per US$. Further, average rupee depreciation of 0.50 per cent per anmum during the construction period and the repayment period has also been considered.
		All expenses are in Indian rupees, hence there is no forex risk during the operations period. The company may consider a suitable hedging mechanism for the payments towards a very small import component of BTG, if required after finalisation of BTG contracts in foreign currency; hence, the risk of rupee depreciation is substantially mitigated.
Interest rate risk	Company	The interest rates assumed for projections are in line with the current market scenario for raising long-term loans. Under the said assumptions, company is expected to be able to service its debt comfortably.

contd...

...contd...

		The sensitivity has been worked out for increase in rate of interest by 50 bps wherein DSCR remains at comfortable level. The 25 per cent of the power proposed to be sold to DISCOM would have interest variation pass through as per the PPA.
Other Risk		
FM risk	Procurers/ Company	Company proposes to take out a comprehensive insurance policy package during the construction/operations period for this project. Under the negotiated PPA with PTC, if purchaser/Central Transmission Utility (CTU) is the affected party on account of FM events during operation and as a result the power is not sold or evacuated, PTC agrees to use reasonable endeavours to buy the contracted capacity for sale to third parties at a minimum price agreed with PTC. In case of higher realisation after adjusting both capacity and energy, charge would be shared equally between PTC and the company. In case of delay due to FM events (except natural FM events) affecting PTC, PTC shall make payment of capacity charges to the company for the period of such events in excess of three continuous or non-continuous months as deemed supply of power. Lenders may stipulate suitable condition that company shall take adequate insurance cover over its assets, offered as security for the facility, against fire and all such other risks as may be required by the lenders/lenders insurance advisor (LIA).
Change in law	Procurers/ Company	The project would have certain protection against changes in law. The definition of change in law refers to the modification, repeal or enactment of any laws, change in any consents, approval or licenses available or obtained having implication on revenue under this agreement, change in interpretation or application of Indian law. Due to change in law, it results in company's revenue or project cost directly attributable to the project; PTC shall provide adjustment to tariff payment

Risk Factor	Relevant Party	Proposed Mitigation Mechanism
Pre-construction Delay		
Finalisation of key contracts	Concerned company	Implementation agreement and the PPA have been signed. The company is expected to sign a fixed price-fixed time EPC contract representing a single point responsibility for the implementation of the project. The contract would be signed prior to disbursements.
Approval, permits and clearances	Concerned company	The company is in the process of obtaining the techno-economic clearance (TEC) from Central Electrical Authority (CEA). MoEF clearance for the project has been obtained on September 21, 2006.
Land acquisition	Concerned company	The process for acquisition of land has already been initiated. The Government of Sikkim (GoS) has agreed to provide government land on a long term lease of 35 years as may be required for permanent works and on short term lease of 15 years for temporary works.
Financing Risk		
Equity	Concerned company	The equity required for the project would be brought in by Lanco Infratech Limited (LITL) and GoS. LITL has already brought in Rs 0.51 bn. It may be noted that promoters would bring in upfront equity of Rs 200 cr. In addition, LITL would also provide an undertaking to bring in the entire equity required for the project. Further, as mentioned earlier, LITL has already raised funds through initial public offer (IPO) on 06.11.2006 and collected Rs 1,037.63 cr. It will take care of the initial infusion of the capital in the company for Rs 200 cr. Rest of the infusion of capital shall be made through internal accruals in years to come from the parent company and other group companies.

contd...

...contd...

Construction Risk		
Geological risks	Concerned company	Central Water Commission (CWC) in consultation with Geological Survey of India (GSI) and concerned company have carried out geological and geotechnical investigations of the project site. Investigations were carried out at the proposed sites for barrage, intake and desilting chamber, head race tunnel, surge shaft and power house. The results of these studies have been considered during the design engineering and location of the project components. Further, considerable comfort can be derived from the fact that Teesta VI is just downstream of National Hydroelectric Power Corporation's (NHPCs) Teesta V project that is in the advanced stages of construction and is expected to be commissioned in 2007.
Plant performance	Equipment supplier/ EPC contractor	The terms of the EPC contract that would be entered into with the EPC contractor would list down the operation parameters and penalties in the event the plant performance does not meet the parameters contracted.
Delay in construction	Concerned company/ EPC contractor	Suitable provisions for LDs for delay in construction will be provided in the EPC contract.
Damage/ Destruction on account of natural disaster/FM	Insurance agency	The company shall procure adequate insurance cover for the project, including erection all risk, marine all risk, advance loss of profit and marine delay policies, prior to disbursements.
Operational Risks		
Equipment under-performance	Concerned company/EPC contractor	Suitable provisions for LDs will be provided in the EPC contract.
Offtake Risks		
Transmission risk	Maharashtra State Electricity Distribution Company Limited (MSEDCL)	The project proposes to supply power to MSEDCL in the western region. Accordingly, MSEDCL and the company would be entering into arrangements for wheeling of power to the offtakers through PGCIL or other transmission utilities. As per the PPA, the risk of non-availability of transmission capacity would be borne by MSEDCL.
Payment risk	Concerned company/ Lenders	The tariff payable is competitive. In addition, the PPA provides for an LC and Escrow as additional comfort.

Lending Rate

Banks and FIs fix their lending rate on their loan considering the following components:

- Cost of funds (Direct + Liquidity cost)
- Credit risk charge – Compensations (banks/FIs) against expected credit losses
- Capital charge – Return on capital allocated to provide for variability of expected losses
- Overheads

In consortium, pricing is decided after critically examining the credit facility and the pricing offered by banks/FIs with their justification linked to their risk rating or credit quality *vis-à-vis* their base rate/benchmark rate.

Base Rate

Interest rate = Benchmark rate + Credit spread

Credit spread varies for a greenfield and brownfield project based on the rating assigned.

The rate of interest shall be determined on the basis of the base rate which will be arrived at considering the average cost of funds, including administrative cost, average return on net worth and cost of guarantee fees, which Resources and Treasury Department will review on quarterly basis and apprise the credit department.

The banks and FIs will also look at the other factors for fixing the price mentioned as under:

i. Credit rating.

ii. Tenor of the facility with reset clause.

iii. Aligning to the competitive scenario.

iv. Spread in terms of cost of funds.

v. Consistent track record and association with the bank/lender.

vi. Creditworthiness of the company/group.

vii. Availability of liquidity and possibility of its deployment at the market rate.

Typically, credit spread over the benchmark rate depends upon following factors

Risk Categories	*Risk Weights (%)*
Promoter's risk	10
Regulation/Policy risk	5
Financial risk	13
Completion/Execution/Maintenance/ Operation risk	50
Business risk	22
Total	100

Reset

On the date of reset, the interest rate shall be governed by the following:

- The base rate or benchmark rate of banks/FIs. (To be reviewed once in a quarter or as and when required.)
- Revised risk profile of the project, as indicated by the migration of the external/internal risk rating.
- Internal risk policy of banks/FIs.

Penal Interest

In terms of extant Reserve Bank of India (RBI) guidelines, banks have been advised about the overall penal/additional interest to be charged by banks, which should not exceed two per cent over and above the rate of interest applicable/normally charged to the respective borrower.

Consequent upon substantial deregulation of interest rates on loans and deposits by RBI, individual banks/institutions have been empowered to formulate policy on lending rates taking into account their cost of funds, the underlying credit risk, etc.

Charging of penal interest contains *inter alia*, the definition, applicability, reasons, quantum of penal interest, amount on which penal interest shall be levied, period for which penal interest has to be charged, rate of penal interest, as well as the competent authority for relaxation/ waiver of penal interest.

Penal rate of interest shall be applicable for all the term loans advanced by the company.

Broad areas where penal interest will be charged by the company are: default in repayment of loans as well as in borrowing covenants/terms of sanction and above the rate of interest applicable/charged to borrowers.

Discretionary powers to relax/waive penal rate shall be vested with the competent authority.

Upfront Fee

In all cases of new accounts, upfront fee/processing charges (non-refundable and non-adjustable) not less than 0.25 per cent (excluding service tax) or as fixed by the respective banks/FIs would be recovered before disbursement.

Prepayment Charges

Prepayment charges are to minimise the effect on net interest income (NII) and asset-liability mismatch in the event of prepayment/non-availment of term loan facility sanctioned.

Guidelines:

- Sanctioning authorities shall stipulate prepayment/commitment charges in sanction terms.
- Prepayment charges shall be applicable not less than 0.50 per cent on the prepaid amount in the event of the agency remitting prepayments voluntarily.
- There will be no prepayment charges in the case the agency remits repayments at the time of reset of rate of interest. Any part prepayment shall be pro rata amounts, unless otherwise agreed to by the lenders.
- Prepayment/commitment charges shall be applicable to new sanctions/renewal.

Commitment Charges

The borrower shall pay to the lenders a non-refundable commitment fee not less than 1 per cent of the amounts undrawn beyond two quarters in variance with the drawdown schedule.

Provided that the borrower may vary the drawdown schedule by giving notice thereof to the lenders not less than 30 days prior to the commencement of the quarter. The fee would be calculated on the basis of the drawings not made and the number of days deviated from the drawdown schedule.

Annual Review Charges

All accounts shall be reviewed annually. The annual review charges may be as described below:

Loan Amount	*Annual Review Charges as Fixed by Banks/FIs*
Up to Rs 100 cr	
Rs 100 cr to Rs 500 cr	
Rs 500 cr and above	

Revalidation Charges

Sanction letter issued by banks/FIs will have a validity period as laid down in their credit policies. In the event the sanction gets lapsed, the borrower needs to remit revalidation charge as specified in their respective service charges manual.

Charges for Modification of Sanction Terms and Conditions

The borrower needs to remit a fee in the event of any modifications to sanction terms and conditions carried out by banks/FIs in line with lead lender or in line with their respective credit policies.

Waiver of Charges

Boards of the banks/FIs either by themselves or through delegations of the power may waive the prepayment, upfront fee, commitment charges, revalidation charges, charges for modification of sanction terms and conditions and review charges based on the merits of the cases in order to align with the lead bank and other lenders in the consortium.

Conclusion

Undertaking infrastructure business in India involves many risks and problems that are mainly due to differences in market conditions, financial models, legal system and culture. Banks/FIs are facing various types of financial and non-financial risks, *viz*., credit, interest rate, liquidity, foreign exchange rate, legal, regulatory, operational, reputational and time horizon. These risks are often interdependent and interlinked. Their identification, assessment and measurement, and corrective steps to control overall level of risks to be undertaken in the projects need to be properly analysed and appraised. The primary responsibility of understanding the risk lies with banks/FIs through their various tools and techniques. Factors which relate to risks are basically of two types: external factors and internal factors. The external factors relate to the state of the economy, swings in equity prices, foreign exchange rates, interest rates, trade restrictions, economic sanctions and government policies etc. The internal factors as outlined in RBI policy are deficiencies in loan policies/administration, absence of prudential credit concentration limits, inadequately defined lending limits for loan officers/ credit committees, deficiencies in appraisal of borrowers financial position, excessive dependence on collaterals and inadequate risk pricing, absence of loan review mechanism and post-sanction surveillance, etc.

Infrastructure sector provides several project models with different risk return implications available for capital participation across all core sectors. Success will lie in analysing risk factors and their mitigating strategies to build a profitable business model that earns a high sustained return on capital. Therefore, lenders must understand the risk return positioning of individual subsectors. They have to build deep expertise to undertake accurate risk assessment, skilled and knowledgeable personnel, who would help the companies to mitigate risk using financial products as well as determine when to opt out of the deal. Thus, the importance of risk quantification and management measures cannot be overlooked. Banks/ FIs assess liquidity and pricing risk through simple gap analysis and the gap is estimated covering their assets and liability. They put in place gap limits for liquidity and pricing risk. It shows that pricing of the product in infrastructure is dependent on the nature, composition and dimension of the various risks related to the project. Thus, risk management is a key differentiator for the lenders in the infrastructure financing arena.

10 Exposure Norms

Exposure

Exposure shall include credit exposure (funded and non-funded) and investment exposure (including underwriting and similar commitments). The sanctioned limits or outstandings, whichever are higher shall be reckoned for arriving at the exposure limits. However in the case of fully drawn term loans, where there is no scope for redrawal of any portion of the sanctioned limit, bank may reckon the outstanding as the exposure.

Capital Funds

Capital funds will comprise Tier-I & Tier-II capital as defined under capital adequacy standards and as per the published accounts as on March 31 of the previous year. The infusion of capital under Tier-I and Tier–II, either through domestic or overseas issue after the published balance sheet date, will also be taken into account for determining the exposure ceilings. Other accretions to capital funds by way of quarterly profits etc., would not be eligible to be reckoned for determining the exposure ceiling. The bank is prohibited from taking exposure in excess of the ceiling anticipation of infusion of capital at a future date.

Unsecured Exposure

Unsecured exposure has been defined as an exposure where the reliable value of the security, as assessed by the bank/approved valuers/Reserve Bank inspecting officers, is not more than 10 per cent *ab initio* (i.e., at the time of sanction) of the outstanding exposure.

'Security' will mean tangible security properly charged to the bank and will not include intangible securities like guarantees, comfort letters, etc.

The rights, licenses, authorisation, etc., charged to the bank as collateral in respect of infrastructure projects financed by the banks/financial institutions (FIs) should not be reckoned as tangible security. Such advances shall be reckoned as unsecured.

However, banks/FIs may treat annuities under build, operate and transfer (BOT) model in respect of road/highway projects and toll collection rights, where there are provisions to compensate the project sponsor if a certain level of traffic is not achieved, as tangible securities subject to the condition that banks' right to receive annuities and toll collection rights are legally enforceable and irrevocable.

The Exposure Norm as per Reserve Bank of India (RBI)

Individual Borrower

Twenty-five (25) per cent of capital funds of the bank in case of oil companies who has been issued oil bonds (which do not have statutory liquidity ratio (SLR) status) by Government of India (GoI) and 15 per cent of capital funds of the bank in all other cases (+5% additional exposure, i.e., up to 20% for infrastructure sector and 30% for oil companies mentioned hereinabove).

Group Exposure

Forty (40) per cent of capital funds is for group exposure. In case of additional exposure of the bank to infrastructure, group exposure is relaxed up to 50 per cent of the capital funds for the purpose. It comprises Tier-I and Tier-II capital under capital adequacy standards.

Further, additional exposure up to 5 per cent of capital funds can, however, be considered (assumed), subject to consent of the borrower and also approved by the bank's board of directors.

The exposure norms as prescribed by RBI are as under:

Segment	*Bank Ceilings*	
Maximum exposure Individual borrower/Group	Exposure	% of capital funds
	To single borrower	15
	To single borrower in case of oil companies who has been issued oil bonds which do not have SLR status by GoI	25
	To single Borrower (with incremental infrastructure exposure)	20
	To single group	40
	To single group (with incremental infrastructure exposure)	50

Lending as Percentage of Total Project Cost, Single and Group Exposure Norm in Case of IIFCL

The total lending by the Indian Infrastructure Finance Company Limited (IIFCL) in relation to non-banking financial company (NBFC)-International Finance Corporation (IFC), shall conform to the following:

i. 20 per cent of the total project cost

ii. Single project exposure norm and group exposure norm as per the applicable RBI guidelines for NBFC-IFC

Exposure Norms based on RBI Guidelines

As per RBI norms for NBFC-IFC, credit exposure to single borrower could be up to 15 per cent of its net owned fund (NOF) and in case of infrastructure projects, this could be increased by additional 10 per cent, i.e., 25 per cent of its NOF. Similarly, credit exposure to a promoter group would be 25 per cent of its NOF which could be enhanced by additional 15 per cent, i.e., 40 per cent (25+15) of its NOF in case of infrastructure projects.

Infrastructure Lending

In terms of RBI master circular on exposure norms dated 01.07.2009, infrastructure lending would include all credit facilities extended in any form to a borrower entity engaged in:

i. Developing.

ii. Operating and maintaining.

iii. Developing, operating and maintaining any infrastructure facility that is a project in any of the following sectors, or any infrastructure facility of a similar nature.

    a. A road, including toll road, a bridge or a rail system.

    b. A highway project including other activities being an integral part of the highway project.

    c. A port, airport, inland waterway or inland port.

d. A water supply project, irrigation project, water treatment system, sanitation and sewerage system or soiled waste management system.

e. Telecommunication services, whether basic or cellular, including radio paging, domestic satellite service (a satellite owned and operated by an Indian company for providing telecommunication service), network of trunking, broadband network and internet services.

f. An industrial park or special economic zone.

g. Generation or generation and distribution of power.

h. Transmission or distribution of power by laying a network of new transmission or distribution lines.

i. Construction for preservation and storage of processed agro products, perishable goods such as fruits, vegetables and flowers including testing facilities for quality.

j. Construction of educational institution and hospitals.

k. Lying down and/or maintenance of gas, crude oil and petroleum pipelines.

l. Any other infrastructure facility of similar nature.

Definition of 'Group'

As per RBI circular relating to banks:

i. The concept of 'Group' and the task of identification of the borrowers belonging to specific industrial groups is left to the perception of the banks/FIs. Banks/FIs are generally aware of the basic constitution of their clientele for the purpose of regulating their exposure to risk assets. The group to which a particular borrowing unit belongs, may, therefore, be decided by them on the basis of the relevant information available with them, the guiding principle being commonality of management and effective control. Insofar as public sector undertakings are concerned, only single borrower exposure limit would be applicable.

ii. In the case of a split in the group, if the split is formalised, the splinter groups will be regarded as separate groups. If banks and FIs have doubts about the bona fides of the split, a reference may be made to RBI for its final view in the matter to preclude the possibility of a split being engineered in order to prevent coverage under the 'Group' approach.

Besides the above, the associates shall include the following:

i. Two concerns having one or more common proprietor being director in a private/public limited company and vice versa shall be taken as one for the purpose of group concept.

ii. Any of the directors of private limited company is the director of another private limited company.

iii. A limited company is subsidiary of another limited company within the meaning of the Companies Act 1956.

iv. Professional directors of the board shall be excluded for the purpose of the concept of the group company.

Foreign Trade Policy defines Group Company as under:

"9.28 Group Company means two or more enterprises which, directly or indirectly, are in a position to:

(i) exercise 26 per cent or more of the voting rights in the other enterprise; or

(ii) appoint more than 50 per cent, of the members of the board of directors in the other enterprise.

For the group companies to claim benefits or have their exports counted for benefits to be claimed by another member of the group, the group company should have been in existence at least 2 years prior to the date of application under any of the export promotion schemes notified in the Policy."

Chapter 3 (988) of the Companies Act defines associates as:

"1) In this Chapter 'associate', in relation to an offeror, means:

(a) a nominee of the offeror,

(b) a holding company, subsidiary or fellow subsidiary of the offeror or a nominee of such a holding company, subsidiary or fellow subsidiary,

(c) a body corporate in which the offeror is substantially interested,

(d) a person who is, or is a nominee of, a party to a share acquisition agreement with the offeror, or

(e) (where the offeror is an individual) his spouse or civil partner and any minor child or step-child of his.

2) For the purposes of subsection (1)(b) a company is a fellow subsidiary of another body corporate if both are subsidiaries of the same body corporate but neither is a subsidiary of the other.

3) For the purposes of subsection (1)(c) an offeror has a substantial interest in a body corporate if:

(a) the body or its directors are accustomed to act in accordance with his directions or instructions, or

(b) he is entitled to exercise or control the exercise of one-third or more of the voting power at general meetings of the body. Subsections (2) and (3) of section 823 (which contain provision about when a person is treated as entitled to exercise or control the exercise of voting power) apply for the purposes of this subsection as they apply for the purposes of that section.

4) For the purposes of subsection (1)(d) an agreement is a share acquisition agreement if:

(a) it is an agreement for the acquisition of, or of an interest in, shares to which the offer relates,

(b) it includes provisions imposing obligations or restrictions on any one or more of the parties to it with respect to their use, retention or disposal of such shares, or their interests in such shares, acquired in pursuance of the agreement (whether or not together with any other shares to which the offer relates or any other interests of theirs in such shares), and (c) it is not an excluded agreement (see subsection (5)).

5) An agreement is an 'excluded agreement':

(a) if it is not legally binding, unless it involves mutuality in the undertakings, expectations or understandings of the parties to it, or

(b) if it is an agreement to underwrite or sub-underwrite an offer of shares in a company, provided the agreement is confined to that purpose and any matters incidental to it.

6) The reference in subsection (4)(b) to the use of interests in shares is to the exercise of any rights or of any control or influence arising from those interests (including the right to enter into an agreement for the exercise, or for control of the exercise, of any of those rights by another person).

7) In this section:

(a) 'agreement' includes any agreement or arrangement."

As per Accounting Standard 18, issued by ICAI (Institute of Chartered Accountants of India):

"10.5 An Associate: an enterprise in which an investing reporting party has significant influence and which is neither a subsidiary nor a joint venture of that party.

10.6 A Joint venture: a contractual arrangement whereby two or more parties undertake an economic activity which is subject to joint control.

10.7 Joint control: the contractually agreed sharing of power to govern the financial and operating policies of an economic activity so as to obtain benefits from it.

10.8 Key management personnel: those persons who have the authority and responsibility for planning, directing and controlling the activities of the reporting enterprise."

Definition of Promoter

Explanation I of sub clauses (k) and (l) of Clause 6.8.3.2 of Chapter VI of the DIP (Disclosure and Investor Protection) Guidelines defines the term 'promoter' to include:

"I.A.1 Promoter

(a) the person or persons who are in over-all control of the company;

(b) the person or persons who are instrumental in the formulation of a plan or programme pursuant to which the securities are offered to the public;

(c) the persons or persons named in the prospectus as promoters(s).

Provided that a director/officer of the issuer company or person, if they are acting as such merely in their professional capacity shall not be included in the Explanation.

In view of the above, a promoter is a person who exercises substantial control over the company or a person who undertakes all necessary steps in the floatation of the company. The relationship between a promoter and a company which he has floated must be deemed to be a fiduciary relationship from the day the work of floating the company started. The status of the promoter is generally terminated when the Board of directors has been formed and they start governing the company

It is submitted that the definition of 'promoter is inclusive in nature and is a term of wider significance, and does not confine itself to *de jure* control'".

The definition of promoter as stipulated in the DIP Guidelines employs the term 'control'. Since the DIP Guidelines fail to define the term, reliance is placed upon the Takeover Code, 1997. Clause (c) of sub-regulation (1) of Regulation (2) defines the term as:

"Control shall include the right to appoint the majority of the directors or to control the management or policy decisions exercisable by a person or persons acting individually or in concert, directly or indirectly, including by virtue of their shareholding or management rights or shareholding agreements or voting agreements or in any other manner."

Nevertheless the term 'control' shall be interpreted in the light of the DIP Guidelines.

Definition of Promoter Group

Explanation I of sub clauses (k) and (l) of Clause 6.8.3.2 of Chapter VI of the DIP Guidelines defines the term 'promoter group' to include:

"I.A.2 Promoter Group

a) Promoter,

b) An immediate relative of the promoter (i.e., any spouse of that person, or any parent, brother, sister or child of the person or of the spouse); and

c) In case promoter is a company:

   i. a subsidiary or holding company of that company;

   ii. any company in which the promoter holds 10% or more of the equity capital or which holds 10% or more of the equity capital of the promoter;

   iii. any company in which a group of individuals or companies or combinations thereof who holds 20% or more of the equity capital in that company also holds 20% or more of the equity capital of the issuer company;

d) In case the promoter is an individual:

   i. any company in which 10% or more of the share capital is held by the promoter or an immediate relative of the promoter or a firm or HUF in which the promoter or any one or more of his immediate relative is a member;

   ii. any company in which a company specified in (i) above, holds 10% or more, of the share capital;

   iii. any HUF or firm in which the aggregate share of the promoter and his immediate relatives is equal to or more than 10% of the total; and;

   iv. all persons whose shareholding is aggregated for the purpose of disclosing in the prospectus under the heading shareholding of the promoter group."

The above definition not only encompasses within its ambit the promoter and his immediate relatives but also takes into account the subsidiary or the holding company or any other company in which the promoter holds 10 per cent or more of the capital of the company. In cases of promoter being a natural person, any HUF or a firm in which the promoters and his immediate relatives possess an aggregate shareholding which is either equal to or more than 10 per cent of the total capital of the company. The definition also tends to include persons whose shareholding is aggregated to satisfy the disclosure requirements in the prospectus.

In the light of the issues raised above, it may be noted that the above definition of 'promoter' is segregated into two parts. The first part deals with the general concept of the term 'promoter' whereas the second part differentiates between promoters as 'natural persons' (including his immediate relatives, companies, HUF and partnership firms in which he possesses the prescribed shareholdings) and as 'corporate promoters' (including the holding companies and its subsidiaries).

Conclusion

Banks/FIs invariably follow the exposure norm which is calculated by them on their capital structure ended on the financial year related to single party exposure and group exposure in terms of RBI guidelines. This exposure norm is mandatory in nature applicable to all the lenders. It is a kind of credit discipline that the lenders have to follow within their capital structure so that they may not be exposed to the limit as prescribed by banks/FIs and to also maintain the sectoral exposure norm to avoid the concentration risk which is vital particularly in infrastructure area. In other words, exposure norms prescribes a cap beyond which lenders will not go for lending.

11 Prudential Norms

In respect of consortium advances, each bank/financial institution (FI) may classify the borrower accounts according to its own record of recovery of interest and installments and other aspects having a bearing on the recoverability of the advances. In regard to stabilisation of commercial production and consequent classification of the company account as standard/substandard assets in respect of term loan to the company under consortium arrangement, the decision of the lender, where the lender is not the lead lender, as to whether the company has achieved regular operation and whether there is a need for rescheduling the repayment of term loan will be in line with the lender.

Project Loan

Project loan is any term loan which has been extended for the purpose of setting up of an economic venture. Banks/FIs must fix a date of commencement of commercial operations (DCCO) for all project loans at the time of sanction of the loan/financial closure. DCCO has a direct bearing on classification of an account to non-performing asset (NPA) category.

(i) A loan for an infrastructure project will be classified as NPA any time before commencement of commercial operations as per record of recovery (90 days overdue to banks and 180 days overdue to non-banking financial company (NBFC) and International Finance Corporation (IFC)), unless it is restructured and becomes eligible for classification as 'standard asset'.

(ii) As asset which has been classified as NPA for a period not exceeding 90 days to the banks and 180 days to the NBFC-IFC would be substandard assets.

(iii) A loan for an infrastructure project will be classified as NPA if it fails to commence commercial operations within two years from the original DCCO, even if it is regular as per record of recovery, unless it is restructured and becomes eligible for classification as 'standard asset'.

(iv) If a project loan classified as 'standard asset' is restructured any time during the period up to two years from the original DCCO, in accordance with the provisions of prudential guidelines on restructuring of advances as prescribed by Reserve Bank of India (RBI), it can be retained as a standard asset if the fresh DCCO is fixed within the following limits and further, provided the account continues to be serviced as per the restructured terms:

a. Infrastructure projects involving court cases up to another four years (beyond the existing extended period of two years i.e., total extension of six years), in case the reason for extension of date of commencement of production is arbitration proceedings or a court case.

b. Infrastructure projects delayed for other reasons beyond the control of promoters up to another one year (beyond the existing extended period of two years i.e. total extension of three years), in other than court cases.

(v) The above is subject to adherence to the provisions regarding restructuring of accounts as per prudential guidelines on restructuring of advances as prescribed by RBI, which would require that the application for restructuring should be received before the expiry of period of two years from the original DCCO and when the account is still standard as per record of recovery. The other conditions applicable would be:

a. In cases where there is moratorium for payment of interest, banks should not book income on accrual basis beyond two years from the original DCCO, considering the high risk involved in such restructured accounts.

b. Banks/FIs shall maintain provisions on such accounts as long as these are classified as standard assets as under:

Until two years from the original DCCO	0.25%
During the third and the fourth years after the original DCCO.	1.00%

(vi) For the purpose of these guidelines, mere extension of DCCO will also be treated as restructuring even if all other terms and conditions remain the same.

Prudential Norms

For prudential norms, RBI's guideline as applicable to NBFC-IFC notified in RBI circular no. DNBS.193/DG (VL)-2007 dated February 22, 2007 are to be followed.

The key features of the prudential norms contained in the aforesaid notification are as under:

i. 'Break-up value' means the equity capital and reserves as reduced by intangible assets and revaluation reserves, divided by the number of equity shares of the investee company.

ii. 'Carrying cost' means book value of the assets and interest accrued thereon but not received.

iii. 'Current investment' means an investment which is by its nature readily realisable and is intended to be held for not more than one year from the date on which such investment is made.

iv. 'Doubtful asset' means:

    a. a term loan, or

    b. a lease asset, or

    c. a hire purchase asset, or

    d. any other asset,

    which remains a sub-standard asset for a period exceeding 18 months.

v. 'Fair value' means earning value and the break-up value;

vi. 'Loss asset' means:

    a. an asset which has been identified as loss asset by the NBFC or its internal or external auditor or by the RBI during the inspection of the NBFC, to the extent it is not written off by the NBFC; and

b. an asset which is adversely affected by a potential threat of non-recoverability due to either erosion in the value of security or non-availability of security or due to any fraudulent act or omission on the part of the borrower.

vii. NPA means:

a. an asset, in respect of which, interest has remained overdue for a period of six months or more;

b. a term loan inclusive of unpaid interest, when the installment is overdue for a period of six months or more or on which interest amount remained overdue for a period of six months or more;

c. a demand or call loan, which remained overdue for a period of six months or more from the date of demand or call or on which interest amount remained overdue for a period of six months or more;

d. a bill which remains overdue for a period of six months or more;

e. the interest in respect of a debt or the income on receivables under the head 'other current assets' in the nature of short-term loans/advances, which remained overdue for a period of six months or more;

f. any dues on account of sale of assets or services rendered or reimbursement of expenses incurred, which remained overdue for period of six months or more;

g. the lease rental and hire purchase installment, which has become overdue for a period of 12 months or more;

h. in respect of loans, advances and other credit facilities (including bills purchased and discounted), the balance outstanding under the credit facilities (including accrued interest) made available to the same borrower/beneficiary when any of the above credit facilities becomes on-performing asset:

Provided that in the case of lease and hire purchase transactions, an NBFC may classify each such account on the basis of its record of recovery.

viii. 'Owned fund' means paid up equity capital, preference shares which are compulsorily convertible into equity, free reserves, balance in share premium account and capital reserves representing surplus arising out of sale proceeds of asset, excluding reserves created by revaluation of asset, as reduced by accumulated loss balance, book value of intangible assets and deferred revenue expenditure, if any.

ix. 'Standard asset' means the asset in respect of which no default in repayment of principal or payment of interest is perceived and which does not disclose any problem nor carry more than normal risk attached to the business.

x. 'Sub-standard asset' means:

   a. an asset which has been classified as NPA for a period not exceeding 18 months;

   b. an asset where the terms of the agreement regarding interest and/or principal have been renegotiated or rescheduled or restructured after commencement of operations, until the expiry of one year of satisfactory performance under the renegotiated or rescheduled or restructured terms:

   Provided that the classification of infrastructure loan as a substandard asset shall be in accordance with the provisions detailed under 'Norms relating to Infrastructure Loan' on page 153.

xi. 'Subordinated debt' means an instrument, which is fully paid up, is unsecured and is subordinated to the claims of other creditors and is free from restrictive clauses and is not redeemable at the instance of the holder or without the consent of the supervisory authority of NBFC. The book value of such instrument shall be subject to discounting as provided hereunder:

Remaining maturity of the instrument's rate of discount

   a. Up to one year–100 per cent

b. More than one year but up to two years–80 per cent

c. More than two years but up to three years–60 per cent

d. More than three years but up to four years–40 per cent

e. More than four years but up to five years–20 per cent to the extent such discounted value does not exceed 50 per cent of Tier-I capital.

Income Recognition

i. The income recognition shall be based on recognised accounting principles.

ii. Income including interest/discount or any other charges on NPA shall be recognised only when it is actually realised. Any such income recognised before the asset became non-performing and remained unrealised shall be reversed.

For the purpose of this paragraph, `net lease rentals' mean gross lease rentals as adjusted by the lease adjustment account debited/credited to the profit and loss account and as reduced by depreciation at the rate applicable under Schedule XIV of the Companies Act, 1956 (1 of 1956).

Loans, Advances and Other Credit Facilities including Bills Purchased and Discounted

The provisioning requirement in respect of loans, advances and other credit facilities including bills purchased and discounted are as under:

i. Loss assets: The entire asset shall be written off. If the assets are permitted to remain in the books for any reason, 100 per cent of the outstanding should be provided for.

ii. Doubtful assets

a. 100 per cent provision to the extent to which the advance is not covered by the realisable value of the security to which the NBFC has a valid recourse shall be made. The realisable value is to be estimated on a realistic basis.

b. In addition to item (a) above, depending upon the period for which the asset has remained doubtful, provision to the extent of 20 per cent to 50 per cent of the secured portion (i.e., estimated realisable value of the outstanding) shall be made on the following basis:

Period for which the asset has been considered as doubtful	*% of provision*
Up to one year	20
One to three years	30
More than three years	50

iii. Substandard assets: A general provision of 10 per cent of total outstanding shall be made.

Norms Relating to Infrastructure Loan

Applicability

i. These norms shall be applicable to restructuring and/or rescheduling and/or renegotiation of the terms of agreement relating to infrastructure loan, as defined in paragraph 2(1)(viii) of these directions which is fully or partly secured standard and sub-standard asset and to the loan, which is subjected to restructuring and/or rescheduling and/or renegotiation of terms.

ii. Where the asset is partly secured, a provision to the extent of shortfall in the security available, shall be made while restructuring and/or rescheduling and/or renegotiation of the loans, apart from the provision required on present value basis and as per prudential norms.

Funded Interest

In the case of funding of interest in respect of NPAs, where the interest funded is recognised as income, the interest funded shall be fully provided for.

Income Recognition Norms

The income recognition in respect of infrastructure loan shall be governed by the provisions of paragraph 3 of these directions.

Treatment of Provisions Held

The provisions held by the NBFC against non-performing infrastructure loan, which may be classified as 'standard' in terms of sub-paragraph (3) hereinabove, shall continue to be held until full recovery of the loan is made.

Eligibility for Upgradation of Restructured Substandard Infrastructure Loan

The substandard asset subjected to rescheduling and/or renegotiation and/or restructuring, whether in respect of installments of principal amount, or interest amount, by whatever modality, shall not be upgraded to the standard category until expiry of one year of satisfactory performance under the restructuring and/or rescheduling and/or renegotiation terms.

Conversion of Debt into Equity

Where the amount due as interest is converted into equity or any other instrument, and income is recognised in consequence, full provision shall be made for the amount of income so recognised, to offset the effect of such income recognition:

Provided that no provision is required to be made, if the conversion of interest is into equity which is quoted;

Provided further that in such cases, interest income may be recognized at market value of equity, as on the date of conversion, not exceeding the amount of interest converted to equity.

Conversion of Debt into Debentures

Where principal amount and/or interest amount in respect of NPAs is converted into debentures, such debentures shall be treated as NPA, void *ab initio*, in the same asset classification as was applicable to the loan, just before conversion and provision shall be made as per norms.

Increase in Exposure Limits for Infrastructure Related Loan and Investment

The systemically important non-deposit taking NBFC may exceed the concentration of credit/investment norms, as provided in paragraph 18 of these Directions, by 5 per cent for any single party and by 10 per cent for a single group of parties, if the additional exposure is on account of infrastructure loan and/or investment.

Risk Weight for Investment in AAA Rated Securitised Paper

The investment in 'AAA' rated securitised paper pertaining to the infrastructure facility shall attract risk weight of 50 per cent for capital adequacy purposes subject to the fulfillment of the following conditions:

i. The infrastructure facility generates income/cash flows, which ensure servicing/repayment of the securitised paper.

ii. The rating by one of the approved credit rating agencies is current and valid.

   Explanation: The rating relied upon shall be deemed to be current and valid, if the rating is not more than one month old on the date of opening of the issue, the rating rationale from the rating agency is not more than one year old on the date of opening of the issue, and the rating letter and the rating rationale form part of the offer document.

iii. In the case of secondary market acquisition, the 'AAA' rating of the issue is in force and confirmed from the monthly bulletin published by the respective rating agency.

iv. The securitised paper is a performing asset.

Conclusion

As discussed above, classification of assets is done taking into account the degree of well defined factors. Banks/FIs should not delay or postpone the identification of NPAs especially in respect of infrastructure accounts having the large sum. The doubts in asset classification arising out of any reasons are to be settled through internal channels within one month from the date on which the account would have been classified as NPA as prescribed by RBI through its guidelines contained in RBI/2011-12/66/DBOD/NO/BP.BC.12/21.04.048/2011-12—July 2012. RBI further states that the availability of security or net worth of borrower/guarantor should not be taken into account. Infrastructure accounts' asset classification should be done borrower wise and not facility wise. If the debits arising out of devolvement of LC or invoked guarantees are parked in a separate account, the balance outstanding in that account also should be treated as a part of the borrower's principal operating account for the purpose of the application of prudential norms.

Asset classification of accounts under consortium arrangements should be based on the record of recovery of the individual member bank and other aspects having a bearing on the recoverability of the advances. Where the remittances by the borrower under consortium arrangements are pooled with one bank and/or where the bank receiving remittances is not parting with the share of other member banks, the account will be treated as not serviced in the books of the other member banks and therefore be treated as NPA. The banks therefore should arrange to get their share of recovery transferred from the lead bank or get an express consent from the lead bank for the transfer of their share of recovery, to ensure proper asset classification in their respective books.

Take out finance: The norms of asset classification will have to be followed by the concerned bank/FI in whose books the account stands as balance sheet item as on the relevant date. If the lending institution observes that the asset has turned NPA on the basis of the record of recovery, it should be classified accordingly. The taking over institution on taking over such assets, should make provision for the account as NPA from the actual date of it becoming NPA even though the account was not in its books as on that date.

Prudential norms are required to be followed by the banks/FIs meticulously and properly.

12 Restructuring of Accounts

Introduction

The basic objective of restructuring is to put in place a transparent mechanism for restructuring of debts of potentially viable entities facing temporary problems due to factors beyond their control. In particular, the policy framework will aim at preserving viable units that are affected by certain internal and external factors and minimise the losses to the creditors and other stakeholders by way of providing timely support through an orderly and coordinated restructuring programme.

It is to be ensured that while taking up restructuring in any account, the ultimate viability/repaying capacity of the borrowers should be kept in view instead of considering temporary/short term restructuring of the account. It assumes greater importance in the context that second time restructuring of any account will downgrade the account as regulatory concessions are not available in case of second/repeated restructuring.

Further, restructured loan accounts which have been classified as non-performing assets (NPA) should be upgraded to the standard category only after observing satisfactory performance of one year from the date when first repayment of interest or installment of principal falls due, under the terms of restructuring package.

Borrowers indulging in frauds and malfeasance shall not be eligible for restructuring. Willful defaulters shall also not generally be considered for restructuring. Where strong justifiable reasons exist for considering restructuring the accounts of a willful defaulter, it should be ensured that the borrower has taken satisfactory steps to rectify the willful default.

i. Restructuring cannot be done with retrospective effect.

ii. If restructuring is taken up, the same should be implemented within 90 days from date of receipt of application.

iii. The restructuring should not be a repeated restructuring.

iv. The restructuring package should have right of recompense clause.

v. The bank/lender(s) should have the right to prepone repayment installments if projections are over achieved.

Asset Classification and Provisioning of Loan Accounts

Banks and financial institutions (FIs) will follow asset classification and provisioning norms for all loan accounts as prescribed by Reserve Bank of India (RBI):

Eligibility Criteria as per RBI Prudential Guidelines

i. The accounts classified under standard, substandard and doubtful categories may be restructured.

ii. The process of restructuring can be initiated in deserving cases, subject to borrower agreeing to the terms and conditions.

iii. No account will be taken up for restructuring unless the financial viability is established and there is a reasonable certainty of repayment from the borrower.

iv. Any restructuring done without looking into cash flows of the borrowers and assessing the viability of the projects would be treated as an attempt at evergreening a weak credit facility.

RBI further lays down that the viability should be determined by the banks/FIs based on the acceptable viability benchmarks determined by them which may be applied on a case by case basis, depending on merits of each case.

Illustratively, the parameter may include:

i. The return on capital employed

ii. Debt service coverage ratio (DSCR).

iii. Gap between the internal rate of return (IPR) and cost of fund.

iv. The amount of provision required in lieu of the diminution in the fair value of the restructured advance.

Accounts can be restructured under the following stages:

i. Before commencement of commercial production;

ii. After commencement of commercial production but before the asset has been classified as substandard;

iii. After commencement of commercial production and the asset has been classified as sub-standard:

Provided that in each of the above three stages, the restructuring and/or rescheduling and/or renegotiation of principal and/or interest may take place, with or without sacrifice, as part of the restructuring or rescheduling or renegotiating package evolved.

Restructuring, Rescheduling or Renegotiation of Terms of Infrastructure Loan

The non-banking financial companies (NBFC) may, not more than once, restructure or reschedule or renegotiate the terms of infrastructure loan agreement as per the policy framework laid down by the Board of Directors of the company as mentioned above.

Treatment of Restructured Standard Loan

The rescheduling or restructuring or renegotiation of the installments of principal alone, at any of the aforesaid first two stages shall not cause standard asset to be reclassified in the substandard category, if the project is re-examined and found to be viable by the Board of Directors of the company.

Provided that rescheduling or renegotiation or restructuring of interest installment at any of the foregoing first two stages shall not cause an asset to be downgraded to substandard category subject to the condition that the amount of interest foregone, if any, on account of adjustment in the element of interest as specified later, is either written off or 100 per cent provision is made.

Treatment of Restructured Substandard Asset

A substandard asset shall continue to remain in the same category in case of restructuring or rescheduling or renegotiation of the installments of principal until the expiry of one year and the amount of interest foregone, if any, on account of adjustment including adjustment by way of write off of the past interest dues, in the element of interest as specified later, shall be written off or 100 per cent provision made there against.

Adjustment of Interest

Where rescheduling or renegotiation or restructuring involves a reduction in the rate of interest, the interest adjustment shall be computed by taking the difference between the rate of interest as currently applicable to infrastructure loan (as adjusted for the risk rating applicable to the borrower) and the reduced rate and aggregating the present value (discounted at the rate currently applicable to infrastructure loan, adjusted for risk enhancement) of the future interest payable, so stipulated in the restructuring or rescheduling or renegotiation proposal.

Corporate Debt Restructuring (CDR) Mechanism

CDR is aimed at preserving viable corporates that are affected by certain internal and external factors and minimise the losses to the creditors through an orderly and coordinated restructuring programme.

Reference to CDR system could be triggered by:

i. Any or more of the creditors who have minimum 20 per cent share in term finance, or

ii. The concerned corporate if supported by a bank, or FIs have stake as in 1 above.

CDR system will have a three tier structure:

i. CDR standing committee and its core group

ii. CDR empowered group

iii. CDR cell

Eligibility Criteria

A loan amount is eligible for CDR provided the initiative to resolve the case under the system is taken by at least 75 per cent of the creditors by value and 60 per cent by number. This mechanism is to be availed by the companies that are hurt due to developments beyond management control.

CDR system will be applicable only to accounts classified as standard and substandard. There may be a situation where a small portion of debt by a bank might be classified as doubtful. In that situation, if the account has been classified as standard/substandard in the books of at least 90 per cent of creditors (by value), the same would be treated as standard/substandard, only for the purpose of judging the account as eligible for CDR, in the books of the remaining 10 per cent of creditors. There would be no requirement of the account/company being sick, NPA or being in default for a specified period before reference to the CDR system. However, potentially viable cases of NPAs will get priority. This approach would provide the necessary flexibility and facilitate timely intervention for debt restructuring. Prescribing any milestone(s) may not be necessary, since the debt restructuring exercise is being triggered by banks and FIs or with their consent.

There have been instances where the projects have been found to be viable by the creditors but the accounts could not be taken up for restructuring under the CDR system as they fell under 'doubtful' category. Hence, a second category of CDR is introduced for cases where the accounts have been classified as 'doubtful' in the books of creditors, and if a minimum of 75 per cent of creditors (by value) and 60 per cent creditors (by number) satisfy themselves of the viability of the account and consent for such restructuring, subject to the following conditions:

i. It will not be binding on the creditors to take up additional financing worked out under the debt restructuring package, and the decision to lend or not to lend will depend on each creditor bank/FI separately. In other words, under the proposed second category of the CDR mechanism, the existing loans will only be restructured and it would be up to the promoter to firm up additional financing arrangements with new or existing creditors individually.

ii. All other norms under the CDR mechanism such as the standstill clause, asset classification status during the pendency of restructuring under CDR, etc., will continue to be applicable to this category also.

The Ministry of Finance, Government of India in May 2012 has advised banks/FIs that loans under CDR should not be restructured to bail out companies with incompetent management. CDR should only be taken where the slippages have been for reasons beyond the control of the management of the company. In case CDR is done in cases that have been spoilt due to the incompetence of the management or where diversion or misuse of funds has taken place, the change of the management must be the first option, the ministry added. The ministry further advises banks/FIs not to convert distress loans into quasi-equity to revive companies. Quasi-equity provides low yielding coupons, and banks/FIs have to make huge provisions on them. It is rightly observed that while restructuring a debt, frequent recourse to long-term cumulative convertible preferences is taken which is likely a grant to the promoter shareholder. No dividend accrues on compulsorily convertible preference shares (CCPS) until the company becomes profitable.

To keep the CDR mechanism on the right track, banks and FIs have to follow stricter norms like:

i. Infusion of higher capital i.e., 20-25 per cent of the CDR amount being sought by the company from the current 15 per cent and to be paid up front.

ii. If diversion and misutilisation of fund is established, the case under CDR should not be entertained.

Provision for Diminution in the Fair Value of Restructured Advances

i. Reduction in the rate of interest and/or reschedulement of the repayment of principal amount, as part of the restructuring, will result in diminution in the fair value of the advance. Such diminution in value is an economic loss for the bank and will have impact on the bank's market value of equity. It is, therefore, necessary to measure such diminution in the fair value of the advance and make provisions for it by debit to profit and loss account. Such provision should be held in addition to the provisions as per existing provisioning norms, in an account distinct from that for normal provisions. For this purpose, the erosion in the fair value of the advance should be computed as the difference between the fair value of the loan before and after restructuring.

Fair value of the loan before restructuring will be computed as the present value of cash flows, representing the interest at the existing rate charged on the advance before restructuring and the principal discounted at a rate equal to the bank's benchmark prime lending rate (BPLR) as on the date of restructuring plus the appropriate term premium and credit risk premium for the borrower category on the date of restructuring.

Fair value of the loan after restructuring will be computed as the present value of cash flows, representing the interest at the rate charged on the advance on restructuring and the principal discounted at a rate equal to the bank's BPLR as on the date of restructuring plus the appropriate term premium and credit risk premium for the borrower category on the date of restructuring.

The provisions arise due to change in contractual terms of the loan upon restructuring which are in the nature of financial concessions. These provisions are distinct from the provisions which are linked to the asset classification of the account classified as NPA and reflect the impairment due to deterioration in the credit quality of the loan. Thus, the two types of the provisions are not substitutes for each other.

ii. In the case of working capital facilities, the diminution in the fair value of the cash credit/overdraft component may be computed as indicated in paragraph (i) above, reckoning the higher of the outstanding amount or the limit sanctioned as the principal amount and taking the tenor of the advance as one year. The term premium in the discount factor would be as applicable for one year. The fair value of the term loan components (working capital term loan and funded interest term loan) would be computed as per actual cash flows and taking the term premium in the discount factor as applicable for the maturity of the respective term loan components.

iii. In the event any security is taken in lieu of the diminution in the fair value of the advance, it should be valued at Re 1/- till maturity of the security. This will ensure that the effect of charging off the economic sacrifice to the profit and loss account is not negated.

iv. The diminution in the fair value may be recomputed on each balance sheet date till satisfactory completion of all repayment obligations and full repayment of the outstanding in the account is done, so as to capture the changes in the fair value on account of changes in BPLR, term premium and the credit category of the borrower. Consequently, banks may provide for the shortfall in provision or reverse the amount of excess provision held in the distinct account.

v. In respect of all restructured accounts where the total dues are less than Rs 1 crore, diminution in fair value will be computed at five per cent of the total exposure, till the financial year ending in March 2011. This position will be reviewed thereafter by RBI.

vi. The total provisions required against an account (normal provisions plus provisions in lieu of diminution in the fair value of the advance) are capped at 100 per cent of the outstanding debt amount.

Diminution in Fair Value Calculation in the Borrowal Account of Rs 1.00 cr. and above

RBI CIRCULAR NO. DBOD NO. BP.BC.No.37/21.04.132/2008-09 Dtd. 28/08/08 and No. BP.BC.No.121/21.04.132/2008-09 Dtd. 09/04/09

Name of the Account: Table D: Applicable for the TL Accounts where interest is being calculated on

1	Rate of interest (RoI)		
2	RoI		
3	Credit rating	RoI	
4	Balance outstanding as on 31.03.2009		

Note: i. Separate sheet should be used facility wise in case of the borrower having multiple credit facility

ii. Put necessary values in the appropriate columns to arrive at result.

Table 12.1

Chart for Fair Value Calculation

Sr. No.	*Month ending*	*Discounting factor*	*Before Restructuring*				
			Op. Bal.	*Repayment*	*Cl. Bal.*	*Intt.*	*Total cash flow*
(1)	*(2)*	*(3)*	*(4)*	*(5)*	*(6)*	*(7)*	*(8)*
0	Mar-10	1			0.00		
1	Apr-10	1.000	0		0.00		0.00
2	May-10	1.000	0.00		0.00		0.00
3	Jun-10	1.000	0.00		0.00	0.00	0.00
4	Jul-10	1.000	0.00		0.00		0.00
5	Aug-10	1.000	0.00		0.00		0.00
6	Sep-10	1.000	0.00		0.00	0.00	0.00
7	Oct-10	1.000	0.00		0.00		0.00
8	Nov-10	1.000	0.00		0.00		0.00
9	Dec-10	1.000	0.00		0.00	0.00	0.00
10	Jan-11	1.000	0.00		0.00		0.00
11	Feb-11	1.000	0.00		0.00		0.00
12	Mar-11	1.000	0.00		0.00	0.00	0.00
13	Apr-11	1.000	0.00		0.00		0.00
14	May-11	1.000	0.00		0.00		0.00
15	Jun-11	1.000	0.00		0.00	0.00	0.00
16	Jul-11	1.000	0.00		0.00		0.00
17	Aug-11	1.000	0.00		0.00		0.00
18	Sep-11	1.000	0.00		0.00	0.00	0.00
19	Oct-11	1.000	0.00		0.00		0.00
20	Nov-11	1.000	0.00		0.00		0.00
21	Dec-11	1.000	0.00		0.00	0.00	0.00
22	Jan-12	1.000	0.00		0.00		0.00
23	Feb-12	1.000	0.00		0.00		0.00
24	Mar-12	1.000	0.00		0.00	0.00	0.00
25	Apr-12	1.000	0.00		0.00		0.00
26	May-12	1.000	0.00		0.00		0.00
27	Jun-12	1.000	0.00		0.00	0.00	0.00
28	Jul-12	1.000	0.00		0.00		0.00
29	Aug-12	1.000	0.00		0.00		0.00
30	Sep-12	1.000	0.00		0.00	0.00	0.00
31	Oct-12	1.000	0.00		0.00		0.00
32	Nov-12	1.000	0.00		0.00		0.00
33	Dec-12	1.000	0.00		0.00	0.00	0.00
34	Jan-13	1.000	0.00		0.00		0.00
35	Feb-13	1.000	0.00		0.00		0.00
36	Mar-13	1.000	0.00		0.00	0.00	0.00

contd...

...contd...

(1)	(2)	(3)	(4)	(5)	(6)	(7)	(8)
37	Apr-13	1.000	0.00		0.00		0.00
38	May-13	1.000	0.00		0.00		0.00
39	Jun-13	1.000	0.00		0.00	0.00	0.00
40	Jul-13	1.000	0.00		0.00		0.00
41	Aug-13	1.000	0.00		0.00		0.00
42	Sep-13	1.000	0.00		0.00	0.00	0.00
43	Oct-13	1.000	0.00		0.00		0.00
44	Nov-13	1.000	0.00		0.00		0.00
45	Dec-13	1.000	0.00		0.00	0.00	0.00
46	Jan-14	1.000	0.00		0.00		0.00
47	Feb-14	1.000	0.00		0.00		0.00
48	Mar-14	1.000	0.00		0.00	0.00	0.00
49	Apr-14	1.000	0.00		0.00		0.00
50	May-14	1.000	0.00		0.00		0.00
51	Jun-14	1.000	0.00		0.00	0.00	0.00
52	Jul-14	1.000	0.00		0.00		0.00
53	Aug-14	1.000	0.00		0.00		0.00
54	Sep-14	1.000	0.00		0.00	0.00	0.00
55	Oct-14	1.000	0.00		0.00		0.00
56	Nov-14	1.000	0.00		0.00		0.00
57	Dec-14	1.000	0.00		0.00	0.00	0.00
58	Jan-15	1.000	0.00		0.00		0.00
59	Feb-15	1.000	0.00		0.00		0.00
60	Mar-15	1.000	0.00		0.00	0.00	0.00
61	Apr-15	1.000	0.00		0.00		0.00
62	May-15	1.000	0.00		0.00		0.00
63	Jun-15	1.000	0.00		0.00	0.00	0.00
64	Jul-15	1.000	0.00		0.00		0.00
65	Aug-15	1.000	0.00		0.00		0.00
66	Sep-15	1.000	0.00		0.00	0.00	0.00
67	Oct-15	1.000	0.00		0.00		0.00
68	Nov-15	1.000	0.00		0.00		0.00
69	Dec-15	1.000	0.00		0.00	0.00	0.00
70	Jan-16	1.000	0.00		0.00		0.00
71	Feb-16	1.000	0.00		0.00		0.00
72	Mar-16	1.000	0.00		0.00	0.00	0.00
73	Apr-16	1.000	0.00		0.00		0.00
74	May-16	1.000	0.00		0.00		0.00
75	Jun-16	1.000	0.00		0.00	0.00	0.00
76	Jul-16	1.000	0.00		0.00		0.00
77	Aug-16	1.000	0.00		0.00		0.00
78	Sep-16	1.000	0.00		0.00	0.00	0.00

contd...

...contd...

(1)	*(2)*	*(3)*	*(4)*	*(5)*	*(6)*	*(7)*	*(8)*
79	Oct-16	1.000	0.00		0.00		0.00
80	Nov-16	1.000	0.00		0.00		0.00
81	Dec-16	1.000	0.00		0.00	0.00	0.00
82	Jan-17	1.000	0.00		0.00		0.00
83	Feb-17	1.000	0.00		0.00		0.00
84	Mar-17	1.000	0.00		0.00	0.00	0.00
85	Apr-17	1.000	0.00		0.00		0.00
86	May-17	1.000	0.00		0.00		0.00
87	Jun-17	1.000	0.00		0.00	0.00	0.00
88	Jul-17	1.000	0.00		0.00		0.00
89	Aug-17	1.000	0.00		0.00		0.00
90	Sep-17	1.000	0.00		0.00	0.00	0.00
91	Oct-17	1.000	0.00		0.00		0.00
92	Nov-17	1.000	0.00		0.00		0.00
93	Dec-17	1.000	0.00		0.00	0.00	0.00
94	Jan-18	1.000	0.00		0.00		0.00
95	Feb-18	1.000	0.00		0.00		0.00
96	Mar-18	1.000	0.00		0.00	0.00	0.00
97	Apr-18	1.000	0.00		0.00		0.00
98	May-18	1.000	0.00		0.00		0.00
99	Jun-18	1.000	0.00		0.00	0.00	0.00
100	Jul-18	1.000	0.00		0.00		0.00
101	Aug-18	1.000	0.00		0.00		0.00
102	Sep-18	1.000	0.00		0.00	0.00	0.00
103	Oct-18	1.000	0.00		0.00		0.00
104	Nov-18	1.000	0.00		0.00		0.00
105	Dec-18	1.000	0.00		0.00	0.00	0.00
106	Jan-19	1.000	0.00		0.00		0.00
107	Feb-19	1.000	0.00		0.00		0.00
108	Mar-19	1.000	0.00		0.00	0.00	0.00
109	Apr-19	1.000	0.00		0.00		0.00
110	May-19	1.000	0.00		0.00		0.00
111	Jun-19	1.000	0.00		0.00	0.00	0.00
112	Jul-19	1.000	0.00		0.00		0.00
113	Aug-19	1.000	0.00		0.00		0.00
114	Sep-19	1.000	0.00		0.00	0.00	0.00
115	Oct-19	1.000	0.00		0.00		0.00
116	Nov-19	1.000	0.00		0.00		0.00
117	Dec-19	1.000	0.00		0.00	0.00	0.00
118	Jan-20	1.000	0.00		0.00		0.00
119	Feb-20	1.000	0.00		0.00		0.00
120	Mar-20	1.000	0.00		0.00	0.00	0.00
TOTAL			0		0.00	0.00	

Sr. No.	*Month ending*	*Discounting factor*	*After Restructuring*							
			Op. Bal.	*Repayment*	*Cl. Bal.*	*Intt.*	*Total cash flow*	*PV of (8)*	*PV of (13)*	*Diminution in fair value*
(1)	*(2)*	*(3)*	*(9)*	*(10)*	*(11)*	*(12)*	*(13)*	*(14)*	*(15)*	*(16)*

Likewise data would be given from 1st April to 31st March as shown in Table 12.1.

Conclusion

Restructuring provides timely package to the debts of viable entities facing problems. Whereas CDR is timely and transparent, mechanism for restructuring of corporate debts fall outside the purview of BIFR, DRT and other legal proceedings for the benefit of all concerned. It facilitates restructuring of advances of borrowers enjoying credit facilities of more than one bank/FI. This mechanism is applicable to infrastructure project where borrowers are generally availing the advance under consortium arrangement. It is a non-statutory mechanism which is a voluntary system based on debtor creditor agreement (DCA) and inter-creditor agreement (ICA). The DCA and ICA shall provide the legal status to the CDR mechanism. The debtors shall have to accede to the DCA, and ICA would be a legally binding agreement among the creditors. The rationale behind CDR is to give the fresh credit cycle to the account depending upon the viability nature of the account.

13 Monitoring, Supervision and Follow-Up *vis-à-vis* Review of Term Loans

Monitoring begins immediately after sanctioning of an advance. It involves a systematic sequencing of activities, like:

i. Execution of documents.

ii. Creation of securities.

iii. Registration of charges.

iv. Obtention of operational data/Statement of stocks and book debts.

v. Fixation of drawing power.

vi. Verification of securities periodically.

vii. Watching the operations in the account.

viii. Watching the recovery of interest and installments as per terms of sanction.

ix. Identifying weakness, if any, in the accounts.

x. Prompting competent authority for initiating corrective action.

Therefore, monitoring is a continuous process to ensure safety of funds by constant vigil/watch on the advance account, from the date of sanction till recovery, in order to maintain its health.

Even though the three terms—supervision, follow-up and review—have distinct meanings of their own, all the three activities can be put under monitoring. In the context of credit department of a bank, monitoring shall encompass supervision and follow-up of activities that follow sanction of credit limits to a borrower like execution of legal documents, creation of securities, creation of charges as required under law, compliance with other terms of sanction, supervision of securities prior to disbursement,

disbursement as per sanction, monitoring the operations in the account, servicing of the credit extended, monitoring recovery as envisaged in the sanctioned terms, identifying the weaknesses in the account, advising appropriate authorities of the weaknesses and finally, keeping a continuous vigil and watch over the credit portfolio of the bank.

In infrastructure, follow-up of projects during its implementation is a specialised task calling for close monitoring and interactions with multiple agencies involved in financing/promotions/consultations and sharing of security.

Before financial closure and the first disbursement, there are certain pre-commitment, pre-disbursement conditions etc., which need to be met. There are also some financial covenants of the guarantors to the project that need to be verified. At the time of sanction, documentation and disbursement, monitoring schedule would be drawn up duly examining its adequacy, and the compliance of the conditions aforesaid would be furnished at periodical intervals. The equity infusion schedule also needs to be followed up to ensure maintenance of debt-equity norms envisaged. The achievement of project milestones with the follow-up report has to be compiled with.

At the time of seeking disbursement of funds for project construction, the project companies are required to submit information on the project status and implementation, listing out the various items of expenditures incurred.

Lenders' engineer (independent engineer wherever appointed) would be visiting the site at periodical intervals and feed information regularly about project progress. The disbursements would be made taking into account the information submitted by the lender independent engineer (LIE), the company and the auditors–wherever feasible, information would be collated.

Compliance regarding pre-commitment conditions/covenants of lenders, which will include:

i. All clearances/permissions like land acquisition, licenses, fuel linkage, rail linkage, etc.

ii. Contract finalisation like shareholder's agreement etc.

iii. Documentation etc.

Compliance regarding pre-disbursement conditions/covenants of lenders, which will include:

i. Loan tie-ups.

ii. Raising equity as stipulated.

iii. Meeting financial parameters.

iv. Security creations.

v. Finalisation of various agreements like engineering, procurement and construction (EPC) contract, raw material supply and transportation, operation and maintenance (O&M) contract, escrow, etc.

vi. Observations, if any, made by credit auditors of bank.

Compliance of other conditions of the lenders during construction phase *viz.*,

i. Regulatory time schedule.

ii. Physical completion schedules.

iii. EPC contract terms and compliance thereof.

iv. Project cost–estimated and actual—commitment of funding, details of escalation, if any.

v. Expenses schedule—estimated and actual—funding thereof.

vi. Liquidated damages, if any.

vii. Debt-quity infusion schedule.

viii. Progress of the project.

ix. Lender engineer's–scope and reports.

x. Issues raised by the LIE in his report(s).

xi. Chartered Accountant's certificate on sources and uses of funds.

xii. Completion test requirements and compliances.

xiii. Insurance and other hedging mechanism.

xiv. Creation of charges on securities etc.

xv. Inter-creditor arrangements and compliances, etc.

xvi. Environmental and license conditions and compliances.

xvii. Cost escalation, if any.

xviii. Cost and time overruns, if any.

xix. Working capital tie-up.

Compliance during post-construction phase, which shall be in line with the normal follow-up including aspects as under:

i. Projections: business, profitability, debt-equity ratio (DER) and actual performance.

ii. Compliances in respect of appointments of key personnel for various functions.

iii. Compliances regarding statutory/tax obligations.

iv. Environmental compliances.

v. Expansions: as per stipulations, conditions on group's expansion, diversifications, cross investments, etc.

vi. Management and decision making systems in regard to joint ventures etc.

vii. Financial covenants and compliances thereof—dividend policy etc.

viii. Certificate regarding non-violation of the covenants as per the common term sheet.

ix. Position of court cases, if any, against the company.

The site visits would also be combined with that of other lenders, and disbursing branch would also be involved. The visits would also ensure interactions with project managers/co-sponsors during the implementation stage and with the working capital bankers in the post-completion stage. Non-compliance of critical covenants that are vital for project viability would be given utmost importance and site visit reports would be submitted with the course of action proposed. When the project implementation is complete, a completion audit would be conducted with the help of lenders' engineer certifying the various parameters of performance envisaged in the project contracts. This will be a source of comfort for the lenders and the project participants as well, including equity holders.

After the construction phase is over, the follow-up of the project would be undertaken as per the terms and conditions stipulated for the loan. It should also be examined whether the actual performance and the cash flows of the project company are in line with the project estimates and appropriate measures initiated for addressing any variations. Any financial irregularity (e.g., default in payment of interest, principal repayments, etc.) observed in the project would be reported. However, the project company's inability to meet the financial covenants stipulated such as current ratio, total outstanding liability (TOL)/tangible net worth (TNW), interest coverage ratio, etc., would be reported to the management as the case may be, as per the procedure laid down by the institute.

Project Monitoring as Part of Disbursement Process

The department shall use mechanism of disbursement to monitor the physical and financial progress during every stage of project implementation. Deviations of material nature, if any, shall be immediately discussed at the joint meeting of the project and outcome/record of such meetings may be maintained by way of report/note prepared by an officer attending such meetings, followed by copy of the minutes of such meetings obtained from the lead bank. The note of progress report has to be submitted to general manager (GM) (credit). Annual review of accounts of all projects will be submitted to the chairman and managing director (CMD)/Board under the structured format of the respective banks/financial institutions (FIs) referred in Annexure A-7.

Post-Sanction/Disbursement Supervision and Monitoring

Objectives

Infrastructure projects are more complex and require close follow-up during the initial phases of commercial operations. In the circumstances, the follow-up during its implementation is a specialised task calling for close monitoring. Monitoring of the project is required at all the stages of project. At the time of sanction, documentation and disbursement, monitoring schedule would be drawn.

Proper monitoring and supervision of the facilities are activities of vital importance with the following broad objectives:

i. Collection of data relating to physical and financial performance of assisted companies;

ii. Analysis of the data/information to assess the performance *vis-à-vis* appraisal estimates;

iii. The shaping of the project *vis-à-vis* the milestones planned as per original schedule.

Site Visits

First Site Visit: The site visits will be arranged by the lead bank or the borrower. It will be desirable that dealing officer should join the first visit before commencing any disbursement. This is only applicable where the site visit is proposed by the lead bank, however, many times disbursements are proposed without having pre-disbursement site visit based on lending confirmation notice (LCN) issued by lead bank. Sometimes site visit is deferred or postponed in some cases; however, the same is undertaken before the next disbursement.

Subsequent Site Visits: As far as subsequent visits are concerned, the dealing officer should ensure at least one visit in a year for each project. In case such visits are not being arranged by the lead bank, then dealing officer may take it up with lead bank and request for such visits. In special circumstances, where such visits are not feasible due to convenience of all lenders or for any other valid reasons, the same is put as a note under monthly progress report submitted to the competent authority.

Report on Site Visits: After each site visit, the dealing officer shall submit a site visit report to the appropriate authority and also obtain the copy of the joint visit from the lead bank. If any adverse developments in project implementation are noticed, the dealing officer should submit a comprehensive note with his recommendation for future actions to protect the lenders interest to the appropriate authority. This report should be filed chronologically and made available for scrutiny by the lenders' auditors.

Monitoring Reports

During the currency of the financial assistance, the lead bank will provide structured information relating to the special purpose vehicle (SPV) to all the banks and FIs in consortium through the following reports:

Implementation Period Progress Report

As a part of understanding amongst lenders at joint meeting, lead bank should obtain regular reports on project implementation. The report shall cover information on physical and financial progress, performance *vis-à-vis* milestones, details of capital expenditure and means of finance, status of approvals, creation of security, pending litigation, etc.

All project implementation progress reports must be accompanied by the following:

i. LIE's report, giving physical status and likely delay in implementation, if any.

ii. SPV's statutory auditor's certificate.

Significant deviations, if any, observed in the performance of the project *vis-à-vis* projections as per the appraisal, including any reappraisal/total review. The reasons for such deviations shall be studied and ascertained.

Operations Period Report

This report must be furnished by all SPVs after project completion and the project is put to operation on a quarterly or semi-annual basis during the currency of the financial assistance. The report seeks information on actual physical and financial performance *vis-à-vis* projections, status of key approvals, status of insurance, pending litigation, etc.

Project Completion Report

Upon the project achieving commercial operation date (COD), dealing officer shall prepare a project completion report. The report should compare (actual vs. appraised) important items such as cost and means of financing, determine reasons for variations, if any, and the likely impact on the project economics.

Annual Report

The SPV must furnish a copy of its audited annual accounts/annual report within six months from the date of closure of its accounting year. The credit department shall review the financial performance, including the auditor's report and directors' report and hold discussions with the SPV to seek clarifications, if any.

Report of External Agencies (Trust and Retention Account (TRA), LIE, Consultants/Auditors)

Lenders' Independent Engineer (LIE)

LIE is appointed to review and report on the progress and other implementation related issues to the lenders. Generally, the LIE visits the site every month/quarter and files his report to lenders. A copy of the LIE's report should be received and reviewed by the dealing officer. And if there is a major deviation, the same should be brought to the notice of GM(credit).

Environmental and Social Monitoring Review (ESMR)

The environmental and social conditions stipulated and related to the project to be verified and to be observed whether they are complied with or not. If not, the reasons are to be assigned to with course of actions.

Auditor's Certificate

Implementation Stage: The end-use of funds is an important requirement of the project monitoring and supervision. Each disbursement request from the borrower should be accompanied by a certificate from the Chartered Accountant of the borrower, certifying the project cost incurred till the certificate date and the means of finance for the same.

Project Completion Report: Upon the project achieving physical completion, the borrower should furnish a certificate from the statutory auditors/independent auditors of the borrower, certifying the completed project cost and the actual means of finance for the same.

Lender's Insurance Advisor (LIA)

The job of LIA would be to ensure that appropriate insurance cover has been obtained by SPV. Lead bank will review that various policies continue to be in force and effect with details of all insurances required *viz.*, validity of these insurances, amount of insurance, nature of cover and list of assets which are insured for the project. Lead bank is to confirm that valid and adequate insurance cover has been obtained on the project and a certificate to this effect should be brought on record by other members of the consortium.

Lender's Legal Counsel (LLC)

The job of LLC would be to ensure whether proper, valid and enforceable documents are drafted, taking into consideration the views of all lenders and get the same properly executed. LLC shall also issue due diligence certificate regarding validity, legality and enforceability of documents to the lead bank, who in turn will issue it to all the members of the consortium.

Project Review

With a view to develop in-house expertise and as an ongoing monitoring process, it is recommended that dealing officer should perform the following:

i. Review of undisbursed sanctions.

ii. Review of disbursed cases.

iii. Performance review of projects in operation.

iv. Planning and policies for irregular accounts.

Review of Undisbursed Sanctions

Cases where disbursement has not commenced within 12 months of sanction would be reviewed and reported to the competent authority.

Review of Disbursed Cases During Implementation Stage

An annual review of all borrowers whose projects are in construction phase shall be reviewed as an ongoing monitoring.

Performance Review of Projects in Operation

i. Review of SPVs: It shall be carried out for monitoring purposes. This will provide guidance for future projects and experience gained may also be actively used for developing future portfolio.

   The review shall look into the following:

   a. The assumptions made at the time of evaluation of the proposal.

   b. Current project status, performance.

   c. Payment track record.

d. Adequacy of security provided by the client.

e. Adequacy of insurance.

f. Compliance with loan covenants.

g. Outstanding issues, if any.

ii. Annual Review of Sanction: All sanction accounts shall be reviewed and a note will be submitted to the Board.

Monitoring of Problem Loan, Based on Early Warning Signals

In spite of sound risk management and appraisal processes, some accounts may develop weaknesses on account of changes in internal or external conditions. Monitoring mechanisms need to be put in place to identify such weak accounts before they turn non-performing assets (NPAs).

Tracking Process

Standard assets with certain financial and/or operational irregularities, as well as borrowers with a weak financial position should be monitored effectively. Certain irregularities have been defined below to identify early warning signals.

Financial/Operational Irregularities

i. Quarterly/monthly interest overdue for more than 30 days.

ii. Principal/instalments overdue for more than 30 days.

iii. Diversion of funds.

iv. Incomplete documentation.

v. Non-compliance of terms and conditions as per the agreement.

Weak Financial Position

i. Poor financial performance in terms of declining sales and profits, cash losses, net losses, erosion of net worth, management of escrow account, etc.

ii. Slippage in the completion of the project stages or getting the required clearances.

The above list is not exhaustive and there may be other signals which can be noticed during appraisals/inspection of the site.

Review of Term Loans

All term loan accounts should be reviewed once in a year to ensure inter alia that:

i. The progress of implementation of the project is as per schedule.

ii. The instalments due have been remitted. If not, the reasons for non-payment should be analysed where the company has gone into operation and payment of instalments of loan has commenced.

iii. Rephasement of instalment where necessary has been arranged.

In cases where the borrower's company has been enjoying a term loan facility, the annual review on the prescribed format of the bank/FIs along with the information on compliance with the stipulated financial covenants, is to be submitted to the authority.

In cases where term loan as well as working credit facility have been sanctioned to the company, review of term loan should form a part of the review/renewal of working capital limits. The proposal should contain a brief write-up containing the following information on term loan:

i. Position of the project.

ii. Position of the account.

iii. Irregularities, if any, during the year under review.

iv. Compliance with terms of sanction.

v. Compliance with financial covenants.

vi. Review of debt servicing capacity as detailed here under:

	Original projections for the year under review	Actual data for the year
Cash approvals		
Maturing term obligations		
Net debt service coverage ratio (DSCR)		

14 Loan Review Mechanism

Banks/financial institutions (FIs) should setup a separate and independent Credit Monitoring Department whose primary function would be:

i. To identify promptly loans which develop credit weaknesses and capture them under special mention accounts (SMA).

ii. To evaluate portfolio quality and isolate potential areas.

iii. To provide information for determination of loan loss provision.

iv. To assess the adequacy and adherence to loan policy and procedures of banks/FIs and to monitor compliance with relevant laws and regulations.

v. To provide top management with information on credit administration including credit sanction process, risk evaluation and post sanction follow-up.

An SMA may briefly have the following main characteristics:

i. An account is considered as 'weak' if it is irregular/overdrawn (except where irregularity is due to interest) for more than 30 days.

ii. External rating of the project.

- External rating below BBB.
- Commercial operation date (COD) delayed beyond 2 years.
- COD delayed beyond 1 year up to 2 years.
- COD delayed up to 1 year.
- Rating below 'BBB' with no extension in COD.

iii. Extension in COD (rating above 'BBB') carrying higher risk weight and higher provision i.e., to the extent of 150 per cent.

iv. COD achieved but rating below BBB.

v. Extension in COD of the project with change in repayment schedule.

vi. Cost overrun in the project.

vii. Time overrun.

Based on the features illustrated above, the department needs to take a view and enhance the level of monitoring the account. Accounts adversely commented upon from the stand point of their quality in the audit report/ inspection report should also be reported in SMA with a plan of actions.

The account shall also be classified as SMA if:

i. There is an overshooting of the cost of the project, as envisaged by the company, by more than 25 per cent without proper arrangement for meeting the excess cost.

ii. Accounts of the borrowers with other banks/FIs are running irregular.

iii. There is a non-compliance of important terms and conditions of sanctions such as: charging of prime/collateral securities, incomplete documentation in terms of creation/registration of charge/mortgage, etc.

Conclusion

Loan accounts have been brought under SMA for various reasons as explained in the chapter. The objectives of the system are to keep the concerned authority informed of the position of the account and also to suggest and initiate timely remedial actions in effective and efficient manner at periodical intervals for the purpose of control and regular monitoring. A proper analysis of reasons leading to non-payment should be properly assessed, analysed and submitted to the authority in structured format. For the accounts reported in SMA due to non-payment of installment/interests, the concerned project should be visited and a detailed report highlighting the ground realities should be submitted. In fact the visits to such project must be accorded a priority. Credit department would have the special responsibility to keep monitoring such accounts and informing about the same to the authority.

15 Securitisation

Introduction

Securitisation involves packaging a designated pool of assets (mortgage loans, consumer loans, hire purchase receivable, and so on) and issuing securities which are collateralised by the underlying assets and their associated cash flow stream. Securitisation is originally oriented by a firm that seeks to liquefy its pool of assets. Securities backed by mortgage loans are referred to as mortgage backed securities; securities backed by other assets are called asset based securities.

Key steps: Securitisation can take place in different ways and assume complex structures. Broadly, the following steps are involved in a securitisation programme.

i. Seasoning–The originator (the firm that seeks to liquefy its assets) identifies its assets to be securitised and packages them in a pool.

ii. Credit Enhancement–The originator or some other agency may enhance the credit quality of the pool of assets to be securitised by providing insurance, often of a limited kind, to the investors.

iii. Transfer to a Special Purpose Vehicle (SPV)–The pool of assets is transferred to a SPV, usually organised as a trust, for valuable consideration. Once the transfer is completed, the assets are taken off the balance sheet of the originator.

iv. Issuance of Securities–The SPV issues securities backed by the pool of assets held by it. These securities are called pass through certificates (PTCs) because cash flows received from the pool of assets are transmitted to the holders of these securities on a prorata basis after deduction of service fee. There may be one or more classes of PTCs with differing priorities. Where there are two or more classes of PTCs, the rules for the distribution of interest and principal repayments derived from the underlying pool of assets, among different classes of PTC holders are specified upfront.

Securitisation of Loan Portfolio

Securitisation is a mechanism by which pools of infrastructure loans are converted into marketable securities to enable investments thereon. The transactions between parties in the infrastructure sector can be broadly classified as those relating to 'primary infrastructure loan market' and 'secondary infrastructure loan market'. The primary market activity mainly comprises creation of infrastructure loans as a result of transactions between the borrowers (infrastructure promoters) and primary lenders. The primary lenders create assets against loans provided by them to the promoters. The loans held as assets, generate cash flows represented by repayments of both principal and interest.

The secondary mortgage market mainly involves the conversion of infrastructure loans into tradable financial instruments and the sale of these instruments to prospective investors. The cash flows which come as repayments from the borrowers to the originators, can be transferred to a third party with simultaneous transfer of assets to an intermediary agency (SPV) designated for the purpose of managing the bought over pool of mortgages. These cash flows are passed on to the investors by the SPV. In the process, the infrastructure loans are converted into securities which are tradable financial instruments and sold to investors. The secondary market is thus made up of securities which are backed by infrastructure loan asset backed securities (ABS) and refers to the transactions between the issuers and investors.

Once the securitised infrastructure loans are sold by the originators *viz.*, the primary lending institutions, they are both derecognised in the originator's books of account and presented in a specific manner. All future transactions in the asset backed financial instruments then take place in the secondary mortgage market, depending upon the depth of the market. The overall liquidity in the capital market and infrastructure finance system would increase with the number of transactions among investors in the secondary mortgage market.

Figure 15.1

Infrastructure Finance: Ideal Market Structure

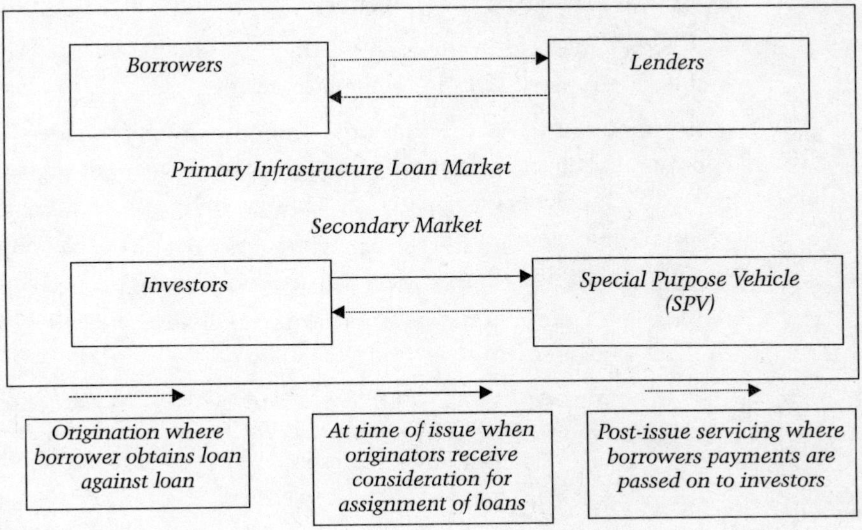

For the purpose of promoting such a transaction, banks/financial institutions (FIs) may consider the following:

i. Assignment and transfer of a pool of infrastructure loans along with the underlying cashflows, from the primary lending institution to SPV.

ii. Securitisation of infrastructure debt: On acquiring the pool along with the underlying mortgages, an express creation of SPV (in the form of a company or a trust) may be made by banks/FIs in respect of the infrastructure debt, appointing itself as the trustee/promoter for the benefit of the investors. Once the assets have been declared property in trust ('the trust'), the trust/company will issue PTCs to investors.

In this process, the infrastructure lenders can securitise their loan portfolio and obtain immediate liquidity for the same for lending more to the sector.

i. Securitisation of the infrastructure loan portfolio can be done by assigning (selling) the same to promoter/trustee (or its designated SPV created for the purpose).

ii. In return, the infrastructure lenders will obtain the consideration for the portfolio which will be equal to the amount of outstanding loans sold/assigned.

iii. The SPV will package the loan portfolio so purchased into ABS and issue the same to capital market investors.

iv. The promoter/trustee will authorise the infrastructure lenders to continue to collect the repayments of the loan along with interest from the borrowers without any change in its procedures or processes, on its behalf.

v. The borrowers (infrastructure companies) will continue to repay the loan in same manner as before with no change in their loan contract/agreement.

It will be the promoter/trustee's endeavour to evolve infrastructure finance solutions suited to the specialised needs of the market.

Securitisation: Benefits

Supportive fiscal measures and the policies of Reserve Bank of India (RBI) have established a systemic framework for specialised infrastructure finance in the country and the sector has been witnessing steady growth in the past few years. In the recent past, with the emergence of the capital market as the central pool of resources for sectoral development, the pre-eminence of securitisation as a viable and sustainable market oriented sourcing mechanism has come to be recognised. With the potential of integrating infrastructure market with the domestic as well as the international capital markets, securitisation also brings a range of specialisations, resulting in efficient and cost effective structures and practices.

The process:

i. Facilitates the mortgage finance intermediaries to leverage their resources to compete effectively;

ii. Enables risk transfer and improves capital adequacy ratio (CAR);

iii. Assists asset-liabilities management and helps sourcing long term funds;

iv. Enables better management of financial spreads and facilitates improvement of return on assets and return on equity;

v. Enables new source of fee based income;

Touchstones

i. 'Bankruptcy remoteness of pool' from the originator (pool of assets to be out of reach of originator(s) and their creditors/ liquidators).

ii. Issuance of securities (ABS) by the SPV to investors collateralised by the underlying infrastructure assets/receivables.

iii. Reliance by investors on the performance of the assets for repayment.

Securitisation: Offers an Alternative

Macro-level Sectoral Benefits

i. An off-balance sheet financing mechanism:

- Legal true sale of assets by originator to an SPV – Assets go off the balance sheet of originators;
- Asset side financing – Can support in generating more loans without additional capital.

ii. Potential to support as an additional source of finance:

- Flow of funds from capital market for financing infrastructure.

iii. Risk diversification:

- Precludes concentration of financial risk within financial sector;
- Risk transfer to multiple third parties (different sectors);
- Securitisation and borrowing are not mutually exclusive;
- Securitisation enhances borrowing abilities.

iv. Creation of a long-term debt market through introduction of ABS.

Banks/Lenders: Benefits to Individual Entities

i. Enables better asset-liability management:

- Securitisation replaces assets having long-term cash flows with cash thereby shortening average maturity of assets.

ii. Regulatory reliefs: More efficient association of capital:

- Possible to redeploy the ABS proceeds for generating more loans with no additional capital.

iii. Overcome exposure limitation:

- Single party/group/sector exposures;
- Later, once sufficient asset base is created, India Infrastructure Finance Company Limited (IIFCL) can securitise its own portfolio to create more head room.

iv. Alternative to take-out financing:

- Potential to overcome limitations in take-out finance.

v. Interest rate sensitivity:

- Securitisation: Tool for interest rate risk management;
- Securitisation helps in overall balance sheet management.

vi. Fee based income:

- Servicing free.

Figure 15.2

Possible SPV Structures

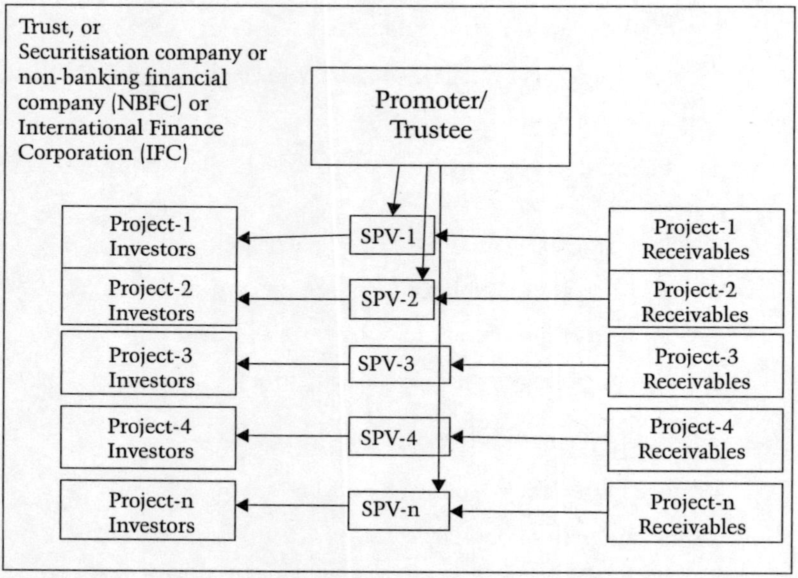

Infrastructure Loans: Structural Issues

Main Issues

i. Long term loans: Asset-liability mismatch

ii. SPV financing: Project's risks with SPV

iii. Multiple levels of Risk-Unconventional Asset cover – Not amenable for resale, reapplication and are not treated as security:

- Construction risk
- Operational risk
- Demand risk
- Network risk
- Technological risk
- Financing risk arises
- Regulatory (sovereign) risk

iv. Long gestation projects with high capital costs and backended project returns

v. Interest rate risk

Safeguards

i. Selection Criteria – After careful consideration

ii. Due diligence and rating

iii. Credit enhancement

iv. Cash flow tranching: Waterfall structures (senior/subordinates)

Securitisation Architecture

i. Promoter/trustee can assume the following roles:

- Trustee/promoter
- Investor in senior class instruments
- Credit enhancer/guarantor/subordinate investor
- Each role – may be mutually exclusive

ii. Exposure will not be on promoter/trustee
- Exposure only to the extent of credit enhancement (limited guarantee) or investment

iii. Project selection criteria: Needs to be stringent
- Construction risk
- Operational risk
- Demand risk
- Network risk
- Technological risk
- Financing risk arises
- Regulatory (sovereign) risk
- Stringency to be based on risks and rating
- Flexible: Relevant and acceptable to lenders

iv. Rating due diligence

Capital Market Issues and Investors

i. Demat of ABS
- Securities Contracts Regulation Act (SCRA) has been amended and demat is permitted

ii. Listing and trading of ABS in stock exchanges
- Listing process is being finalised by Securities and Exchange Board of India (SEBI)

iii. Existing investors
- Insurance companies
- Banks
- Financial institutions
- Mutual funds

iv. Potential investors
- Pension funds/provident funds

The success of a new financial instrument, such as Infra ABS, is mainly dependent on its ability to satisfy the needs of the investors in terms of safety, liquidity and adequate returns. A major problem faced by the infrastructure finance market today is the lack of a secondary market. Absence of a secondary market for securitised paper or its inactiveness may make the sale of the securities difficult and hence may not provide exit routes to the investors, thus making it an unattractive instrument. This risk can be reduced by developing an active secondary market. Market making is vital for managing this form of risk.

Listing on the Stock Exchanges: The listing of the Infra ABS on the stock exchanges will facilitate secondary market development. There are several problems associated with the listing of the ABS as of date. Availability of information of the issuer (i.e. the SPV) and of the underlying assets is essential. The ABS can be issued in dematerialised form. Investments in ABS by mutual funds, though subject to their individual investment policies, will greatly add to the trading depth of the instrument. Once ABS paper is in profusion in the market, establishment of an infra mutual fund that has a specific mandate to invest in ABS paper may be encouraged. Further, with clarity in listing requirements of the NSE and the gradual trading of ABS papers, there will be increased secondary market activities leading to better liquidity. Also, awareness building about the Infra ABS product and the risks involved will also help build the market on sound lines.

Development of an effective secondary market for infra assets backed securities will require, amongst others, the following facilities/mechanisms:

i. Dematerialisation of securitised assets: A depository holds securities in dematerialised form. It maintains ownership records of securities in a book entry form and also effects transfer of ownership through book entry. Dematerialisation of securities has resulted from the reforms in the secondary capital markets. It has helped reduce the incidence of bad deliveries and has removed the problems relating to non-delivery/loss/mutilation of physical shares. Further, the effective transaction costs have been reduced on account of reduction/elimination of stamp duties. Electronic transfer of securities has also eased the process of transfer. The dematerialisation of asset backed securities (ABS) will not only enhance the initial participation of the investors but will also improve the trading volumes directly flowing from the benefits of the electronic process. Further, dematerialisation will also facilitate splitting of the certificates and reducing the lot size thereby improving its trading in the market.

ii. Effective custodial/depository services for such assets: The transparency and efficiency of secondary market trading in asset backed securities will also depend upon efficient custodial/ depository services. Further, quality of custodian and depository services for asset backed securities is likely to increase the investor base. Custodians and depository participants also act as information dissemination agents in the investment markets. Competition and regulatory development have facilitated reduction in custodial charges and improvements in standard of services. Depository facilities have extended the length and breadth of the investment facilities to hitherto inaccessible markets in different parts of the country. Depository facility also has favourable implications for stamp duty payable on transfer.

iii. Listing of securities or re-purchase mechanism: The presence of a market with a wide reach, a large number of investors, high visibility, transparency and investor confidence will help the cause of secondary market trading in the infra asset backed securities. The present stock markets will certainly provide suitable, readymade platforms on which these securities can be traded on screen on-line. The electronic order matching system, and transparent pricing and matching mechanisms enables the market participants to see the full market on a real time basis. The system has also brought together investors across regions irrespective of their geographical locations. Technology has delivered these trading platforms to the door steps of the investors. It has promoted equal access to information and transparency. A sound secondary market infrastructure to provide a ready platform for successful launches of Infra ABS and its acceptance among investors is desirable.

iv. Presence of market makers: Many securities have seen no depth despite being listed on the stock exchanges on account of absence of interest of promoters, lack of quotes and other drawbacks. This issue can be addressed through the services of market makers who may provide two way quotes for the securities thus, providing momentum to the trading process and depth to the market. Market making mechanism has proved beneficial in various cases as it has helped provide the much-needed initial impetus to trading on the stock markets.

v. Effective settlement mechanism: Once traded, the ABS will require efficient clearing and settlement and therefore will need to be sensitised and customised to these processes and platforms. An interactive mode will be necessary both at the institutional level as well as the instrument level for quick integration. High levels of demat settlements will give depth to trading of mortgage backed securities in the secondary market and will also help to develop a transparent price discovery mechanism.

vi. Conducive regulatory, legal and taxation framework: Any instrument that is not backed by a clear and conducive regulatory, legal and taxation framework will not generate investor interest. The risk awareness of investors is further heightened when these issues are not clearly addressed by the respective authorities. The infra ABS market will also require a clear cut regulatory, legal and taxation framework. The issues that need to be addressed may relate to defining true sale, qualifications of a special purpose vehicle trust, taxation treatment of the income of the conduit and the investors. Further, legal issues of stamp duty also need to be clarified to weed out any doubt that the investor might harbour. Unless the issues are clearly addressed, the participation in the secondary market process will remain limited.

vii. Development of a benchmark yield curve: The market can expand rapidly by developing benchmark yield curves that will allow the risk-adjusted pricing of the ABS. The development of a liquid market in ABS depends upon the presence of a reliable benchmark yield curve that can guide the pricing of the securities. The pricing of the ABS, as has been the experience can be a complex process on account of the periodic redemption factor. However, once the benchmark yield curve is developed, it will enable the investors to take a view on the instrument and trade in the same.

viii. Mark to market norms: Currently there are no mark to market norms for securitised instruments. The Fixed Income and Money Markets' Dealers Association (FIMMDA) has been advocating, among other things, the norms for mark to market of ABS. This is dependent on the development of investors' understanding of the product and close monitoring of the behaviour of the instrument to be able to establish a trend pattern or predictablity model which will have a bearing on the expectations of the investors and consequently the pricing and valuation of the instrument.

ix. Confidence building measures: As detailed above, the investors' primary concerns are liquidity, safety and stability of cash flows. They also need to be protected against imprudent and undependable SPVs. The credibility of the sponsor of the ABS and integrity and the fiduciary responsibility of the SPV are important determinants of the investors' comfort. Besides the issues discussed above, the confidence building measures should include:

- Safety net in the form of a credit default guarantee from reputed institutions.
- Structuring the product to give even cash flows/stable cash flows.
- Disclosure standards for investor protection.
- Defining the SPV's responsibilities towards the investors.
- Putting in place a regulatory mechanism for enforcement of standards, codes of conduct etc., for investor protection.
- Putting in place regulatory guidelines on treatment of securitised assets for risk-weightage and capital adequacy requirements, exposure norms, provisioning, disclosure standards, appraisal norms, internal rating, model terms and conditions, standards of documentation, etc.

16 Documentation

Introduction

As there are a number of parties involved in a project besides the borrower and the lender, like the contractors, fuel suppliers, transporters, etc. legal contracts and documentation are intricate and complex. Further, generally, in all projects, overseas parties are involved in contractual obligations necessitating both Indian and overseas legal counsels. The documents are drafted separately for each project as each project requires a distinct set of documents for protecting various interests. The documentation process involves integration of commercial and legal aspects which is evident from the project structure as given in Figure 16.1.

Figure 16.1

Project Structure

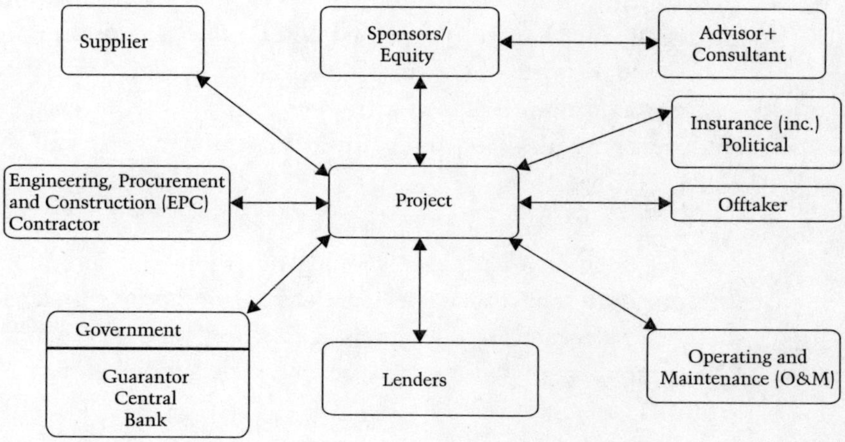

As infrastructure projects are financed on non/limited recourse, contracts/agreements distribute risks amongst the parties to the project.

The contracts also structure the flow of money/revenues through various accounts to enable the lenders to capture them effectively. Insurance contracts providing against risks such as force majeure, termination, delay, etc., are an important part of documentation in a project and are required to be examined critically by the legal counsel.

Besides, as lenders to the project shall be sharing the security and the benefits of contracts assigned to them, contracts/agreements are drafted amongst them keeping in mind the commercial and legal aspects of lenders *inter se* relationship and the collective interest of the lenders *vis-à-vis* the project.

Core Documents for Contractual Framework

Contractual framework in project finance originates with the 'core' documents, which would provide the basis on which the project is being implemented. On the basis of the 'core' documents, contractual relationships are entered into, which finally ties down each party in the project to other.

i. Generally the lead bank with consultation of all participating lenders appoints a reputed law firm, as lenders legal counsel (LLC), to draft and prepare the required financing and security documents (loan documents). However, in those cases where banks/financial institutions (FIs) enter as new lender through the route of downsell of loan by the existing lenders with deed of accession or novation, then it requires to appoint an independent advocate for drafting of required loan documents and due diligence report.

ii. LLC generally certifies and prepares the due diligence report that all the documents are legally valid and enforceable and proper stamp duties have been levied thereon. Sometimes, there is no LLC/advocate for the aforesaid purpose, then, independent advocate is appointed for the specific due diligence report on the banks/FIs point of view.

iii. Lead bank/LLC ensures the compliance of the know your customer (KYC)/anti money laundering norms/guidelines and obtains all required documents from borrower/promoters/ sponsors in regard thereto.

iv. LLC informs the status of compliance regarding the applicable permits, permissions, approvals and clearance required for the project.

The objectives of documentation in project finance, besides establishing the debt and its enforceability, are:

i. To assume only measurable or measured risks.
ii. To have control over key project decisions.
iii. To take control of the project in case of default.
iv. To monitor the project both during the construction and operation stage.

Classification of Documents

The essential documents/agreements required for developing an infrastructure project can broadly be classified into project document and finance document. Project and finance documents together are referred to as transaction documents.

Project Documents

The documents that cover the various aspects of implementing the project are called project documents. Project documents can be broadly classified as under:

Concession Agreement

The concession agreement is an agreement with the government/ statutory body granting the right to the project vehicle to develop the project.

Shareholders' Agreement

The shareholders' agreement is an agreement between the sponsors/ investors for management of the project vehicle and development of the project. This agreement is crucial from the lenders' perspective, as it would determine the extent of commitment of each investor and the intention with regard to management and control of the project. The main point to be examined here is the distribution of risks between the investors and the promoters.

This agreement should bind the shareholders to invest in the project vehicle. Further, the lenders would like to ensure that the main project developers are not vested with the right to exit. Thus, this agreement should contain clauses prohibiting the promoters/sponsors to sell the shares for a particular period, no charge, pledge, lien, encumbrances or securities in shares.

EPC Contracts

The EPC contract is an agreement between the project vehicle and the construction contractor for construction of the project/facility. It's a critical project document and also relates to the management of risks in the construction period. As stated above, the construction phase is a stage of high risk on account that failure to complete the construction would have significant repercussions. This document is examined by the lenders in great detail for *inter alia*, i) time frame for construction of the facility of the project is to be linked with the concession agreement, ii) standards and specifications as to which infrastructure facility is to be designed/ constructed, commissioned and tested as per the concession agreement—mechanism for monitoring the project, coordination between various suppliers and contractors, management and settlement of disputes, terms of payment, etc.

O&M Contracts

The O&M contract is an agreement between the project vehicle and the O&M contractor. This agreement should provide that the operator shall carry out all scheduled maintenance, payment mechanism, issuing of bills to consumers for the service provided, etc.

Finance Documents

Documents/agreements that govern the financing of the project are referred to as financing documents. Major financing documents are as under:

i. Common loan agreement/term loan agreement/facility agreement/ rupee facility agreement.

ii. Inter-creditor agreement.

iii. Trust and retention account agreement/Escrow agreement.

iv. Hypothecation agreement/Deed of mortgage.

Common Loan/Facility Agreement

This is one of the key loan documents signed between the lenders and the borrower, capturing the entire common term sheets of all the lenders and other terms and conditions normally stipulated for the facilities sanctioned to the borrower. Since the term sheets given by the lenders are not all inclusive and cover the critical terms only, proper drafting of this agreement is paramount as it delineates the rights and obligations of the lenders and the borrower for the loan facilities being extended. If debt includes facilities in different currencies or are lender specific, separate facility agreements will be entered into.

The key points to be covered under this agreement are:

i. The amount borrowed

ii. Term of the loan and repayments.

iii. Interest rates.

iv. Conditions for drawdown.

v. Use of the proceeds.

vi. Financial covenants.

vii. Security structure

Inter-creditor Agreement

Any financing agreement involving a number of lenders and a single borrower requires an inter-creditor agreement. The parties to this agreement are all the lenders under different loan agreements—lenders with loans of different maturity and sometimes even subordinate lenders.

The purpose of an inter-creditor agreement is to provide procedures, agreements and understandings on:

i. Co-coordinating priorities in loan repayments.

ii. For accelerating the maturities of loans.

iii. For establishing loss sharing, etc.

The intention in this agreement is to prevent disputes between creditors which might jeopardise the interest of all the creditors. When the loan is going bad, each lending institution tries to protect itself in the best possible way and obtains an advantage over the other creditors. The procedures in the inter-creditor agreement forestall this. Under this agreement no lender can take legal action except by following the procedures laid down in the agreement. Further, at least two-third or half of the lenders, based on the principal balances, are required to agree for any action. This agreement is also beneficial to the borrower as it has to deal with only one lender—lenders' agent.

Trust and Retention Agreement

This is an agreement between the lenders and the borrowers for controlling the project revenues. The agreement would contain various deposit sub-accounts into which various amounts, equity, loan, etc., would be credited. The agreement would also contain withdrawal sub-accounts through which the borrower would withdraw the amount for various purposes.

Security Agreement

The main security agreements are the hypothecation deed and/or the indenture of mortgage. The lenders have a first *pari passu* charge on all movables, immovable property of the borrower. Further, in this agreement, all documents/contracts are assigned to the lenders. The objective of this agreement is to permit the lenders to step in and control the project. Security in project finance is for a defensive purpose—to prevent third parties from interfering with the project.

Sector Specific Documentation

Besides the documents mentioned above, certain sector-specific documentation is also required, as explained in the Table 16.1.

Table 16.1

Sector List of Main Sector-specific Documents

S.No.	*Sector*	*Documents*
1.	Power	Fuel supply agreement, power purchase agreement, fuel transport agreement
2.	Roads	Concession agreement, traffic study, multipartite agreement
3.	Ports	Concession agreement, traffic study, O&M agreement
4.	Oil & Gas	Fuel supply agreement, offtake agreement
5.	Airports	Operations management and development agreement (OMDA)
6.	Special Economic Zone (SEZ)	State support agreement, shareholders' agreement

Conclusion

Infrastructure projects, particularly PPP's follow standard documents at all stages from bidding to award of concession and finally their execution to ensure transparency in the allocation of risk, clarity in the obligation of concessionaire and minimisation of possibilities of the disputes arising from the agreement. To underpin this approach the Planning Commission of India has published the list of documents like model concession agreement for different sectors in PPP's—national highways/state highways/O&M of highways/national highways (six laning)/urban rail transit systems/non-metro airports/greenfield airports/port terminals/operation of container trains/redevelopment of railway stations and procurement cum maintenance, transmission of electricity, etc. Some of the provisions in the model concession agreement (MCA) relate to improvement of the project in the area of monitoring and dissemination of information.

PPP's are long term commitments by concessionaire and project authority. Their successful delivery also depends upon sound and robust documents, which infrastructure projects follow invariably. These documents discuss in detail the mechanism by which the objective of the project can be achieved. The clauses used in these documents are tailored to meet the specifics of a particular project. For instance, the PPA is considered a core document in power sector, whereas the concession agreement in highway project operated on BOT basis fulfills the same objective. The provisions relate to requirements as per various enactments and contractual obligations. Requirements which initiate from the contractual documents are the submission of performance security, copies of project agreements including financing documents, the EPC contract, the O&M contract, etc. An important pre-cursor is that financial closure is done prior to the fulfillment of the conditions precedent. Some of the conditions can be waived fully or partially, wherein certain other documents cannot be compromised like environmental clearances, write of way for alignment, permission to enter upon and utilise the site. Hence, the documents required for the particular project need to be assessed, analysed and executed cautiously, carefully and duly.

17 Road Sector

Road sector in India has witnessed significant investment in recent years. Public private partnership (PPP) is gradually proving to be a success mechanism for developing and maintaining the national highways. Therefore, a clear risk sharing and regulatory framework to sustain the interest of private participants has been spelt out in the model concession agreement (MCA). The features of the revised MCA are given below.

Risk Framework of MCA

As an underlying principle, risks have been allocated to the parties that are best suited to manage them. Projects risks have therefore been assigned to the private sector to the extent it is capable of managing them. The transfer of such risks and responsibilities to the private sector would increase the scope of innovation leading to efficiencies in cost and services.

The commercial and technical risks relating to construction, operation and maintenance (O&M) are allocated to the concessionaire, as it is best suited to manage them. Other commercial risks, such as the rate of growth of traffic, are also allocated to the concessionaire.

Key Concessionaire Risk/Obligations

i. Construction Risk: The concessionaire is required to commence construction works when the financial close is achieved or on an earlier date that the parties may determine by mutual consent. The concessionaire shall not be entitled to seek compensation for any prior commencement and shall do it solely at his own risk.

ii. O&M Risk: Concessionaire to operate and maintain the project facility (as specified in the concession agreement); failure to repair and rectify any defect or deficiency within a specified period shall be considered as breach of responsibility.

iii. Financial Risk: The concessionaire shall, at its cost, expenses and risk, make some financing arrangement as would be necessary to finance the cost of the project and to meet project requirements and other obligations under the agreement in a timely manner.

iv. Traffic Risk: The MCA provides for increase or decrease of the concession period in the event the actual traffic falls short or exceeds the target traffic. It also provides for termination of the agreement if the average daily traffic in any accounting year exceeds the design capacity and continues to exceed for three subsequent accounting years.

Key National Highways Authority of India (NHAIs) Risk/Obligations

i. Land Acquisition Risk: NHAI is responsible for acquiring the requisite land for the project highway.

ii. Approvals: NHAI will provide all the reasonable support and assistance to the concessionaire in procuring applicable permits/ permissions required from any government instrumentality.

Key Common Risk

Force Majeure Risk—means occurrences in India or all of non-political event(s), indirect political event(s) and political event(s), which include the following:

Non-Political Event

i. Act of God, epidemic, extremely adverse weather conditions or radioactive contamination or ionising radiation, fire or explosion.

ii. Strikes or boycotts.

iii. The discovery of geological condition, toxic contamination or archaeological remains on the site.

iv. Any event or circumstances of a nature analogous to any of the foregoing.

Indirect Political Event

i. An act of war, invasion, armed conflict or act of foreign enemy, blockade, embargo, riot, insurrection, terrorist or military action.

ii. Civil commotion or politically motivated sabotage which prevents collection of toll/fees.

iii. Industry-wide or state-wide or India-wide strikes or industrial action which prevent collection of toll/fees.

iv. Any public agitation which prevent collection of toll /fees.

Political Event

i. Change in law.

ii. Compulsory acquisition by any governmental agency of any project assets or rights of concessionaire or the contractors.

iii. Unlawful or unauthorised or without jurisdiction revocation of or refusal to renew or grant, without valid cause, any consent or approval required by developer.

Road Development Policy

The Government of India (GoI) has adopted a road development policy to attract private sector participation. The features are as under:

i. The government has permitted 100 per cent foreign equity in construction and maintenance of roads, highways, tunnels, etc.

ii. Grant up to 40 per cent of project cost to make project viable.

iii. 100 per cent tax exemption in any 10 consecutive years within a period of 20 years after completion of construction provided the project involves addition of new lanes.

iv. Agreements to avoid double taxation with a large number of countries.

v. Concession period up to 30 years.

vi. Right to charge tolls on certain (toll) projects. These tolls are indexed to a formula linked with the wholesale price index (WPI)

vii. The government permits duty free import of high capacity equipment required for highway construction.

viii. Government support for land acquisition, resettlement and rehabilitations.

Viability Gap Funding (VGF) Scheme

The VGF scheme provides financial support in the form of capital grant for PPP projects in various infrastructure sectors. It is intended to support projects which are commercially unviable but have high economic benefit.

Traffic Estimate and Forecast

Traffic growth on a road facility is generally estimated on the basis of:

i. Historical trends.

ii. Future development along the project road.

iii. The economic outlook of the states most influencing the traffic on the project road.

Hence, future traffic estimation necessitates an assessment of the past growth of the economy, identification of the factors which influence the travel pattern on the road and of the main activities in the area generating or attracting traffic.

The traffic that is likely to use the project road is estimated on the basis of the traffic and travel characteristics gathered through primary as well as secondary surveys. The traffic on the project road would normally consist of the following components:

i. Normal traffic.

ii. Induced/new generated traffic.

iii. Diverted traffic.

An equally important study is toll revenue projections. Thus, the different categories of toll tickets as given hereunder to be looked into:

i. Traffic paying normal toll rate (single trip).

ii. Traffic paying return journey rates.

iii. Traffic paying monthly pass rates.

iv. Traffic paying local concessional rates.

v. Exempt traffic.

In any forecast, there is an inherent element of uncertainty and it is not possible to measure risk in a strictly statistical sense. A border line is drawn, quantifying the main risks that could have an impact on forecast.

i. Low case: with regard to lower than projection economic performance of the country linking project road.

ii. High case: more optimistic economic outlook of future year.

iii. No diversion.

iv. Maximum diversion.

Environmental Issues in Road/Highway Sector

The major issues can be summed up as follows:

i. Impacts on forest land.

ii. Roadside tree cutting.

iii. Road widening impacts on sensitive locations.

iv. Redevelopment and rehabilitation issues of construction sites in post construction phase.

v. Construction camps/Construction plants.

vi. Safety issues.

vii. Community severance issues.

viii. Impacts on coastal areas, if applicable.

Major Hurdles in Road Sector

i. Delays in:
   - Acquisition of land.
   - Obtaining clearances and approvals from various agencies/ authorities.
   - Availability of state support agreement (SSA).

ii. Toll survey needs to cover the following factors:
   - Savings in vehicle operating costs:
     - Fee paying traffic.

    - Local users.
    - Exempted vehicles.
  - Savings in time.
  - Savings in distance covered.

ii. Time gap between preparation of detailed project report (DPR) and bid invitation.

iii. Poor performance of some contractors.

Corrective Measures in Road Sector

i. To ensure proper planning of land acquisition:
  - Forest and defence lands: approvals and clearances.
  - Compensation to be factored, wherever displacements are there.
  - Toll survey.
  - To factor competing routes while estimating expected toll.

ii. Project management:
  - Past track record.
  - Arms length distance between EPC contractor and promoters.

iii. Lenders' perspective:
  - Whether project is annuity-based.
  - Collaterals/Additional security.
  - Debt Equity Ratio: required equity and to be brought upfront.

iv. Risk mitigation planning/Project insurance.

Conclusion

Proposals related to road sector in infrastructure projects are getting quick disposal from the banks/FIs particularly when they are annuity backed. It is a fact that despite the risk obligations arising out of construction risk and O&M risk (relating to concessionaire to operate and maintain the project facility as specified in the concession agreement) there is robust growth in

PPP investments in road sector. Investment in other sectors such as power, irrigation, port and urban development are relatively meagre. To maintain this tempo it would be more practical if the feasibility report should be done at the end of the government at its own cost and after determining the alignment and completing the land acquisition it should relocate the utility services and thereafter invite competitive bids. This process will definitely attract both private companies as well as FIs/banks to expedite the process at their respective ends. Sometimes it is found that the project is not viable on toll basis alone. The government may consider giving cash subsidy to the project provided the project is otherwise considered necessary. Projects funded with a larger equity would require higher tariff levels to sustain their return on equity (ROE), however, banks/FIs are unlikely to agree to lower equity proportions which need to be relooked. One more issue needs to be thought of to maintain the pace of development in the road sector and to remove the fund crunch, i.e., foreign equity participation of up to 100 per cent may be allowed in BOT National Highway Project. Participation of up to 51 per cent may be approved automatically to arrest the fund crunch. This will also have a bearing on concentration risk, the banks and FIs are facing with regard to the road sector. To maintain the pace of the economic growth in our country, development of road sector is a must.

18 Power Sector

Power sector in our country requires huge amounts of funds. The Planning Commission of India has set up a target of 1,00,000 MW for the Twelfth Five Year Plan (2012 to 2017). The commission holds that 'it is an ambitious target but is achievable.' Power sector investment will guide the entire target. The total investment in the power sector itself, including generation work in progress, will be around US $ 300 billions (Rs 13.5 lac crores). Undoubtedly this target of growth is vital for the prosperity of the country.

Financing power projects is a critical and strategic issue because its characteristics are different. It requires large amount and long terms funds which involves high amount of risks. Debt is the major source of financing of power projects. Nowadays projects are financed by using:

i. Off-balance sheet financing method, or

ii. Non-recourse financing method.

Financing Power Projects: Debt Financing

There are several methods of financing power projects globally such as project financing, leasing of infrastructure, structure financing, public private partnership (PPPs), etc., but in our country the methods used are as under:

i. Equity financing.

ii. Debt financing.

iii. PPPs.

iv. Leasing of infrastructure.

v. Venture capital.

Here focus should be on debt financing and its influencing factors on debt financing. Debt is often structured in form of senior debt or subordinated debt. Mezzanine finance refers to a kind of financial instruments that are primarily in the form of debt but also share qualities of equity capital. Mezzanine finance includes convertible bonds and preferred stock. The debt shall need to be tapped from various domestic and international sources which shall include direct market borrowing, banks/financial institutions (FIs) and multilateral/bilateral credits. The most common type of debt financing is borrowing from banks/FIs which can be quick and relatively inexpensive.

The second type of debt financing is corporate debt or bonds. A bond is a security sold to an investor. It is a contractual obligation between the issuer and the holder. The issuer promises to make interest payments to the holder at specific dates and to return the principal at a certain date (maturity). Only established companies get this capital. Trade debt financing is a fancy phrase for extending accounts payable. The objective here is to delay payments of the payables beyond the sales and accounts receivable collection cycles. However, the most common type of debt financing as explained earlier is borrowing from banks/FIs which is not quick these days. From the project point of view, there are a number of hurdles for the availability of the debt to finance the power project.

Requirement for Setting-up/Operating Power Station

The basic requirement for setting up and operating a power station is availability of suitable and adequate fuel, land, water, infrastructure facilities like road and rail head, and suitable access for power evacuations.

Land requirements for coal fired, thermal power station can broadly be classified under the following heads:

i. Plain area.

ii. Township.

iii. Ash disposal (bottom ash or fly ash).

iv. Other requirements for intake water pipe routes, ash disposal route, conveyor/railway and road access, transmission corridor, etc.

Fuel requirement, availability and transportation and also evacuation at what level should be elaborated. The basis of technical parameters of the plant and ancillary equipment are to be discussed. (Brief parameters of the built turbine generator, cost and their availability on the site.)

Project Cost

Project cost estimate and financial aspects have to be looked into on the following basis:

i. Main equipments and ancillary plants and equipments.

ii. Price of coal and cost of transportation.

iii. Time schedule.

iv. Manpower.

v. Taxes/Duties/Insurances.

Figure 18.1

Parties in a Power Project

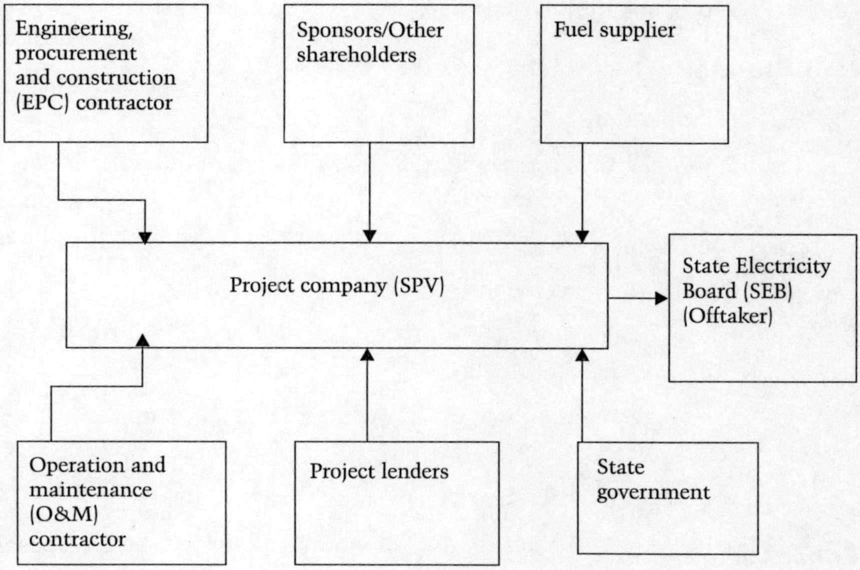

Statutory Clearance Approvals and Permits

i. Approval from Central Electrical Authority (CEA) for cost of the project.

ii. Techno-economic clearance from CEA.

iii. Techno-economic clearance from SEB.

iv. Notification to be issued under Section 29(3) of Indian Electricity (Special) Act, 1948.

v. Water availability from the Central Water Commission/state government.

vi. Pollution clearance (water and air) from State and Central Pollution Control Boards.

vii. Environment and forest (E&F) clearance from Ministry of Environment and Forest (MoEF)/state government.

viii. Civil aviation clearance for the height of chimney from the National Airport Authority.

ix. Rehabilitation and resettlement of displaced families from Land and Acquisition Department, MoEF/state government.

Non-Statutory Clearances

i Allotment of project.

ii. Power purchase agreement (PPA)/Memorandum of Understanding (MoU).

iii. Land availability and allotment of land from state government.

iv. Concession agreement.

v. Fuel linkage from Ministry of Petroleum and Natural Gas/ Ministry of Coal (MoC).

vi. Sales agreement for fuel from suppliers, i.e., petroleum companies/ coalfield.

vii. Fuel transportation agreement.

Other Clearances

i.. Reserve Bank of India (RBI) clearance for foreign investment.

ii. External commercial borrowing (ECB) clearance.

iii. Foreign exchange permission from RBI for ECB.

iv. Permission for license for capital goods import from Ministry of Petroleum/MoC.

v. Approval for handling and storage facilities of fuel from the Chief Controller of Explosives.

vi. Approval for power evacuation, borrow earth permit, permission for installation of crusher, asphalt plant, license for use of explosives, license for setting up batching plant, and approval of the railway authorities in the form of a general arrangement drawing that would enable the concessionaire to construct road over bridges/under bridges at level crossings on the project highway etc., should be in order.

vii. Power fuel supply agreement (FSA), source of power fuel, government policy for power project, foreign regulatory in case of imported coal based power project should be evaluated.

Coal Quality

Coal quality is the key factor in the variable cost. The specific coal consumption depends upon the quality of coal received. There is a lot of uncertainty in the quality of coal. The machine is designed for a certain GCV (gross calorific value) of coal. If that quality is not fed, the load will come down. There is a need of blending of coal when low quality coal is received.

Coal Transportation

Coal transportation is a critical issue. For non-pit head stations, generators have to depend on railway transports. Most of the time, railways are not able to provide racks for transportation of coal. As a result, generators have to look for alternative method which cost more than Rs 1,500/tonne.

Captive Coal Blocks

Government has allotted many coal blocks to the companies. Some of these are regionally explored; meaning the reserves as announced is only tentative. The development of coal block requires many approvals both from the state government and the central government (Ministry of Environment and Forest, Ministry of Coal and Ministry of Power). The usual practice is that the company receives a letter of assurance with validity period from the coalfields. Under the terms of the letter of assurance, the price of coal shall be as per the price notified by Coal India Limited from time to time. In addition, the company is required to complete certain milestones within stipulated months of the date of issue of the letter of assurance. In the event, the company does not complete any of the required milestones and fails to furnish an additional commitment guarantee, or if the company fails to fulfill all the required milestones, Central Coalfields shall have the right to cancel or withdraw the letter of assurance. Further the company has to sign the fuel supply agreement with Central Coalfields within three months of the expiry of the letter of assurance or satisfactory achievement of the required milestones, Central Coalfields shall have the right to encash the commitment guarantee.

Coal *vis-à-vis* FSA

Coal continues to be the main source of generation of power; however, its availability is a key factor nowadays. It is therefore necessary to address the issues and concerns related to FSA. The supply side constraints are a serious impediment for the coal fired power plants. Coal companies are not signing FSAs with developers who have been issued letters of assurances over years back. They are signing in some projects that are about to be commissioned, that too for only 50 per cent of the quantity assured earlier on the basis of which the developer would have calculated the projected balance sheet and obtained the debt capital. If 50 per cent coal is to be through imports, the cost of imports would go up substantially. This will result in heavy losses unless the tariff can be revised which is not easy in the case where PPA has already been signed.

An FSA between a fuel supplier and a special purpose vehicle (SPV) ensures that risks associated with inadequate quality/quantity of fuel is passed on to the fuel suppliers. The fuel suppliers compensate the SPV for any alternate fuels that may need to be purchased by it or pay consequential damages to the SPV which are essentially all the losses suffered by the SPV under the PPA and other project documents on account of a default by the fuel supplier under an FSA.

Environmental Issues in Power Sector

Hydro Power

i. Compensatory aforestation in lieu of forest land diverted for the project.

ii. Catchment area treatment (CAT) to minimise erosion in the catchment of the reservoir, thereby reducing siltation in the reservoir.

iii. Rejuvenation of dumping sites and quarry sites, using engineering and biological measures.

iv. Green belt plan, conservation measures, etc., to conserve flora and fauna native to the ecosystem of the area.

v. Dam break analysis and disaster management plan for downstream areas vulnerable to flooding in case of dam breach.

Thermal Power

i. Ash disposal and solid waste management.

ii. Water availability.

iii. Installation of Flue gas desulphurisation unit if high sulphur content coal is used as fuel.

iv. Commitment for control of particulate emissions.

v. Water conservation measures.

Major Hurdles in Power Sector

i. Land acquisition issues.

ii. Resettlement and rehabilitation of project affected people.

iii. Fuel linkage.

iv. Verification of the coal agreement, if entered into.

v. Rising cost of imported coal *vis-à-vis* its effect on PPA.

vi. Boiler turbine generator issues.

vii. Lack of standardisation of product specifications for transmission and distribution (T&D) equipment across different utilities.

viii. Slow pace for adoption of new technology by domestic manufacturers.

ix. Low investment in research & development (R&D).

x. Inadequate testing facilities for high voltage (HV) equipment.

xi. Lack of water dependability study.

xii. Tariff revision in line with cost of generation.

Social Issues in Road and Power Projects

i. Land acquisition.

ii. Loss of livelihood (especially the road side commercial structures).

iii. Partial impact on structures.

iv. Resettlement and rehabilitation issues.

v. Acquisition of large compact areas (which sometimes causes submergence of the whole village in case of hydro power project).

vi. Loss of livelihood.

vii. Issue of social responsibilities towards local communities.

viii. Opportunity of employment during construction.

ix. Likely impact on tribal population, wherever applicable.

The Planning Commission's Working Group for the Twelfth plan has pegged the requirement for coal imports at 213 MT by 2017. The fresh estimates made by consulting firm Mercados suggest that only about 114 MT of imported coals can be absorbed by the country's power plant on account of blending constraints, specifically in the form of technical limitations at boilers in existing stations. It is equally important that the imported coal requirement may face logistical constraints due to inadequate first mile connectivity of the ports with railway network and critical congestion within the railway network itself. Any further increase in the coal import requirement for power generation would face major difficulties in reaching the generation centres, thus leading to stranded assets and sub-optimal performance.

Corrective Measures in Power Sector

i. Land acquisition issues
   - Forest and defence lands: approvals and clearances.
   - Compensation to be factored, wherever displacements are there.

ii. Resettlement and rehabilitation of project affected people
   - Suitable implementation plan may be worked out in consultation with various stakeholders and project affected people.

iii. Fuel linkage
   - To execute FSA with suppliers such as coalfields (domestic as well as foreign) at an early stage.

iv. Verification of the coal agreement, if entered into, by a reputed law firm.

v. Tariff revision in line with cost of generation.

Power Project Risks

The power projects suffer from a number of risks—typical and critical in their nature. Even the big players like Lanco group and GMR group are facing problems related to the land acquisition, environmental clearances funding, manpower, etc.

Types of Risks

Company can control	*Company cannot control*	*Within Financier's control*
Operating	Supply	Syndication
Technical	Market	Funding
Cost	Infrastructure	Legal
Management	Environmental	
Participant	Political	
Engineering	Force majeure	
Completion	Foreign exchange (FX) currency	

Typical Risk Allocation at Three Stages

Development	*Construction*	*Operations*
Technical feasibility	Schedule	Market changes
Commercial/Financial feasibility	Cost	Capacity/Production shortfalls
Project economics	Performance	Fuel/Material supply
Permits and authorisations	Design changes	Interruption and cost escalation
Third party intervention	Interest rate	O&M
Political change	Escalation	Interest rate
Sponsor risk	Consequential damages	Currency depreciation
Contractor risk	Force majeure/Country risk	Statutory change
Lender risk	Currency changes	Civil unrest/Strikes
Host government and offtaker risk	Availability of foreign exchange	Third party liability
		Plant residual value

Power Purchase Agreement (PPA)

The salient features of a PPA are as follows:

i. The PPA establishes the condition under which the SPV would sell power to the distribution companies of the states.

Under the PPA, the distribution companies guarantee a minimum offtake from the SPV, if it fails to do so, a minimum payment will be made by the distribution company. Typically, the minimum payment would cover all the fixed charges incurred by the project including depreciation, interest on term loan, fixed O&M expenses, and return on equity.

ii. A payment and security mechanism that ensures availability of payment on time is established in PPA.

iii. The PPA also lays down the formula for computing tariffs which in addition to the fixed charges, also includes variable costs such as fuel costs and also an incentive for performance.

iv. The PPA also envisages termination under conditions of sustained default by either the SPV or the distribution company in performing their respective obligation or under conditions of forced majeure. It also allows an exit to the project's shareholders and lenders in the event it is terminated by providing for a distribution company of the facility and laying down different buyout prices that would be payable by the distribution company under different termination conditions. It also ensures that appropriate remedy periods are available prior to affecting a termination.

v. The lenders consider the PPA as an important project document and evaluate the sufficiency of the negotiated tariffs, specially if the elements of the fixed charges is predetermined and not cost based.

vi. The lenders also evaluate the requirement of interconnection facilities and take a view on the ability of the distribution company to complete the same prior to the commercial operation date (COD) of the project. Amongst the key provisions of the PPA is the security and the credit enhancement, and lenders also need to be satisfied with the same. Project lenders also ensure that under different events of termination and consequent distribution company's buyout, the committed buyout price includes outstanding debt and interest.

In view of the above, it is observed that:

a. Life of PPA is greater than debt amortization period.
b. PPA guarantees a revenue stream for the project.
c. Defines rights and obligations of both parties.
d. Highly specialised legal document.
e. Backed by state government guarantee.

Conditions Precedent to Disbursement

Lending proposals under power, in particular, thermal based power require closer scrutiny over the terms of sanctions before the first disbursement. Hence, conditions precedent, forming part of term sheets issued by the lenders should specify the following:

i. Completion of acquisition of the land for the project.
ii. Complete tie-up of the project equity and satisfactory execution of the shareholder's agreement.
iii. Completion of front-end engineering design by reputed engineering consultants and finalisation of a technical configuration for the project.

iv. Execution of the EPC contract.

v. Completion of environmental impact assessment studies and receipt of clearances from the MoEF and Pollution Control Board.

vi. Execution of FSA.

vii. Execution of PPA.

viii. Equity subscription as per terms.

ix. Creation of securities.

x. Assignment of all project contracts to lenders.

xi. Others on case to case basis.

Figure 18.2

Tier Payment and Security Mechanism

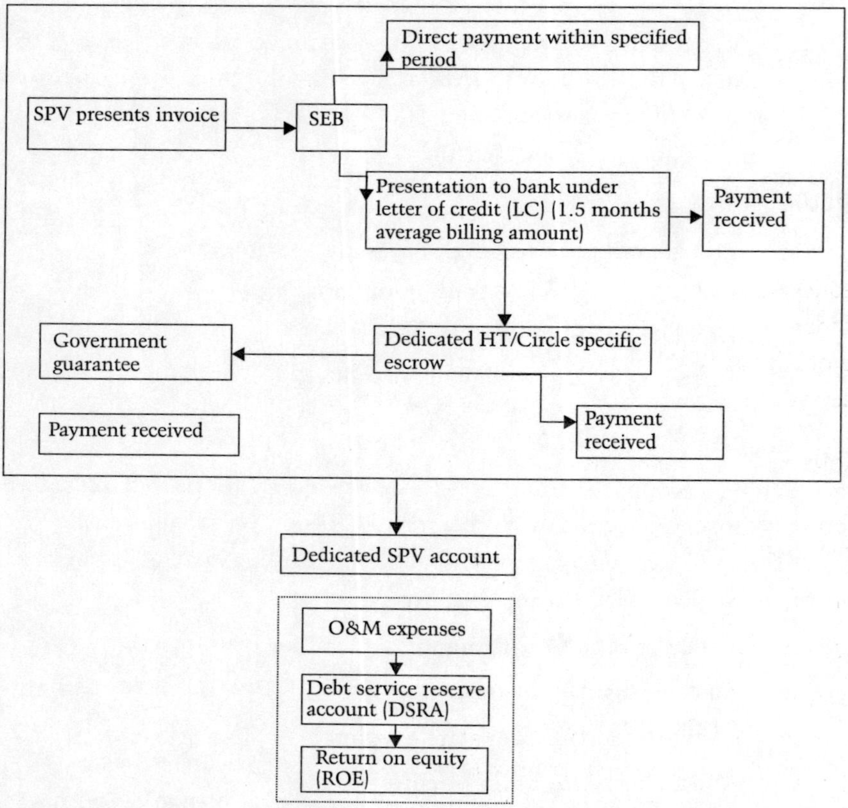

Ultra Mega Power Projects (UMPPs)

UMPPs are very large sized projects. These projects will meet the power needs of a number of states and distribution companies located in these states and are being developed on a build, own and operate (BOO) basis. They are identified on the basis of tariff based competitive bidding. PFC (Power Finance Company) has been identified as a nodal agency for this initiative and the Ministry of Power has laid down rules regarding technology:

i. The UMPPs use super critical technology with a view to achieve higher levels of fuel efficiency which results in saving of fuels and lower green house gas emission.

ii. Flexibility in unit size subject to adoption of specified minimum super critical parameters.

iii. Integrated power project with dedicated coal blocks for pit head projects.

iv. Coastal projects to use imported coal.

Bidding Process

The bidding process involves two stages. The first stage involves request for quotation (RFQ) containing qualifying criteria for selection of bidders. The second stage invites request for proposal (RFP) from the bidders so qualified. After evaluation of the RFP documents, the successful bidder is identified on the basis of the lowest levelised tariff.

Role of the Ministry of Power

The Ministry of Power, Government of India, is playing a key role for ensuring:

i. Coal block allotment/Coal linkage.

ii. Environment/Forest clearances.

iii. Water linkage.

iv. Required support from state governments and their agencies.

v. Working out allocation of power to different states from UMPPs in consultation with the states.

vi. Facilitating PPA and proper payment security mechanism with state governments/state utilities.

vii. Monitoring the progress of shell companies with respect to predetermined timeliness.

SPV in UMPPs

PFC has to set up separate SPV to act as authorised representative of the procurers (distribution companies of the power procuring states). UMPPs follow a competitive tariff based bidding process in which an SPV is set up to reduce risk perception and increased investor confidence. The SPV takes care of regulatory requirements such as land acquisition and environmental clearances, and transfer these to the winning bidder.

Role of the State Governments

States hosting the UMPPs and other power procuring states are playing a proactive role. They play their roles regarding:

i. Implementation of the rehabilitation and resettlement plan.

ii. Authorisation to the PFC/SPV to carry out the bidding process on behalf of the distribution utilities.

iii. Participation through its representative in various committees set up for undertaking the competitive bidding process.

iv. Facilitating signing of the PPA.

v. Ensuring proper payment security mechanism with the distribution utilities.

Renewal Energy (RE)

Banks and FIs finance RE project developers assessing the credit worthiness of the companies. Sectors being financed are: solar energy, wind energy, hydro energy, biomass, power generation, waste to energy. Proposal relating to above sector for debt is to be appraised after going through the high level outline of the project, technology, lifespan, total Capex (capital expenditure), required debt amount, subsidy support, contract review and related risks and their mitigation.

External Cost of Power Generation

The cost of renewal energy systems (RBS) is very site specific. Since they are designed to tap into existing natural flows of energy, it is obvious that a particular RBS will be cheapest where the appropriate flow exists. Thus, hydro electric systems will be practical and economically viable where there is a flow of water. Similarly solar power will be economical only where solar energy is abundantly available. The cost of a biomass-based system depends on the availability and cost of the biomass, if this is already onsite as waste, as in a cane sugar mill, the operation is much cheaper than when biomass has to purchased and transported to site.

Tariff Structure of Renewable Energy (RE)

The tariff for renewal energy technologies shall be single part tariff consisting of the following fixed cost components as per CERC regulations/ tariff norms: 1) return on equity; 2) interest on loan capital; 3) depreciation; 4) interest on working capital. The commission has issued comprehensive tariff regulations for renewal energy which ensures assured returns with full cost recovery during debt repayment period for full useful life in case of solar and small hydro power projects. It also provides longer tariff visibility for solar projects. This is expected to promote development of green energy. The tariff period varies depending upon type of renewal projects. The tariff period for RE shall be 13 years, for solar PV and solar thermal power projects, the tariff period shall be 25 years.

Capital Cost of Renewal Projects

Renewal energy system generally has large initial capital cost and small operational costs; and fossil fuel plant has the reverse especially if there are no emissions preventions. Capital cost of solar power is in the range 14.2-15.2 crore per mw, while biomass is the cheapest as shown in Figure 18.3. Cost of solar power per unit production is the highest and the cost of hydropower is the lowest.

Figure 18.3

Capital Cost per MW

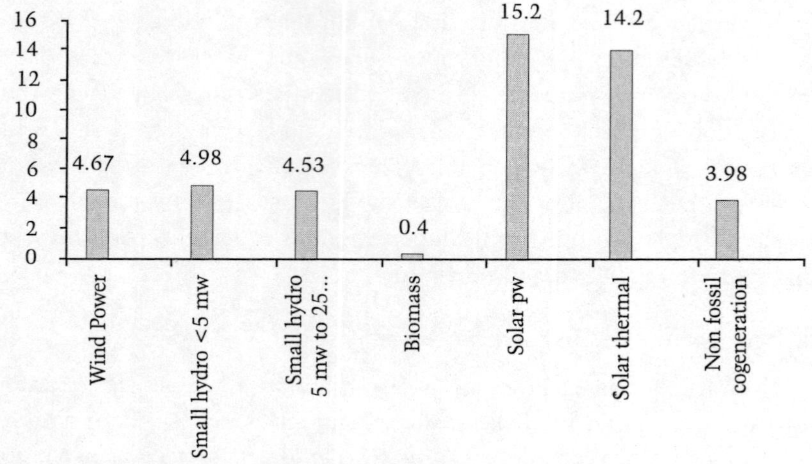

Source: *CERC Annual Report 2009-10.*

Indian Renewal Energy Development Agency Ltd (IREDA)

IREDA, established as a public limited govt. company under the Company's Act 1956 has been notified as a public financial institution under section 4A of the Company's Act 1956 and registered as NBFC with RBI. The main objectives of IREDA are:

1. To give financial support to specific projects and schemes for generating electricity and/or energy through new and renewal sources and conserving energy through energy efficiency.
2. To maintain its position as a leading organisation to provide efficient and effective financing in RE and energy efficiency/ conservation projects.
3. To increase IREDA's share in the RE sector by way of innovative financing.

Hydro Power

Hydro power is the cleanest source of energy. As the fuel is water, the generation cost is low. However, it is saddled with problems. The hydro power projects are difficult to execute. They are located in hilly areas and in difficult terrain and thus face the problem of adverse geological conditions and natural calamities. Resettlement and rehabilitation issues have been another contentious issues. Lack of infrastructure is another stumbling block. Transmission of power involving huge distance to the load centres in north and west is a challenge which puts an upward pressure on the transmission costs.

Conclusion

Power is one of the most important infrastructural requirements in the economic development of fast growing economy like India. To sustain the GoI's outline growth rates and the rising consumerism, the power sector needs to grow with at least similar outline rates (8%-9%) or more. Despite this kind of need, financing to power sector is still a concern both for the promoters and the lenders, even though equity market in India has shown a positive response towards companies venturing into the power sector. The over subscription of equity issues of corporate like, Adani, NHPC and PFC shows that many new private companies can use this public mode of financing for their investments in power sector. While the equity market offer tremendous opportunity for power giants like Reliance, Adani, Tata Power and NTPC, the small and medium segment companies have to rely on more innovative financing mechanisms for funding their investments need. The major issues impacting the financial investments in the power sectors—poor financial health of state utilities/delays in finalising competitive bids/delays in getting clearances/appropriate fiscal incentives not available to channelise savings/not tapping of long term funds available with PF, pension and insurance funds/capital is being raised for green field projects only and long term price hedging instruments do not exist in the power market—need to be solved on priority basis to ensure the growth of volume.

Rapid economic growth in infrastructure, aggravated by population explosion in urban conglomerations has precipitated the need for quality, uninterrupted power. To keep pace with such demand, the sector will need investments of about Rs 24 lakh crores by 2017, which may be realised if careful risk assessment is done on the key points like, ATNC losses (Aggregate Technical & Commercial), single window clearance system for approvals, training of manpower and improvements in demand side management (DSM). Too many clearances like, coastal clearances, MoEF's clearances, land clearances, Pollution Control Board clearances, etc., should be given through single window clearances system, so that the developers do not run from pillar to post. In particular, coal linkage approval must be given to serious and sound developers on an urgent basis considering their track record. The delay in getting these clearances is also responsible for increase in project cost. The challenge faced by the power sector in terms of high transmission & distribution (T&D) losses, lack of consumer education, political interference and inefficient use of electricity adds to the problem. The ATNC losses in various states are very high. The problem is further compounded by losses arising due to theft and pilferage, poor billing and tariff collection.

Lenders, these days are not willing to lend on the basis of project specifications, cost and promoter's strengths. Keeping in view the non-availability of coal and gas and shortfall in CIL (Coal India Limited) supply, they are focussing their financing on promoters' ability to arrange coal from alternate sources, project location amenable to alternate supply and ability of promoter to sell power from the higher cost source to the utility. Whether the project is based on the fuel linkage or not, is the core concern for the lenders. These days lenders are more selective and careful in lending to power sector particularly in generation area and issues like assessing fuel at reasonable cost—source as well as transportation—and the condition of utility has become central to their decision on funding new power projects.

19 Airport

The Government of India (GoI) in April 2008 approved the policy of Greenfield airports enabling greenfield projects to be set up on public private partnership (PPP) basis. The Planning Commission has developed a model concession agreement for greenfield airport, allowing the state government to take up the development of such airports through PPP.

A greenfield airport can be developed and operated either by Airports Authority of India (AAI) or by a private company that has been given a licence by Directorate General of Civil Aviation (DGCA). A greenfield airport to be set up by AAI would preferably be constructed under PPP mode. Foreign direct investment (FDI) up to 100 per cent is permitted through automatic approvals. If required, a capital grant up to 20 per cent of the project cost can be provided through viability gap funding (VGF) scheme. In the case of private operator, financing, construction and operation of the airport shall be the responsibility of the private company. The state government or any entity of the state government can also apply for a licence to DGCA for the development and operation of the airport. The state government may provide various incentives like land at concession rate, concession/exemption of state taxes, real state development right around the airport but cannot enter into any concession agreement with a private operator as they do not have the power to grant airport concession under the AAI Act. It is only the AAI which is authorised to enter into a concession agreement with a private entity as per the Act. For any greenfield airport, all the requisite clearances related to defence, air, traffic services, customs, immigration, etc., shall be the responsibility of the private operator.

Measures for making the greenfield airport project viable:

i. Land and external infrastructure provided by the state government for the airport on lease through land lease agreement with a variety of combinations such as token lease, moratorium on lease, deferred payment lease, etc.

ii. The state government may also enter into a state support agreement such as grant, infrastructure loan, interest free loan, etc.

iii. The central government may levy an advance development fee (ADF) on embarking passengers at the existing airports or for the development of new airports on terms and conditions as per ADF rules framed by the ministry.

iv. The greenfield airport operator may be allowed to levy a user development fee (UDF) at the new airport subject to the regulatory regime enforce.

v. Aeronautical charges which may be levied at the airport shall be as approved by the government/regulator.

vi. Passenger service fee (PSF) levied at all airports would be applicable to greenfield airport also.

Financing proposals for airports depends upon a number of factors like location, economic activity and connectivity, which are deemed to be key for a successful airport. Land acquisition, availability of raw materials at the assured cost, availability of utilities (power and water etc.), market competition and potential are equally important factors to assess the feasibility of the airport project. Financial health and creditworthiness of the parent companies forming special purpose vehicle (SPV) is to be critically looked into.

Risk

Like any other public service facility, airports are also exposed to infrastructure risks of constructions, operations, financing, etc.

Risks	*Risk Factors*
Project completion risk	Project completion risk: Completion within schedule and budgeted cost.
	Assured supply of construction inputs.
	Land acquisition.
	Required regulatory clearances.
	Quality of workmanship.
	Environmental compliance.

contd...

...contd...

Risks	*Risk Factors*
Technology risks	Cost and time comparison with other similar projects.
	Risks with new/unproven technology.
	Infrastructure support for construction.
	Availability of raw materials at assured cost
	Availability of utilities—power, water, etc.
Market risks	Market capacity and potential.
	Cyclicality/Recessionary trends in demand.
	Competition from new entrants.
	Price risk: Volatility, product price depreciation.
	Breakthrough technologies causing technological obsolescence.
	Change in user preferences and product quality
Legal risks	Collateral and security strongly enforceable.
	Structure of arbitration mechanism.
Financial strength	Project debt: Equity (Norm-Maximum of 3.275)
	Project debt service coverage ratio (DSCR) (Norm-Minimum of 1)
	Project loan life coverage ratio (LLCR) (Norm-Minimum of 1.1)
	Total outstanding liabilities (TOL)/tangible net worth (TNW)
	Contingent liabilities.
	Foreign exchange risk.
Corporate governance, management quality	Transparency in related party transactions.
	Management: Track record and competence, succession issues.
	Financial discipline: Strict control on cash flows.
	Strict control on more borrowings.
	Accounting quality: Revenue recognition, depreciation policies, etc.
Project external risks	Risks due to acts/policies of the government.
	Risks arising due to change in taxation policies/custom duty changes.
	Risks arising due to external factors like WTO, global economic changes, etc.
	Claims arising due to operating accidents.
	Risks of disruption due to labour trouble, force majeure events, etc.

Conclusion

In airports too, private participation has been encouraged. In line with the global transition, the government took action to shift funding pattern from budgetary allocation to private financing. Accordingly government approved, long term leased route for airports owned and operated by AAI. Under the Eleventh Plan, great emphasis had been placed on the PPP for the development of airport equipped with world class facilities. The projected investment in airport during the said plan was Rs 30,968 crore, where major contribution was envisaged from the private sector amounting to Rs 21,630 crore, i.e., 69.25 per cent. The private companies in this sector have shown its print. Delhi and Mumbai airports are being modernised under the PPP programme in addition to greenfield airports at Hyderabad and Bengaluru.

Financing pattern to airport is different from other sectors. There are lots of grants/concessions provided by the government including equity participations, lease of land at very nominal rent. Even stamp duty payable on land lease is exempted. Exemption is also given with regard to property tax and construction materials. Banks/FIs are finding airport proposals more secure if the company is found otherwise in order.

20 IIFCL Credit Products

India Infrastructure Finance Company Limited (IIFCL) was set up by Government of India (GoI) to provide long-term finance for viable infrastructure projects to promote and develop top class infrastructure in India.

The IIFCL funds viable infrastructure projects through the following modes:

i. Long-term debt;

ii. Refinance to banks and financial institutions (FIs) for loans, with tenor exceeding 10 years, granted by them.

iii. Any other mode approved by government from time to time.

IIFCL mandate include:

i. Providing long-term finance to commercially viable infrastructure projects.

ii. Giving overriding priority to public private partnership (PPP) projects.

iii. Supplementing available long-term debt resources.

Figure 20.1

Sector-wise Funding by IIFCL

Transport	• Road and bridges • Railways • Seaports • Airports • Inland waterways • Other transportation projects
Energy	• Power • Gas pipelines
Urban Infrastructure	• Urban transport • Water supply • Sewage • Solid waste management • Other physical infrastructure in urban areas
Special Economic Zone (SEZ) and Tourism	• Infrastructure projects in SEZs • International convention centres and other tourism infrastructure projects
Other	• Cold storage chain • Warehouses • Fertiliser manufacturing industry

Present Offerings of IIFCL

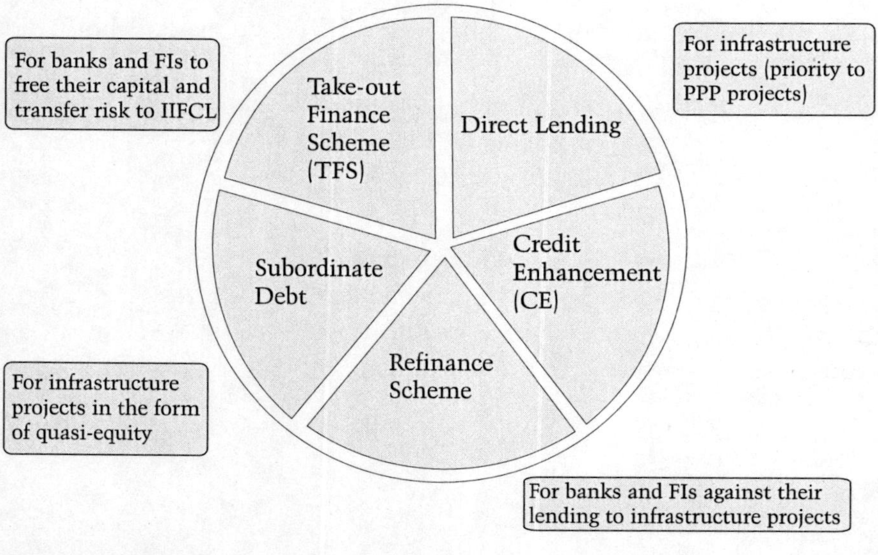

In addition to above, ECB is also extended through IIFCL (UK)—a subsidiary of IIFCL. The guidelines on ECB have been rationalised. The features of these guidelines are given hereunder.

ECBs will be available for capital expenditure under the automatic route for the purpose of maintenance and operations of toll systems for roads and highway provided they form part of the original project.

The project companies desirous of refinancing an existing ECB have now been permitted to raise fresh ECBs at higher all-in-cost/ reschedule and existing ECBs at a higher all-in-cost under the approval route provided the enhanced all-in-cost not exceed the all-in-cost ceiling prescribed as per the extant guidelines. Further, the companies in the power sector are allowed to utilise 40 per cent of fresh ECBs raised towards refinancing of rupee loan(s) availed by them from the domestic banking system under the approval route provided that at least 60 per cent of the fresh ECBs projected to be raised for fresh capital expenditure is for infra projects.

Infrastructure companies have been permitted to avail ECBs for the payment of rupee loan(s) availed of from the banking system and/or fresh rupees capital expenditure under the approval route subject to the conditions as mentioned:

i. The companies should be in the infrastructure projects.
ii. They should earn consistently during the past three financial years.
iii. They are not in the RBI default list or caution list.
iv. Such ECBs should only be utilised for repayment of rupee loan(s) availed for capital expenditure incurred earlier and are still outstanding in the books of the banks or for fresh capital expenditure.

It may be noted that refinancing of buyer's credit for import of capital goods in the infrastructure will be placed under the automatic route subject to certain conditions as laid down by RBI. It is also decided to increase the maturity of such buyer's credit to maximum 5 years.

Direct Lending

The total lending by the IIFCL to any project company shall not exceed 20 per cent of the total project cost (TPC). Loans will be disbursed in proportion to debt disbursements from FIs. The IIFCL will release funds to the lead bank as and when due. The lead bank consortium will make disbursements on behalf of the IIFCL and seek reimbursement which shall be made within one month of receiving a demand, with necessary particulars, from the lead bank.

Recently, to expedite the process of loan requirement through a single window concept, a consortium arrangement has been made with a number of members, where a project appraised by any member of the consortium will be acceptable to others. The members of the consortium are as follows:

i. State Bank of India (SBI).

ii. Punjab National Bank (PNB).

iii. Bank of Baroda (BoB).

iv. Bank of India (BoI).

v. Canara Bank.

vi. Union Bank of India (UBI).

vii. Industrial Development Bank of India (IDBI).

viii. Life Insurance Corporation of India (LIC).

ix. IIFCL.

The arrangement is aimed at providing total financial assistance under one go.

IIFCL offers direct financial assistance to the various infrastructure projects. Such assistance is based on the framework stipulated under the Scheme for Financing Viable Infrastructure Projects by a SPV called IIFCL Ltd (known as SIFTI). Financial support to the extent of 20 per cent of TPC or 80 per cent of the lead bank's share whichever is lower, is extended to the project company. IIFCL is however not authorised to play the role of the lead bank.

Subordinate Debt

Following are the salient features of subordinate debt:

i. Applicable for projects awarded through competitive bidding.

ii. The project to be approved by the PPPAC (Public Private Partnership Appraisal Committee).

iii. The concession agreement should provide for an escrow account.

iv. Sub-debt provided up to 10 per cent of project cost.

v. Tenor in excess of 10 years.

vi. Subordinate debt shall not be converted into equity.

vii. No separate appraisal; IIFCL accepts lead bank's appraisal.

viii. Eligible sectors as per SIFTI (Scheme for Financing Viable Infrastructure Projects through Special Purpose Vehicle).

Take-out Finance Scheme (TFS)

The TFS was conceptualised and initially launched in 2010 pursuant to the announcement in the Union Budget 2009-10 to stimulate public investment in infrastructure, effectively address the asset-liability mismatch (ALM) of commercial banks arising out of financing long term infrastructure projects and free up capital for financing new infrastructure projects. Under the scheme, IIFCL can take out infrastructure loans to the projects which have achieved the COD from the books of the banks/FIs as per its norms. Since the take out sans construction risks, IIFCL offers lower rate of interest depending upon its policies followed time to time. The scheme extends to benefit the stakeholders *viz.*, the lenders and the project developers which would enable increased flow of funds to the infrastructure sector.

The existing term loans of banks and FIs in infrastructure projects can be taken out by IIFCL, with benefits to the infrastructure project company and outgoing lenders.

Eligibility Condition under TFS

Following are the conditions which govern the TFS:

i. Project to have been funded under the consortium arrangement, having a common loan agreement.

ii. The residual tenor of the loan to be taken out by IIFCL should be at least six years.

iii. Actual debt service coverage ratio (DSCR) to be at least 1.0.

iv. Take-out of only those loans which are classified as standard in the books of the lenders.

v. Priority will be given to projects under PPP arrangement.

Extent of Take-out by IIFCL

Following equation can be used in this regard:

Amount of Take-out = Maximum (75% of residual debt of lead bank) + Maximum (100% of residual debt of other lenders in the consortium)

Total amount of take-out in a project will be limited by Minimum (30 per cent of TPC, less IIFCL outstanding loan by way of direct lending and 50% of residual debt on the date of tak-eout).

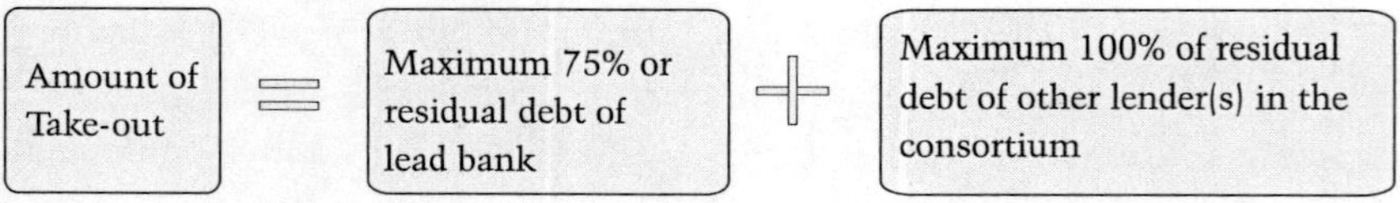

Tenor of Take-out Finance

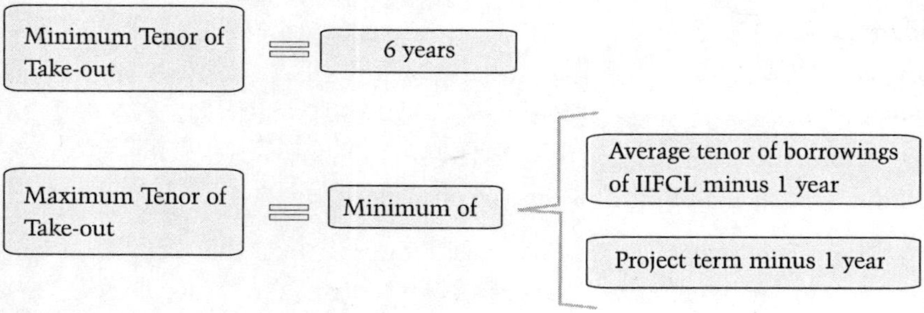

Lead bank is to retain a minimum of 10 per cent of its exposure till the last repayment of the taken out loan.

Timing of Take-out

IIFCL can take out loans:

i. Immediately on commercial operation date (COD), in case of PPP for roads (annuity basis).

ii. For other projects, at least one year after:

  a. COD or

  b. Provisional COD or

  c. When toll starts/revenue generates.

Key Points for the Implementation of TFS

Following are the salient features of TFS:

i. Either the borrower or the lender can request IIFCL for take-out.

ii. No objection certificate (NOC) is required from the lender whose loan is to be taken out and also from the rest of the consortium.

iii. Approval from the concessioning authority.

iv. After the loans are taken out, IIFCL will become a party to the inter-creditor agreement.

v. A take-out agreement is to be signed between IIFCL, lender(s), and the borrower.

In the month of September 2011, IIFCL signed memorandum of understanding (MoU) with LIC and Infrastructure Development Finance Company (IDFC) to provide take-out finance to banks and other eligible lenders, in the presence of Hon'ble Finance Minister. The key features of the MoU are:

i. Identified project lender(s) will offer eligible infrastructure projects for availing take-out financing to IIFCL in respect of mutually agreed accounts.

ii. Provide for take-out finance of 50 per cent of TPC by IIFCL, IDFC and LIC in the ratio of 30:20:10 instead of extant limit of 30 per cent of TPC by IIFCL alone.

iii. Quadripartite agreement to be entered into between the parties.

With this MoU in place, TFS (Revised) of IIFCL will facilitate banks to take more exposure in new projects, which in turn will help in bridging the gap in infrastructure financing.

Refinance Scheme

Objective

i. To facilitate the flow of funds in an increasing manner for the development of infrastructure.

ii. To provide refinance for term loans sanctioned by banks and public financial institutions (PFIs) for only new commercially viable projects in road, port, railways sectors, competitively bid power projects and UMPPs.

Eligibility

i. Banks and PFIs are eligible for refinance from IIFCL.

ii. PFIs notified under Section 4 (A) of the Companies Act, 1956.

iii. Projects for which bids are submitted on or after 31.01.2009 only.

Extent of Refinance: Up to 80 per cent of the loan amount disbursed by the banks/PFIs to infrastructure projects.

Exposure Limit: Exposure to banks will be capped by IIFCL's single party and group exposure norms.

Rate of Interest (RoI): IIFCL will charge ROI 2.50 per cent less than the ROI being charged by banks in the project, subject to the condition that our minimum ROI should be 7.85 per cent.

Tenor of Refinance: 10 years with a reset after 5 years, if the GoI is considering to allow an extension with reset for 5 more years.

Repayment of Refinance: The repayment of refinance would be linked with the repayment schedule of the loan fixed by the consortium in a manner so as to ensure total repayment of refinance amount within a period of 10 years.

IIFCL Direct Sanction where Refinance is Available: IIFCL to sanction 10 per cent of the project cost as against 20 per cent where refinancing facilities are available for such projects.

Other Terms of Refinance:

i. Upfront fees: No upfront fee to be levied.

ii. Prepayment: Refinance instalment is permitted to be prepaid only in cases where the borrowing units have prepaid the corresponding loan instalments.

iii. Additional Interest: Failure to service interest or debt would attract the provisions of the general agreement which will attract one per cent additional interest.

iv. Inspection: Periodic inspection post disbursement of refinanced accounts scrutiny.

Thus IIFCL offers its refinance assistance to the various infrastructure lenders as laid down in the scheme in order to enhance their leveraging capacities.

Credit Enhancement

The Concept

Credit enhancement is an innovative product for Indian infrastructure sector initiated by IIFCL. The aim is to facilitate raising of long-term funds from investors such as insurance companies and pension funds (PFs) for infrastructure sector by providing credit rating enhancement through partial credit guarantee of bond issue by the infrastructure project developer.

The Need

Around 72 per cent of infrastructure special purpose vehicles (SPVs) in India is rated in the BBB and A categories, while an estimated 18 per cent–20 per cent of infrastructure SPVs is rated in the sub – investment grade. Also, the potential investors have low risk appetite and regulatory restrictions. Credit enhancement would lead to an improvement in ratings of infrastructure SPV bonds raised by developers and enable major players with long-term funds like insurance and PF getting enthused to subscribe to such bonds.

Figure 20.2

Credit Enhancement: The Structure

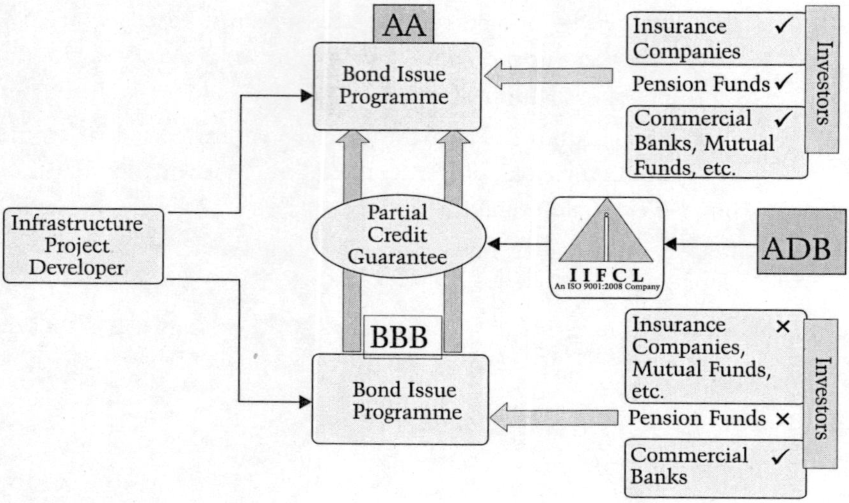

Figure 20.3

Credit Enhancement: The Mechanism

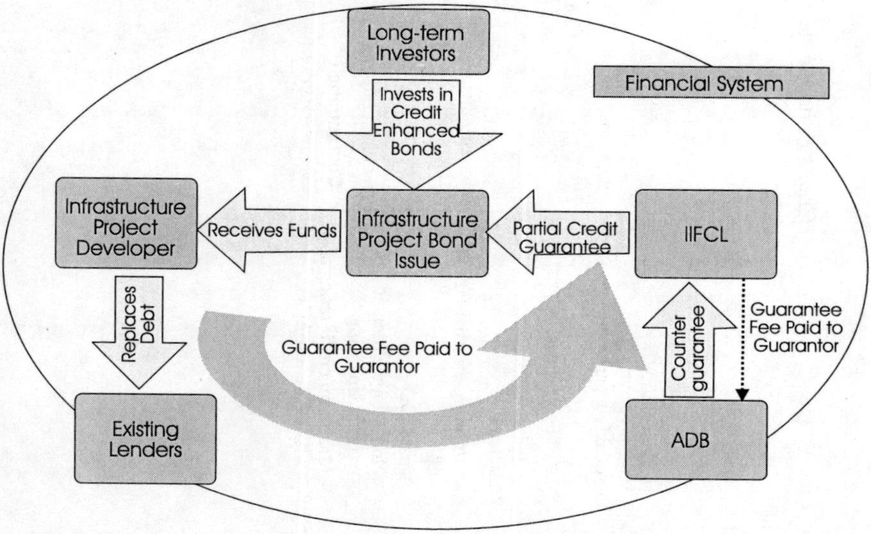

Table 20.1

Credit Enhancement (CE) Framework and Management Cycle

Proposal request processing and eligibility	Appraisal process	Documentation Process	Credit enhancement administration and management	Credit enhancement portfolio administration and management

- Pre-qualifying criteria
  - SIFTI guidelines
  - Credit enhancement scheme
  - Minimum external rating: BBB
  - Post COD
  - Non-recourse/Limited recourse financing
  - Maximum credit rating post enhancement: AA(SO)
  - Minimum average maturity for project bonds: 10 years
- Unconditional and irrevocable guarantee by IIFCL
- IIFCL's independent appraisal
- Checklist for information requirements
- PF/Credit group to map IIFCL's risk profile
	- Selection, due diligence, analysis and mitigation of risks
	- Structuring of enhancement extended
	- Vetting independently by risk group
	- Concentration risk addressed (group/single party/ sector/rating)
	- Rating and risk related pricing for each project
		- Documentation:
		  - Credit enhancement specific documents
		- Harmonisation with consortium finance and project documents
		- Security
		  • Valuations
		  • Timeframes
		  • Charge
		  • Enforceability
			- Management information system (MIS) for renewals, resets and compliance
			- Security/Collateral revaluation
			- Site visits
			- End use
			- Project review and alerts
			- Ageing schedule
			- Monitoring
			- Lender insurance agent (LIE) reports
			- Back-stop guarantee by Asian Development Bank (ADB)
			- Sharing of information with bond investors
			- Assessment of projects from beginning
				- Average returns from credit enhancement portfolio
				- Tracking diversification of portfolio *viz.*, promoter groups/ sectors/rating
				- Identifying credit migration
				- Tracking performance and trend analysis of companies/sectors
				- Impact analysis on IIFCL balance sheet

Figure 20.4

Credit Enhancement: Key Features

Sector Eligibility	• The infrastructure project should be from the infrastructure sectors as defined under SIFTI.
Minimum Standalone Rating	• The standalone credit rating of the infrastructure project to be credit enhanced should be at least BBB (before Credit Enhancement by IIFCL).
Project Tenure	• The infrastructure project should have achieved COD as on the date of guarantee/credit enhancement by IIFCL for the project bonds to be issued by the infrastructure project.
Tenure of Bond Issue	• The minimum average maturity period of the project bonds to be 10 years with or without a lock-in of 5 years.
Extent of Credit Enhancement	• Within the following limits: – 40% of TPC – 50% of total bond obligations
Backstop Guarantee to IIFCL	• ADB has principally agreed to provide backstop guarantee of up to 50% of IIFCL exposure.
Security	• 50% of credit enhancement by IIFCL to be backed by sponsor/holding company in form of corporate guarantee.
Guarantee Fee	• The guarantee/credit enhancement fee will be charged by IIFCL for extending guarantee/credit enhancement to the project bonds.
Independent Credit Appraisal	• Credit appraisal of the identified projects be carried out by a reputed appraising institution.

Risk Framework

i. Credit Enhancement Risks

   a. Default by issuer on bond obligations (coupon and principal)/ guarantee fees.

   b. Counterparty (sponsor) moral hazards.

   c. Dovetail sectoral policy and regulations/guidelines for the credit enhancement risks.

ii. Risk Sharing: Between the following parties

   a. Promotor(s)/issuer (sponsor) of the credit enhancement bond.

   b. Guarantor (IIFCL).

   c. Reinsurer (ADB) to the extent of guarantee reinsured.

   d. Concession authority.

iii. Broad Risk Mitigations

   a. In-built risk mitigants: Post-COD, Minimum BBB, etc.

   b. Rating methodology: Rating is done on RAM (Risk Assessment Model) based on risk weights assigned to various projects and policy parameters to arrive at rating number or symbol to fit a probability of default.

   c. Dovetailing documentation with other lenders.

Benefits for Developers

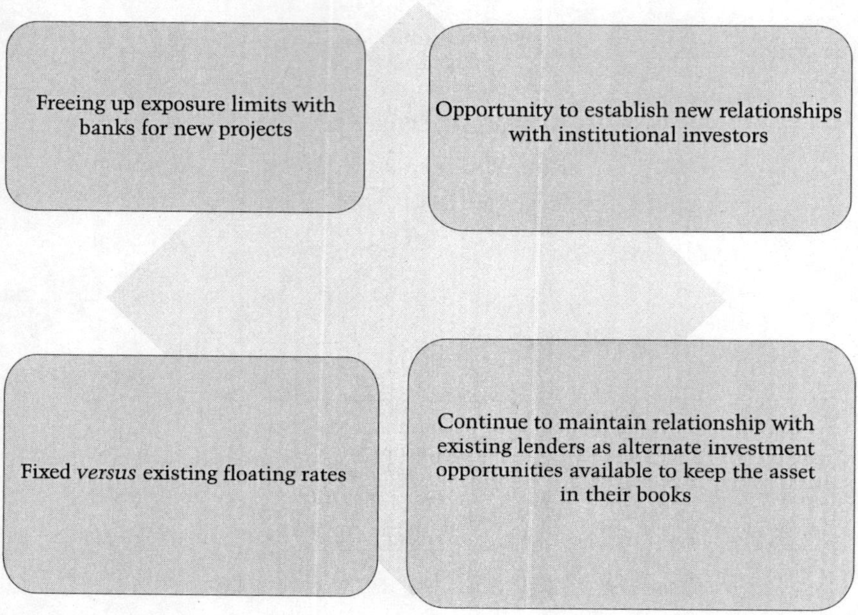

Benefits for Investors

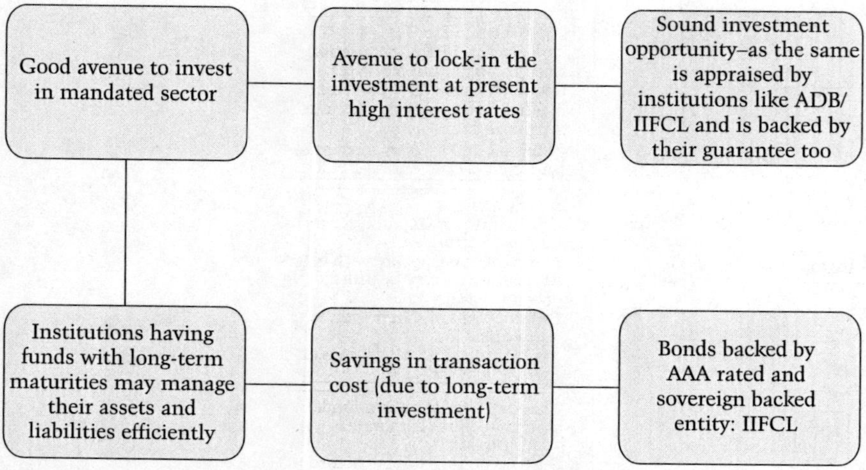

Benefits for Banks

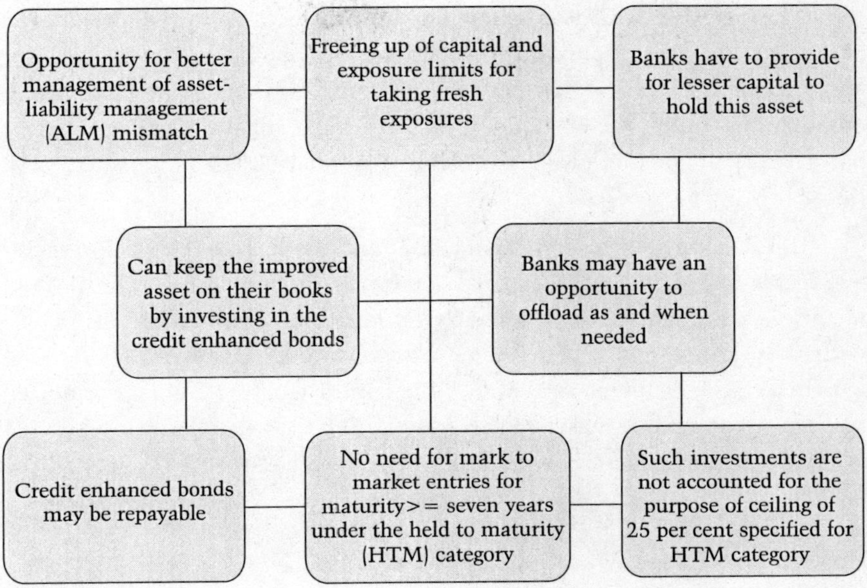

Value Proposition

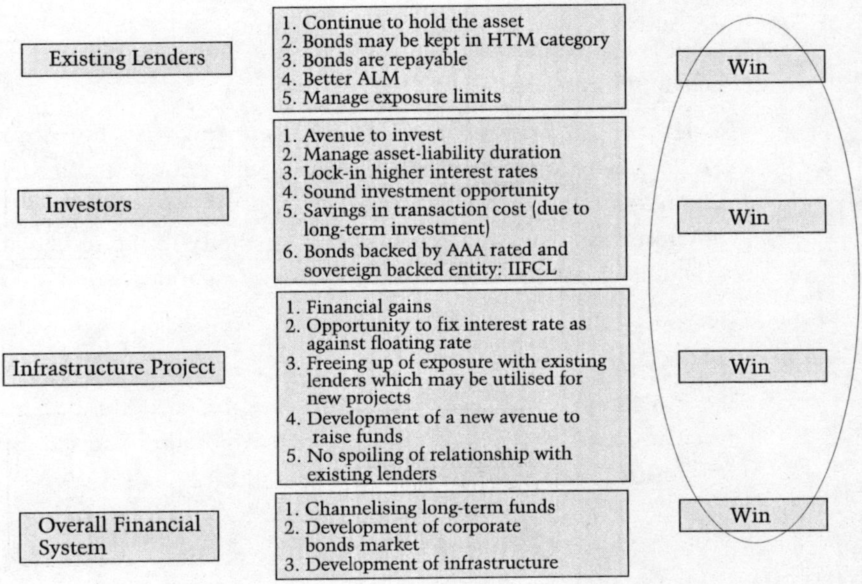

PMDO

The purpose of pooled municipal debt obligation (PMDO) facility is to finance municipal corporations, urban local bodies, local authorities and such other agencies as may be approved by the Credit Committee constituted under the PMDO or entities that are designed as eligible participants under the Jawaharlal Nehru National Urban Renewal Mission (JNNURM).

IIFCL along with IDBI Bank, Canara Bank and IL&FS Financial Services Limited is among the four sponsors of the facility. The PMDO facility is administered by a Credit Committee constituted in accordance with the Memorandum of Agreement (MoA) dated October 13, 2006, in which IIFCL is a member. IL&FS Urban Infrastructure Manager Limited has been appointed as Asset Manager while IL&FS Trust Company Limited is the security trustee and trust and retention account (TRA) agent to the facility.

Role of the Asset Manager

The Asset Manager shall perform the following functions:

i. Manage, operate and monitor the PMDO facility in accordance with this agreement.

ii. Identify borrowers and opportunities that have the potential to be sub-projects.

iii. Carry out an appraisal and due diligence of each borrower and/or sub-project from all relevant perspectives including but not limited to financial, technical, legal, commercial and environmental so as to establish the feasibility of the proposed sub-project and identify critical issues relating to the same.

iv. Formulate the risk rating framework to evaluate proposed sub-projects.

v. Formulate the evaluation report on the proposed sub-project on the basis of its appraisal and place it before the Credit Committee for its approval.

vi. Issue sanction letter to the borrower(s) conveying the sanction of the term loan along with its terms and conditions, as approved by the Credit Committee.

vii. Negotiate, finalise and execute the financing documents on behalf of the lenders and obtain acknowledgement of debt from the borrower(s), as may be required from time to time.

viii. Send copies of executed financing documents to all the lenders.

ix. Ensure that the conditions precedent for disbursement to respective sub-projects have been complied with on the basis of which a certificate would be issued to the lenders, certifying compliance of the conditions precedent.

x. Submit timely reports to lenders apprising them of the sub-project(s) which have been sanctioned by the Credit Committee under the PMDO facility, including a term sheet and information memorandum/appraisal report for that sub-project.

xi. Issue drawdown notice to the lenders, stating the amount, purpose and date of disbursement under a given sub-project, which shall be submitted to the lenders seven days in advance of making disbursements to the respective sub-projects.

xii. Engage professionally skilled and/or experienced personnel to provide the necessary advisory and managerial support and/or guidance for executing its responsibilities effectively.

xiii. Monitor the implementation of the project by borrowers and advise the borrower(s) on the reform actions to be undertaken by them as stipulated by the Credit Committee.

xiv. Ensure assistance is provided to borrowers in managing the bidding process for appointing reputed contractors/firms.

xv. Submit quarterly reports to the Credit Committee on the progress of each sub-project, expenditures undertaken and credit monitoring for the tenor of the term loan.

xvi. Submit quarterly reports to the lenders, apprising them of the conduct of the PMDO facility and the physical/financial progress of the sanctioned sub-projects with respect to expenditures undertaken, contractors appointed, extent of completion of the sub-project and such other information as deemed fit by the Credit Committee.

xvii. Provide the lenders with financial statements of each borrower by the Asset Manager within 90 days from the end of each financial year. In the event the borrower is an urban local body, budget statements of such entities would be provided upon its approval by their council.

xviii. Waive and/or modify 'conditions precedent' for documentation and/or disbursements, etc., depending on the exigency of the situation in order to expedite execution of loan documentation and disbursement, so that project implementation is timely achieved. Provided, however, that waiver and/or modification of such 'conditions precedent', shall not result in dilution of security and they are not of a material nature relating to the loan tenor, interest rate, quantum of loan, securities prescribed and project means of finance, and provided that the Asset Manager keeps the Credit Committee informed of such actions in the immediate subsequent meeting of the Credit Committee and the reasons necessitating the same.

xix. Issue any other waiver, consent, authorisation, approval or permission for and on behalf of the lenders or the security trustee with prior authorisation of the Credit Committee

xx. Oversee covenant compliance for term loan(s) as laid down in the common loan agreement.

xxi. Assist security trustee and TRA agent, in accordance with this agreement, in ensuring payment of dues to the lenders and to initiate action for recovery of dues of the lenders for and on behalf of the lenders.

xxii. Give notice to the security trustee of any litigation or governmental proceedings pending or to the extant material threatened against the borrowers or with respect to any sub-project, promptly on receiving notice thereof.

xxiii. Recommend to the Credit Committee with regard to the extension of the term of the PMDO facility.

xxiv. Recommend to the Credit Committee, the debt service reserve to be maintained by the borrower(s).

xxv. Rework the pro-rata allocation of the PMDO facility after final close and recommend it to the Credit Committee for its approval. On receipt of such approval the Asset Manager shall intimate the same to the lenders.

xxvi. Convene the meetings of the Credit Committee and carry out such other administrative procedures as may be required by the Credit Committee.

xxvii. Receive and deal with any request or proposal for waiver, modification, relaxation, consents, authorisations, approvals, extension of time, NOC or other indulgence sought by the borrowers with regard to any of the terms or conditions of the financing documents, provided that ratification thereof is sought in the immediate next meeting of the Credit Committee.

xxviii. Issue letters ceding second charge in favour of the working capital lenders to sub-projects, at the request of the borrowers and as per the directions of the Credit Committee from time to time.

xxix. Carry out any activity/function incidental or ancillary to the above functions.

Role of the Credit Committee

The credit committee is responsible for:

i. Detailed credit evaluation and final credit approvals for the proposals submitted by the Asset Manager. This would include:

   a. Review of management and business model of each borrower and its sustainability as prepared by the Asset Manager.

   b. Review of financial position of the borrower and the guarantor, if any, the borrower's past payment record to its existing lenders, and borrower's present and future prospects and financial projections as prepared by the Asset Manager.

ii. Supervision of any contract management activities undertaken by the Asset Manager.

iii. Reviewing the PMDO facility's lending policy and performance.

iv. Reviewing the risk rating framework, for evaluation of proposed sub-projects, as formulated by the Asset Manager.

The credit committee shall consider:

i. Approving the recommendations of the Asset Manager with regard to the debt service reserve to be maintained by the borrower in the debt service reserve account (DSRA).

ii. Deciding the additional sectors and additional category of borrowers for providing funding under PMDO facility as stated in clause 1.5 and clause 2.2 (x) to 2.2(xii) of the concession agreement.

iii. Deciding with respect to administration of the PMDO facility, including reset of interest rates and the term of the facility, including extension of the tenor of the PMDO facility by an additional three years subject to provisions of Clause 3.2 and 3.3 of the concession agreement.

iv. Increasing the commitment to each sub-project up to 20 per cent of its corpus.

v. Providing its approval for the proposals submitted by the Asset Manager on various matters, including interest rate and security structure for the sub-projects.

vi. Deciding on nomination of nominee director on the board of borrowers from time to time to represent the lenders.

Conclusion

IIFCL extends credit facility under the ambit of SIFTI giving priority to PPPs. It also provides the loan to a private sector company under non-PPP category provided it has under taken a project where the service to be provided is regulated or the project is being setup under MoU arrangement with the central government/state government or a public sector undertaking, however, total landing for non-PPP project shall not exceed 20 per cent of the lending programme of the company in any financial year. IIFCL is also not authorised to play the role of the lead bank. It is to note that the tenor of the loan of IIFCL should be larger than that of the longest tenor of commercial debt by at least two years and projects setup on non-recourse basis should only be eligible for financing. IIFCL also provides innovative financing solutions to the infrastructure sector through credit enhancement, take out finance scheme, setting up of a project development company and an infrastructure debt fund. The company's resolve is to address institutional and market related gaps and catalyse long term funds to meet the financing requirements of infrastructure sector.

IIFCL, a wholly owned subsidiary of the GoI is positioned centrally in the infrastructure finance system between the industry comprising infrastructure finance intermediaries and infrastructure project promoters and the government.

Annexures

Annexure A-1

Registers Regarding Proposal (Received and Disposed of)

									Month ________2012
Proposals Generated by ________									
Sr. No.	*Name of the proposals*	*Date of receipt*	*Promoter/ Developer*	*PPP/ Non-PPP/ MoU*	*Sector*	*Date of NBC*		*Cleared by NBC or not*	*Date of intimation to the company*

Annexure A-2

Report on Consortium Meeting during the Month

Sr. No.	*Name of the projects*	*Date of consortium meeting*	*Consortium meeting report submission date*	*Important issues impacting the a/c (if any)*	*Officer attended the consortum meeting*	*Key features of the companies presentation*	*Remarks*		

Record Note on Consortium Meeting Dated ------

Project name:

Project background:

Conduct of account:

Issues deliberated in the meeting:

The minutes of the consortium meeting and copy of presentation by the company official are enclosed.

Submitted for taking on record.

Attending officer

Annexure A-3

Proposal for New Business Committee

(Name of the Proposal)

Sr. No.	*Particulars*	*Details*	
1	Nature of the project (PPP/Non-PPP/PSL)		
2	(a) Sector (b) State (c) Project (d) Project cost		
	(e) Means of Finance	Particulars	Amount (Rs crore)
		Total	
	(f) Request for loan amount from banks/FIs		
3	(a) Name of the company/ SPV/Promoter/ Group		
	(b) Shareholding pattern	Promoter	% share
		Total	
4	MoU/PPA		
5	Credit rating by external agency		
6	Single borrower exposure - Proposed borrower exposure		
7	Group borrower exposure - Proposed borrower exposure - Exposure norms (current)		
8	Track record of the borrower (including existing exposure with banks/FIs)		
9	Brief about the proposal (strengths/weakness and mitigants/IRR/D:E ratio, etc.)		

Annexure A-4

Site Visit Report

I. Name of the Officer :

II. Date of Site Inspection :

Sr. No.	*Particulars*	*Remarks*
1.	Name of the company/SPV	
	Promoter/Group	

	Promoter % share

Sr. No.	*Particulars*	*Remarks*
2.	Nature of project	
	Sector	State
3.	PPP/ Public sector/Private sector	
4.	Risk rating by external agency Risk rating by IIFCL	
5.	Cost of the project (Rs/crore)	Means of finance (Rs/crore)

Particulars
EPC cost
Preliminary and preoperative Expenses
Supervision expenses
Financing charges
IDC
Contingency provisions
Working capital
Total

Particulars	Amount
Equity	
Subordinated debt	
Senior debt	
Total	

Sr. No.	*Particulars*	*Remarks*
6.	Lead bank	
7.	Total amount of term loan	

Debt allocation to various banks/lenders – (Rs/crore)

Name of the lending institution	*Allocated amount*	*Disbursement made so far*	*% share of disbursement*	*RoI (%)*

Total				

8.	Whether all the terms and conditions of sanction have been complied with	
9.	Last visit by banks/FIs and comments (Name of the officer and date of visit)	
10.	Lender's engineer/Lead bank/banks/FIs comments on the overall performance of the company/project	
11.	Whether the company is regular in servicing of dues? (Interest and principal)	
12.	Penal interest rate charged by other consortium members Any other charges levied by other bank	
13.	Status of equity –	
	Equity brought in	
	Promoters contribution	
	Unsecured loans from promoters	
	Total	
14.	Status of ESSF issues	
15.	Present status of project	
	Status of land acquisition	
	Scheduled financial progress	
	Actual financial progress	
	Scheduled physical progress	
	Actual physical progress	
16.	Whether audited balance sheet received from the company?	
17.	Latest LIE report received and name of the LIE.	
18.	Audit objections, if any, of other banks	
19.	Planned/Revised COD	
20.	Comments/Observations	

Submitted for information and record

Annexure A-5

Format of the Periodic Environmental and Social Report

	Aspects
	Project Status
Project information	• Progress of the project • Alternations to project parameters and relevant clearances • Communications with regulatory authorities • Expansion plans
	Compliance with Bank/FI Conditions
	Provide a statement on compliance with banks/FIs conditions on environmental aspects of the project as may have been stipulated in the loan agreement.
	Resource Profile
Resource use	• Fuel (quantity consumed, transportation risks) • Water utilisation • Electricity • Other resources utilised (Quantitative information on resource consumption since last reported need to be provided. In case of reporting for the first time, latest annual consumption figures may be provided.)
	Environmental Profile
Air emissions and air quality	• Emissions from various sources • Air quality at work place • Air quality around the project site • Compliance with regulatory requirements
Effluents and liquid discharge and water quality	• Effluent quantity and space quality • Monitoring results of effluent and water quality • Compliance with regulatory requirements
Noise generation and noise levels	• Noise monitoring from various sources • Noise monitoring at work place • Noise around project site • Compliance with regulatory requirements
Waste generation and disposal	• Waste generation from various sources • Waste disposal methods • Status of disposal site
Pollution control aspects	• Performance of pollution control equipment/ systems

Review of emergency management	• Staff and resources • Plan testing

Site Health and Safety

- Accident and incident records
- Internal procedure for internal audits and summary of major findings
- Work area monitoring results for chemical agents as well as physical agents (noise, dust)

Social Aspects

- New development and land acquisition
- Public consultation and community relations
- Current status of resettlement and rehabilitation (R&R) and income generation activities, if applicable
- Status of utilisation of R&R budget
- Community welfare activities
- Details of any public protest/complaints/ litigation and how they have been addressed or being addressed with present status
- Details of any new developments around the project vicinity such as human settlements, new industries, etc.

Summary of Compliance with Environmental Regulations

- Compliance with conditions of the air and water consents and the environmental clearance as applicable
- Compliance with Factories Act and state factories' rules
- Compliance with provisions of all applicable health and safety legislation
- Details of any notices or communication received from the State Pollution Control Board/factories inspectorate and other regulatory bodies

Environmental Management

- Organisation structure
- Staff and resources
- Achievements
- Environmental training/Awareness programmes

Supporting Documents Provided

	Documents	*Enclosed (Yes/No/N.A.)*
1	Environment monitoring report, if available. Else lab reports supporting the environment and emissions data or information provided in the forestery and environmental resources (FER)	
2	Copies of any updates/changes related to state/central environmental clearances/consents along with the copies of the application made.	
3	Details of protests, lawsuits, strictures fines, etc., against the project since inception of the project, issued either by courts, regulators, government or other bodies.	
4	Records of any public consultation documentation as well as any complaints made by the local communities.	
5	R&R monitoring report including status and impact of income restoration activities.	
6	Any other documents of relevance.	

Declaration by the Project

We hereby declare that all the information provided and referred to in this procedure for environmental and social review (PESR) is authentic and that we have not withheld any pertinent information pertaining to environment, health, safety and social matters of the project.

Name and designation of the official	
Signature	
Date	

Annexure A-6

Monthly Report

Credit Department:

Direct Lending

- No. of proposals received: Cleared by NBC: Not cleared by NBC
- During the month, the company received -- proposals requesting aggregate loan of --- crore and these are under process. The mode-wise details of proposals received are as under:

Mode	No. of projects	Loan requested (Rs crore)
PPP		
Non-PPP		
Total		

Gross and Net Sanctions

Sector-wise Details of Gross Sanctions

(Rs crore)

Mode	*Cumulative as on 31st March 20__*	*During Month___ 2012@*	*During 20— to 20__*	*Cumulative as on Month__ 2012*
Road				
Power				
Airport				
Port				
Urban Infrastructure				
PMDO				
Others				
Total				

- At the end of ----, net sanctions of the company in --- projects amounted to ---- crore. The sector-wise details of net sanctions are in Annexure I.

Mode-wise Details of Net sanctions

(Rs crore)

Mode	*Cumulative as on 31st March 20__*	*During Month___ 2012@*	*During 20— to 20__*	*Cumulative as on Month__ 2012*
PPP				
Non-PPP				
PSU				
PMDO				
Total				

Sector-wise Details of Net sanctions

(Rs crore)

Mode	*Cumulative as on 31st March 20__*	*During Month___ 2012@*	*During 20— to 20__*	*Cumulative as on Month__ 2012*
Road				
Power				
Airport				
Port				
Urban infrastructure				
PMDO				
Total				

Financial Closure

- At end of ----, financial closure has taken place in --- cases with net sanction amount of ---- crore involving project cost of ---- crore.

Disbursement

- With further disbursement of ---- crore during the month, the cumulative disbursement of the company as on ----- amounted to -----crore.

Mode-wise Disbursement

(Rs crore)

Mode	*Cumulative as on 31st March 20__*	*During Month___ 2012@*	*During 20— to 20__*	*Cumulative as on Month__ 2012*
PPP				
Non-PPP*				
PSU				
Total disbursement				

Sector-wise Disbursement

(Rs crore)

Mode	*Cumulative as on 31st March 20__*	*During Month___ 2012@*	*During 20— to 20__*	*Cumulative as on Month__ 2012*
Road				
Power*				
Airport				
Port				
Urban infrastructure				
Total disbursement				

- Site visits have been undertaken in --- projects out of --- projects where disbursements have been made.

Details of Site Visits

Cumulative as on 31st March 20__	*During Month___ 2012@*	*During 20— to 20__*	*Cumulative as on Month__ 2012*

(Status as on ----)

Sector-wise Gross Sanctions

(Rs crore)

Sector	*No. of projects*	*Project cost*	*Gross sanctions*
Road			
Power			
Airport			
Port			
Urban infrastructure			
PMDO			
Total			

Sector-wise Net Sanctions

(Rs crore)

Sector	*No. of projects*	*Project cost*	*Net sanctions*
Road			
Power			
Airport			
Port			
Urban infrastructure			
PMDO			
Total			

- Net sanction = Gross Sanction (-) Loans cancelled (-) Unallocated loan amount in case of projects where financial closure has been achieved

Management information system (MIS)

Sector-wise Loan Sanctioned

(Rs/crore)

Sr. No.	Name of the company	Project	Date of sanction	NHAI/ SH	Project cost	Gross sanctions by banks/ FIs	Net sanctions by banks/ FIs	Date of first disbursement	Loan documents signed	PPP/Non-PPP/ Public	COD	ROI (%)	Disbursed till... -2012	Reset clause
Road														
1														
		Sub-total			0.00	0.00	0.00						0.00	
Airport														
1														
2														
		Sub-total			0.00	0.00	0.00						0.00	
Power														
1														
2														
		Sub-total			0.00	0.00	0.00						0.00	

contd...

...contd...

Port

1													
2													
	Sub-total			0.00	0.00	0.00						0.00	

Urban Infrastructure

1													
2													
	Sub-total				0.00	0.00	0.00						0.00
	Total (A)				0.00	0.00	0.00						0.00

PMDO

Sr. No.	*ULB name/ Borrower*	*Sector*	*Project cost*	*Banks/ FIs share*	*Banks/ FIs share*	*Date of first disbursement*	*Loan documents signed*	*PPP/Non-PPP/Public sector*	*COD*	*ROI (%)*	*Banks/ FIs disbursed*	*Reset clause*
1												
2												
		Total (B)	0.00	0.00	0.00						0.00	
	Grand Total (A+B)		0.00	0.00	0.00						0.00	

State-wise Loans Sanctioned

(Rs/crore)

Sr. No.	*Name of the company*	*Project*	*Promoter*	*Project cost*	*Gross sanction by banks/FIs*	*Net sanction by banks/FIs*	*Banks/FIs loan as % of project cost*
1.	Name of the State						
1							
	Sub-total			0.00	0.00	0.00	
2.	Name of the State						
1							
2							
	Sub-total			0.00	0.00	0.00	
	Grand Total						

Promoter-wise Sanctions

(Rs/crore)

Sr. No.	*Name of the company*	*Project*	*Sector*	*Promoter*	*Project cost*	*Gross sanction by banks/FIs*	*Net sanction banks/FIs*
	Name of the promoter						
1							
2							
3							
	Total						
	Name of the promoter						
1							
2							
3							
	Total						

Banks/FIs share as %age of Total Project Cost and Lead Bank Share as %age of Total Debt

(Rs/crore)

Sr. No.	*Name of the company*	*Sector*	*Appraised by*	*Project cost*	*Total debt*	*Banks/FIs share in total debt*	*Banks/FIs debt %age of total project cost*	*Lead bank*	*Lead bank's share in total debt*

Sector-wise, Project-wise Amount Disbursed

	Project name	*Sector*	*State*	*Project cost*	*Loan allocated*	*Amount disbursed*	*Mode*
Road							
1							
Total				0.00	0.00	0.00	
Power							
1							
Total				0.00	0.00	0.00	
Port							
1							
Total				0.00	0.00	0.00	
Airport							
1							
Total				0.00	0.00	0.00	
Urban Infrastructure							
1							
Total (A)				0	0.00	0	
						0.00	
PMDO							
1							
Total (B)				0.00	0.00	0.00	
Total (A+B)				0.00	0.00	0.00	

Site Visit by Banks/FIs—Status as on Month___ 2012

(Rs in crore)

Sr. No.	*Name of the company*	*Project*	*Sector*	*State*	*Project cost*	*Net sanction by IIFCL*	*Loan documents signed*	*Site visited on*

Annexure A-7

Memorandum to be Submitted to the Competent Authority under Review of the Account

Item No. :

Pre–COD/Post-COD

PPP/Public sector/Non-PPP

Sub: Annual Review
A/c name with sanctioned amount

(All figures in Rs crore unless specified otherwise)

Date of sanction	
Date of last annual review	
Sector	
Lead bank	
Total project cost	
Total debt	
Loan sanctioned	
Loan sanctioned by lead bank	

1. Borrower profile:

Name of company (SPV)	
Promoter group	
Shareholding pattern	Promoter / % share Total / 100%

Status of Equity brought in by the Promoters:

Particulars	Required	Brought in
Total		
Equity in terms of CLA		

2. Project details:

Project site location	
Project description	
Concession authority/MoU	
Date of signing concession agreement (CA)/MoU	
Concession period/Project term	
Scheduled COD	
Reasons for delay in COD *vis-à-vis* planned	

Total cost of the project
(Rs in crore)

Particulars	Amount
Total	

Source of finance -
(Rs in crore)

Particulars	Amount
Total	

Total amount of term loan

Debt allocation and disbursements of various banks/FIs

Bank/Lender	*Allocated amount*	*% share*	*Disbursement*	*% share*
Total				

3. Rate of interest	
a. ROI at time of sanction with reset clause	
b. Current ROI	
c. Date of last reset	
d. Date of next reset	

4. Assessment with credit rating	*Earlier*	*Present*	*Upward/ Downward*

5. Status of revenue collections	*Projected*	*Actual performance*	*%age performance*

6. Debt service coverage ratio (DSCR)	
a. At the time of sanction	
b. At the time of review	

7. Compliances of terms and conditions	
a. Whether conditions precedent at this stage are complied with	Yes/No
b. If not, status of compliance	
c. Documentation	Complete/Not completed
d. Date of execution of documents	
8. Sanctions and approvals	
a. Whether all sanctions and approvals have been obtained	Yes/No
b. If not, status of pending sanctions/approvals	
9. Land acquisition	
a. Whether land has been acquired fully	Yes/No
b. If not, status of land acquisition	

10.	Fuel supply linkages (where applicable)	
	a. Whether fuel linkage has been completed	Yes/No
	b. If not, status of fuel linkage	
11.	Remarks in lenders independent engineer (LIE) report	
12.	Date of last site visit	
13.	Banks/FIs comments on the overall performance of the company/project based on site visit report/ consortium meeting/LIE report	
14.	Whether company is regular in servicing dues	Yes/No
15.	Whether the account has been restructured	Yes/No
16.	If yes, date of restructuring	
17.	Status of environment and social safeguards framework (ESSF) compliances	
18.	Last date of review by the board	
19.	Due date for review by the board	
20.	Present status of project	
21.	Comment on operation of the unit/account	
22.	Outstanding issues, if any	
23.	Efforts put in by the borrower for resolution and completion of the project	
24.	Department's justification/recommendation	

The note is placed for review of the account.

Dated

Annexure A-8

Single Party and Group Exposure

Name of the group/party

Group/party exposure

Total single party exposure/Total group exposure

Sr. No.	*Name of the company*	*State*	*Sector*	*Nature of limit*	*Direcrt lending/ others*	*Sanction during the year*	*Amount sanctioned*	*Amount disbursed*	*Repayment made*	*Amount O/s as on 31.03.12*	*Lead bank*	*COD achieved on*	*External rate*	*Group status a/c wise*	*Rank*

Annexure A-9

Memorandum to the Board

Item No.:

Toll/ Annuity

PPP/Public Sector/ Non-PPP

Sub:	Proposal for Sanction of Rs ________ To ______________ under Direct Lending

Executive Summary

1.	Name of borrower (SPV)		
2.	Sector		
3.	a. Project (in brief)		
	b. Location		
	c. State		
4(a)	Promoter(s) group		
4(b)	Whether the company/director is/are in the defaulter list of RBI/CIBIL/ECGC defaulter's list. If yes, details and reasons for taking up the exposure.	Yes/No	
5.	Total project cost (as appraised)		
6.	Means of finance		
6(i)	Equity and upfront as per project information memorandum (PIM)		
6(ii)	NHAI grant		
6(iii)	Debt		
	a. Senior		
	b. Subordinate		
7(a)	Lead lender/Lead arranger		
7(b)	Proposed lenders		
8.	Appraiser		
	Techno-economic viability (TEV) report		
	EPC		

9.	Lead lender's share	
10.	Loan sought	
11.	Concessioning authority/MoU	
12.	DBOFT/BOT (annuity/toll)/PPA	
13.	Status of land acquisition a. Defence land b. Forest land c. No. of bridges d. No. of railway over bridge (ROB)/railway under bridge (RUB) e. Connectivity	
14.	Key project parameters a. DER b. DSCR c. IRR d. Scheduled COD e. Concession period f. Project term g. Door-to-door loan tenor h. Average maturity of loan	
15.	Rating a. External/date b. Internal/date	
16.	Exposure as applicable a. Single party b. Group exposure	
17.	Whether exposure norms complied	Yes/No
18.	Proposed ROI	a. Align to lead bank Or b. Reset clause
19.	Whether scheme compliant	Yes/No

Details of the Project

Date of receipt of proposal	
New business committee clearance	Yes
Credit appraisal grid clearance	Yes

Date:

25. Borrower profile:

Name of company (SPV)	
Project site location	
Project description	
Registered/Corporate office address	
Concessioning authority/MoU	
Date of signing CA/MoU	
Concession period/Project term	
Scheduled COD	

Board of Directors

Sr. No.	*Name of the director*	*Designation*	*%age stake*
1.			
2.			
3.			

Shareholding Pattern

Shareholder	Shareholding %age
Total	100.00%

Whether Listed Company: Yes/No

Group Exposure:

Sr. No.	*Name of company*	*Limit (Rs/crore)*	
		Existing	*Proposed*
Total			

Outstanding/Overdues Position in respect of Group Companies:

Sr. No.	*Name of the company*	*Net sanction (Rs/crore)*	*Proposed sanction (Rs/crore)*	*Loan O/s (Rs crore)*	*Overdue, if any (in Rs)*	*Status of the project*
1						
2						
3.						
4						
5						
Total						

External Rating of Company (SPV):

The borrower shall got itself rated within six months from first disbursement by an external credit rating agency acceptable to the lenders.

Delay beyond six months shall attract additional interest as decided by consortium.

Promoters Details:

a. Background:

b. Financials:

c. External ratings:

d. Past performance/Track record:

e. Comments:

About the project:

Current status (including land acquisition status/fuel linkages)

- Land acquisition
  - a. Defence land
  - b. Forest land
  - c. No of bridges
  - d. No. of ROB/RUB
  - e. Connectivity
- Fuel linkages
  - a. Agreement- vetted by legal department

Permissions and approvals

Implementation schedule

CA/MoU/PPA: Salient Features:-

Traffic/Tariff/Demand study:-

Project cost (As appraised):

Item	Rs/crore	%
Total project cost		100.00%

PPPAC cost:

Justification:

Means of finance:

(Rs/crore)

Means of finance	*Amount*
Equity	
• Promoters' equity	
• Grant	
• Other(s)	
Rupee term loan	
Total	

Observations on promoters equity contribution:

Viability gap funding (if any):

Summary of financials:

a. Projected profit and loss A/c
b. Projected balance sheet
c. Projected cash flow statement

Comments on financials:

Sensitivity analysis *vis-à-vis* IRR:

Risk rating summary:

Credit rating	Based on financial year	Single scale rating
Current		

Rating information/Key risk issues:

Top level risk entity name	Score
Overall Rating	
Environment risk	
Business risk	
Completion risk – build phase	
Execution risk – build phase	
Critical risk – build phase	
Financial risk – build phase	

Risk analysis and mitigation:

Terms and conditions of sanction:

Compliance with the scheme :

i)	3.1 (c)	Lead bank share	
ii)	3.1 (d)	Loan tenure	
		Average maturity	
iii)	5.2	Competitive bidding	Yes/No
iv)	5.3	Non-recourse basis	Yes/No
v)	6.1	Whether appraised by lead bank/lead arranger	
vi)	6.3	Monitoring and periodic evaluation	
vii)	7.5	Disbursement through escrow account	
viii)	7.7	Security (in brief)	

Compliance with credit risk policy guidelines:

Sr. No.	*Parameters*	*Credit norms (Rs/crores)*	*Proposed sanction (Rs/crores)*
1.	Minimum project lending	NA limit (for this sector)	
2.	Single project exposure	As per the norms limit w.r.t. appraised project cost (%)	
3.	Lead bank share	` _____	
4.	Individual exposure limit	As per the banks/FIs norms	
5.	Group exposure limit	As per the banks/FIs norms	

Banks/FIs directors (if any) deemed to be interested in the proposal: None

Observation:

Annexure A-10

NBFC–IFC: Information Submission to RBI

Half yearly statement of capital funds, risk assets/exposures and risk asset ration, etc., as at end of March/September 20..

Form NBS 2

PART - F

Asset Classification

I. Aggregate of credit exposures categorised into:

Item name	Item code	Amount
(i) Standard assets	411	
(ii) Sub-standard assets :		
(a) Lease and hire purchase assets	412	
(b) Other credit facilities	413	
(iii) Doubtful assets	414	
(iv) Loss assets	415	
Total (411 to 415)	410	
Note: (item 410 should tally with CT200)		

II. Aggregate provisioning in respect of I above as per the directions prescribed

Item name	Item code required	Provision required	Actual provision made

(A) Loans, advances and other credit facilities

(i) Sub-standard assets :

(a)	Entire amount taken to the credit of profit and loss account before the asset became NPA and remaining unrealised [Para 3(2) of the directions]	421
(b)	10% of the balance of outstanding dues	422

(ii) Doubtful assets :

(a)	Entire amount taken to the credit of profit and loss account before the asset became NPA and remaining unrealised [Para 3(2) of the directions]	423

PART - H

Particulars regarding concentration of advances including off balance sheet exposure and investments to parties including those in Part G above

Item name	Item	Amount	Code
i) Loans and advances including off balance sheet exposures to any single party in excess of 15 per cent of owned fund of the NBFC. (Details to be enclosed in Appendix No.)		610	
ii) Loans and advances including off balance sheet exposures to a single group of parties in excess of 25 per cent of owned fund of the NBFC. (Details to be enclosed in Appendix No.)		620	
iii) Investments in a single company in excess of 15 per cent of the owned fund of the NBFC. (Details to be enclosed in Appendix No.)		630	

Item name	Item	Amount	Code
iv) Investments in the shares issued by a single group of companies in excess of 25 per cent of the owned fund of the NBFC		640	
v) Loans, advances to (including debentures/ bonds and off balance sheet exposures) and investment in the shares of single party in excess of 25 per cent of the owned fund of the NBFC		650	
vi) Loans, advances to (including debentures/ bonds and off balance sheet exposures) and investment in the shares of single group of parties in excess of 40 per cent of the owned fund of the NBFC		660	

Notes :

(1) All these exposure limits are applicable to the NBFC's own group as well as to the borrower/investee company's group.

(2) Investment in debentures for this purpose shall be treated as credit and not investment.

Item name	Item code	Provision required	Actual provision made
(b) 100% to the extent not covered by realisable value of security plus 20 to 50% of the secured portion for the period the asset has remained doubtful	424		
(iii) Loss assets :			
(a) Entire amount taken to the credit of profit and loss account before the asset became NPA and remaining unrealised [Para 3(2) of the directions]	425		
(b) 100 % of the outstanding balance	426		
Total: (item No.421 to 426)	ST426		

24.11

NBFC–IFC – Information Submission to RBI

Annual Statement of capital funds, risk assets/exposures and risk asset ration, etc., as at end of March 20..

Form NBS 7

PART - F

Asset classification

I. Aggregate of credit exposures categorised into:

Item name	Item code	Amount
(i) Standard assets		411
(ii) Sub-standard assets :		
(a) Lease and hire purchase assets	412	
(b) Other credit facilities	413	
(iii) Doubtful assets	414	
(iv) Loss assets	415	
Total (411 to 415)	410	

Note: (item 410 should tally with CT200)

II. Aggregate provisioning in respect of I above as per the directions prescribed

Item name	Item code	Provision required	Actual provision made
(A) Loans, advances and other credit facilities			
(i) Sub-standard assets :			
(a) Entire interest amount taken to the credit of profit and loss account before the asset became NPA and remaining unrealised	421		
(b) 10% of the balance of outstanding dues	422		

(ii) Doubtful assets :

(a) Entire interest amount taken to the credit of profit and loss account before the asset became NPA and remaining unrealised 423

Item name	Item code	Provision required	Actual provision made

(b) 100% to the extent not covered by realisable value of security plus 20% to 50% of the secured portion for the period the asset has remained doubtful 424

(iii) Loss assets :

(a) Entire interest amount taken to the credit of profit and loss account before the asset became NPA and remaining unrealised 425

(b) 100 % of the outstanding balance 426

Total: (item No.421 to 426)	ST426		

Annexure A-11

Format for Review/Renewal with Modifications/ Rectification/Additional Sanctions

Proposal for	:	New Sanction/Review/Renewal/Enhancement/ Modification/Ratification
Sector	:	
Nature of Industry	:	
Future outlook of the industry for which proposal is being placed	:	
Industry exposure		(Amt. in Rs. crore)
Permitted exposure as per CRMC for FY 2010-11	:	
Outstanding exposure in the sector as per RMCB statement for the quarter ended	:	
NPA in the sector as per RMCB statement for the quarter ended		
Proposed exposure	:	
Credit rating	:	
Status of the account	:	
Whether reported under Special Watch List during the period under review	:	
Whether restructuring exercise undertaken in the past	:	

Memorandum to the Board

Executive Summary

Date:

1.	Name of the Branch & Zone
2.	Name of the Borrower
3.	Group
4.	Name of Promoters
5.	Activity
6.	Location of Corporate Office/Unit/Factory
7.	Dealing with our Bank Since

8. Details of Credit Facilities				(Rs. in crore)
Nature of Credit Facilities	*Existing*	*% share*	*Proposed*	*% share*
WC (CC) limit				
Term loan				
Total funded facilities				
Non-fund based WC limits				
Total limits (Fund based + Non-fund based)				

9. Group Exposure-Name of the other group companies						
Name of the Company	*Total Exposure from the Banking System*	*Our Exposure to the Group*				*% of our share*
		Domestic	*Investment Exposure*	*Overseas*	*Total*	
Total Group Exposure (Including Proposed Exposure)	(Annexure is attached marked as Annex-I).					

10. Interlocking of Funds among Group Companies

Shareholding	
Inter-locking of funds	
NPAs among associate concerns	
Transactions with related parties	

10 A.	Consortium Banking (with Name of Lead Bank & Other Banks)			
11.	Stock Market Perception (If Listed)			
Shares listed in SE	Face Value (Rs.)	Latest market value with date (Rs.)	52 week high (Rs.)	52 week low (Rs.)
BSE/NSE				
12. A	Rating with Score Internal External			
12.B	Rating Migration	Existing	New	
13.	Risk Weight (%)	Existing Level	Expected for 2009	Expected for 2010
14.	Provision Required (%)			

15.	Rate of Interest	Existing	Proposed
	Concession in Service Charges Proposed (If Any):		
Justification For Concessions in Interest Rate & Service Charges, If Any:			
16.	Repayment		

17. Present Position of Accounts with our Bank including Adhoc Limits (If Any)

Rupees in Crores

Nature of limit	*Limit*	*Value of security (our share)*	*Drawing power based on latest stock statement for the m/o*	*Balance outstanding as on*	*Irregularity*	*Remarks*
Term loan						
CC/WCDL/EPC						
Total fund based						
Bank guarantee						
L/C.						
Total non-fund based						
Grand total						

18. Financial Parameters (in Brief):			(Rs. in crore)
Past three years audited	*31st March*	*31st March*	*31st March*
TNW			
TOL/TNW			
Effective TOL/TNW			
Current ratio			
Non-current assets			
Net sales or revenue			
PBDIT			
Net profit [PAT]			
Cash accruals			
DSCR			

Details of non-current assets:			
Particulars	*31st March*	*31st March*	*31st March*
Investment in shares			
Security deposits			
Debtors more than six months			
Other non-current assets			
Total			

Brief Comments on Financials Parameters:

19. Policy Deviations, If Any

Parameters	*Requirement*	*Compliance Position*
Justification for acceptance for policy deviation:		

20.	Whether Names are in Default List	
	ECGC SAL as on	
	RBI WFD List as on June'09	
	RBI Defaulter List as on Sept'08	
21.	Whether the Company/Directors are related to any Senior Officials/Director of Our Bank or Other Bank.	
22.	Non-Compliace of Major Terms and Conditions of Last Sanction	
23.	Comment on Operation of the Account & Unit	
24.	Position of Audits/Inspections	

Type of audit	*Date of audit*	*Deficiency reported, if any*	*Status of compliance*
Credit audit			
Legal audit			
Stock audit			
AFI			
Central statutory auditors			
LFAR			
Others specify			
Qualifications, if any, in the audited balance sheet as on			

25	Details of Sanctions/Modification of Terms of Sanction (If Any) for Last One Year	

26a	Brief Description of the Proposal	
26b	Comments, if any, given by the branch/ZO/FGM office	
27	Security (In Brief)	
28a	BLNBC Cleared on	BLNBC Cleared the proposal on with following observation:
28b	CAG Cleared on	CAG-I cleared the proposal on With following observation:
29	Department Views *vis–a-vis-* Justifications/Recommendation	
30	Competent Authority	Board

General Manager

Enls:

Anneure A-12

Memorandum to the Board

(Regular Proposal)

Date:

1. Controlling Branch	
2. Account Profile	
2.1 Name of the account/borrower	
2.2 Group	
2.3 Main activity	
2.4 Sector (Private/Public/PSU/Jt. Sector)	
2.5 Main management personnel/promoters	
2.6 Major change in management since last sanction, if any	
2.7 Credit rating	Internal: External:
2.8 Track record of the promoters/directors with reference to default list ECGC SAL as on RBI WFD List as on June'09 RBI Defaulter list as on Sept'08	

3. Past Financial Brief	For Existing company

Rupees in crores

Past three years audited	*31st March*	*31st March*	*31st March*
TNW			
TOL/TNW			
Effective TOL/TNW			
Current Ratio			
Non-Current Assets			
Net Sales or Revenue			
PBDIT			
Net Profit [PAT]			
Cash Accruals			
DSCR			

Brief Comments on Financial Parameters-

3.1. Projected Financials in Brief (For newly formed company)-

Rs. in crore

Particulars	*FY*	*FY*	*FY*	*FY*	*FY*	*FY*	*FY*
TNW							
TOL/TNW							
Current Ratio							
Net Sales							
PBDIT							
PAT							
Cash Accruals							
FACR							
Avg. DSCR Minimum DSCR							
IRR							
Break Even point							

Note: The projected financials to be given up to the tenor of the facility proposed.

3.2. Sources & Application of Fund (Rs. in crores)

	31.03.08 (Aud.)	*31.03.09 (Est)*	*31.03.10 (Proj.)*
Long term sources			
Long term application			
Long term Surplus/(deficit)*			
Short term sources			
Short term application			
Short term surplus/(deficit)			

* Tally with NWC figure shown under salient financial indicators

4. Share Holding Pattern as on:

Authorised capital:

Issued/subscribed/Paid up capital:

Name of the Promoters/ Major Shareholders	*No. of Shares*	*Amt. in Rs. Crores.*	*% Holding*
Promoters Holding			
Promoters			
Related Parties/Body Corporate			
Out of above			
Other Closely Held Companies			
Total Promoters/Groups			
Non-Promoters Holding			
Others: Private Corporate Bodies			
Grand Total			
Promoter shares pledged with Bank/FIs may be commented upon			

4.1 Top Ten Shareholders:

Sl.	*Particulars*	*Number of Shares Held*	*Face Valueholding INR Cr*	*% of Holding*
1				
2				
3				
4				
5				
6				
7				
8				
9				
10				
	Total			

5. Salient Past Financials/Particulars of the Major Group Companies/ Main Sponsor/Promoter Company:

Details about Sponsor/Promoter/Group/Associate Concerns (Operative/active companies):-

Name	*Activity*	*Bankers*	*Standard of Asset/Opinion of Banks*

Salient Financials of Group/Promoter Companies (based on past audited BS):
(Rs. in crores)

Companies/Firms	*Years*	*Sales*	*PAT*	*TNW*	*DE Ratio*	*Current Ratio*
	2007					
	2008					
	2007					
	2008					
	2007					
	2008					

6. Compliance with Corporate Governance:

7.1 In case of NBFCs compliance with

RBI norms & guidelines:

7.2 In case of HFCs compliance with

NHB norms & guidelines:

7. Sanction Particulars	*Date*	*Authority*
Last Sanction (Regular/adhoc)		MCB
Last Review		
Present proposal is within the powers of		
Is the proposal for take over from other bank/institution (if yes, reasons there of in brief)		

8. Exposure of Other Banks (Rs in crores)

Name of the Bank/FI	*Sanctioned Limit*			*Balance Outstanding*		
	Term Loan	*WC Fund Based*	*WC Non-fund Based*	*Term Loan*	*WC Fund Based*	*WC Non-fund Based*
Total						

Credit opinion from the existing bankers about the facility availed by the company is to be obtained before disbursement (in case of new connection).

9. Value of the Account (Rs in crores): In case of Existing Accounts

(For new account, value of the account from group companies may be furnished)

(Rs. in Crores)

Particulars	*For the Previous Year*	*For the Current Year from 01.04 to*
Interest earned		
Exchange & commission earned		
Other charges recovered		
(Out of which processing charge/ Up front fees)		
Total value		
Avg. utilisation of fund based limit	%	%
Comments on pro rata share: Whether pro rata business routed through our bank		

10. Brief details of the proposal:

10a Proposal for Sanction	Rupees in crores	
Nature of facility	Existing	Proposed
Term loan		
FLC/ILC (as sub limit of term loan)		( )
Working capital fund based (CC/WCDL/ EPC/FBP)		
Working capital non fund based (BG-Performance/financial)		
Working capital non-fund based (ILC/FLC)		
Total fund based		
Total non-fund based		
Total exposure		

10(b) Proposal for approval for modification/amendments:

11. Exposure in Crores	Borrower		Group	
Prudential exposure	Existing	Proposed	Existing	Proposed
Domestic credit				
Overseas exposure				
Investments				
Total				
Excess over bank norms				
Excess over RBI norms				

Explanatory Note if exposure level exceeds prudential norms:

12. Sharing Pattern of Credit Facilities

Rs. in crores

Existing under consortium/sole/multiple banking Proposed under consortium/sole/multiple banking						
Particulars	*Existing*			*Proposed*		
	Total	*Our Bank*	*%*	*Total*	*Our Bank*	*%*
For term loan						
For working capital						
Fund based						
Non fund based						
Total						

13. Details of Primary & Collateral Securities along with Personal/Corporate Guarantee:

Security	*Existing (Rs. in crores)*		*Proposed (Rs. in crore)*	
Term loan	*Nature*	*Value*	*Nature*	*Value*
Primary	1st *pari-passu* mortgage & hypo. charge over the land & building, plant & machinery and other immovable & movable fixed assets(both existing & future) of the company with other term lending banks and institutions at (location)	As on -our share %	1st *pari-passu* mortgage & hypo. charge over the land building, plant & machinery and other immovable & movable fixed assets of the existing & expansion project of the company (both existing & future) at (location)	After the completion of the project: Our share:
FACR proposed to be maintained at during the entire tenor of our facility.				
For Fund based WC (primary):	Hypo. Charge on current assets: Details to be mentioned On exclusive/ *pari-passu* 1st/2nd charge basis with existing/proposed WC lenders	Our share on the security: DP available based on latest stock statement (Not more than 1 month old from the date of proposal)		(Our share %)

WC-Non Fund Based (BG) Extension of charge on the current & fixed assets as above	Counter Guarantee On *pari-passu* 1st/ 2nd charge basis with existing/ proposed) WC lenders Cash margin %	Residual value after meeting DP& margin: Our bank's share: Value:		
Non Fund Based (ILC/ FLC) Extension of charge on the current & fixed assets as above	Documents to title of goods On *pari-passu* 1st/ 2nd charge basis with existing/ proposed WC lenders Cash margin (%)	Residual value after meeting DP& margin: our bank's share: Value:		
Collateral security for term loan facility	1. Mortgage & hypo. Charge on land & building & other immovable & movable fixed assets other than project assets 2. 2nd *pari passu* hypo. charge on the entire current assets of the company's proposed project at (1st charge with WC lenders)	Residual value: Our bank's share:		
Collateral security for Working capital facility	1. Mortgage & hypo. charge on land & building & other immovable & movable fixed assets other than project assets 2. 2nd *pari passu* hypo. charge on the entire fixed assets of the company's proposed project at (1st charge with term lenders)	Residual value: Our bank's share:		

Details of land & buildings & other properties mortgaged in favour of our bank/consortium are enclosed as per Annexe –. Whether free hold/leasehold/agril. property. The valuations made by (whether bank empanelled?). Wherever two valuations required, dates, name etc.		
Personal guarantee/ corporate guarantee	*Name with PAN NO.*	*Net Worth (Rs. In crores) as on*
Personal guarantee		
Corporate Guarantee		

* Latest Personal balance sheet & income tax return of the guarantors for the year-ended____are to be submitted along with latest address.

Guarantee from ECGC	To be covered under Both WTPCG & WTPSG of ECGC	To be continued

14. Comments on Financing Arrangement:

	Sole/multiple/ consortium	*Leader bank/lead arranger/syndicated by*	*Major financing banks*	*Present status of tie up*
Term loan				
WC				

15. Expected Date of Financial Closure;

16. Pricing		Existing	Proposed
Credit Rating		..... As per BS dated	.... As per BS dated Or based on green field rating module-
Interest	Card Rate	Term loan-CC	Term loan-CC
Prepayment charges			
Processing charges/upfront fees/Commission charges/ Lead bank charges/ Commitment charges			

Reasons for Concessions Proposed:

17. Compliance	
17.1. Terms & conditions of last sanction	Complied/not complied.
17.2. The policies of RBI	Complied/not complied
17.3. Policy compliances:	

Parameters	Requirement	Compliance
Credit Rating	At least B+ with more than 2/3rd marks in management rating	Credit rating
Industry		
Credit Information Report from the Existing Bankers	Should reveal satisfactory conduct & asset classification as standard.	
(For take over/new accounts)		
Take over norms : For take over account		Complied/Not complied
Promoter's contribution	25% (minimum)	Complied/Not complied
DSCR	1.50 (Min.)	Complied/Not complied
Current Ratio	Min. 1.17	Complied/Not complied
TOL/TNW	3.5:1 (maximum)	
	Term debt equity incl. proposed borrowing should not exceed 3:1	Complied/Not complied
Prudential Exposure limit	Single/individual-Rs. Crores Group crores	Complied/Not complied

Comments if there is/are deviations from policy compliance: Mentioned in Gist Sheet

18. Comments on Standard Conditions Modified/Withdrawn and Additional Conditions Imposed.

19. Deptt.'s Views of the Proposal:

While going through the Memorandum we have observed as under:

I) BLNBC has cleared the proposal on____with the following directions:

Branch/ZO since submitted the proposal after compliance of the aforesaid BLNBC directions/with following deviations:

Branch/ZO since approached for acceptance of the proposal with deviations in NBC direction due to following reasons/justifications:

Considering the justifications provided, we may accept the proposal.

II. Brief comments on nature of activity/industry/market scenario.

III. Brief comments on present position of account/conduct of the account.

IV. Brief comments on the past financials of the proposed borrower from audited BS. In case of existing borrowers study the achievement made against estimates considered at the time of last assessment.

V. Brief comments on the performance of the borrower in key performing areas of current financial year (3 months/6 months/9 months) and % achievements made against current year estimates.

Particulars	*Estimated earlier*	*Achievement as on*	*% on achievement*
Sales			
PAT			

VI. Compare the performance of the borrower with that of companies having synergies in activity/industry avg.

20. For Term Loan/Project Finance

Assessment Term Loan:

Total Project Cost	*Amount*	*Means of finance*	*Amount*

a. The project/rationale/infrastructure availability (pre sanction inspection done by & reports). TEV study conducted by .... who are the consultants.

b. Brief remarks on the promoters/company/group company with their past experience/strength/ source to bring in equity/unsecured loan as mentioned in the proposal. How much equity the Promoters will bring in upfront (%/entire equity) before seeking any disbursements from the lenders.

c. Brief comments on cost of the project - comparable with other similar projects/industry average.

d. Compartive Analysis with Industrial Units having Synergies in Activity

Source (Rs. In crore) (for qtr./yr ended)

Players/Name of the Company	Sales	PBDIT Margin (%)	PAT Margin (%)
Industry as a whole (Avg.) As per RM,Deptt. , HO, circular	-		
The company (Last audited)			
The company projections			

Comments;

e. Brief comments on Present status of the project (Initial/advance) : Both physical & financial progress including statutory & regulatory clearances. How much amount so far invested & source. What is the tie up position?

f. Brief comments on Assumptions taken into considerations while arriving at projections in CMA/profitability projections- Realistic/achievable.

The details of assumptions of economic variables, the future Projected Profit & Loss Account, Balance Sheet, and Cash Flow Statements have been drawn & are provided as part of Annexe -

g. Brief comments on key project parameters like DSCR, IRR, BEP etc.

h. Sensitivity Analysis :

The impact of changes in key variables of the project on the debt serving ability of the company has been estimated on the basis of estimates considered. The variables like raw material price, selling price, interest on loan, decrease in capacity utilisation etc. has been considered in the sensitivity calculation and the same are as under:

Sensitivities	*Factor*	*Project*	
		Min. DSCR	*Avg. DSCR*
Base Case			
Increase in Project Cost by			
Increase in Operating Cost by			
Reduction in Selling Price by			
Reduction in Capacity Utilisation by			
Increase in Interest Rate by			

Comments:

21. For New/Enhancement in WC Limits

   a) Brief comments on sales projections: Justified/achievable in relation to past performance/ production capacity/market demand etc.

   b) Justification of holding levels: In line with operating cycle /industry avg.

   c) Brief comments on WC non-fund based requirements

22. Different risk factors & mitigation mechanism:

23. Any other issue/ material Information:

24. Recommendation:

In view of the foregoing, we recommend for sanction of following facilities/Limits in favor of M/s consortium arrangement subject to Terms and Conditions as contained in the enclosed memorandum/Annexe.

Nature of facility	*Existing*	*Proposed*
Term Loan for expansion/new project (under multiple/consortium/sole) at an ROI of		
With sub-limit as ILC/FLC for capital goods	( )	( )
Working capital fund based(CC/WCDL /EPC /FBP): For existing/proposed activity-(under multiple/consortium/sole) at an ROI of		
Working capital non fund based (BG-Performance/financial): For existing/proposed activity-(under multiple/consortium/sole)		
Working capital non fund based (ILC/FLC)		
For existing /proposed activity-(under multiple/consortium/sole)		
Total fund based		
Total non-fund based		
Total exposure		

General Manager

25. Draft Resolutions

The Management Committee of the Board may kindly consider passing the following resolutions:

The Board considered the memorandum No. dated in respect of the account M/s —account with branch, and resolved that the under mentioned fund-based/non fund based facility /limit on the terms and conditions as contained in the memorandum be and is hereby approved

Nature of facility	*Existing*	*Proposed*
Term Loan for expansion/new project (under multiple/consortium/sole) at an ROI of .... With sub limit as ILC/FLC for capital goods	( )	( )
Working capital fund based(CC/WCDL /EPC /FBP) – For existing/proposed activity-(under multiple/ consortium/sole) at an ROI of		
Working capital non fund based (BG-Performance/financial)-For existing /proposed activity-(under multiple/consortium/sole)		
Working capital non fund based (ILC/FLC)		
-For existing /proposed activity-(under multiple/consortium/sole)		
Total fund based		
Total non fund based		
Total exposure		

General Manager

Annexure A-13

Project Information: Takeout Finance—IIFCL

Sr. No.	*Particulars*	*Comments*
1.	Name of the project/SPV	
2.	Is there any concession agreement signed for the project? If yes, then name of the concessioning authority. (A copy of the same to be attached.)	
3.	If no, concession agreement existing, whether MOU with any government agency or PPA has been signed and still valid? (A copy of the same to be attached.)	
4.	PIM (Project Information Memorandum) circulated to banks at the time of first syndication for the tying-up of the debt.	
5.	Scheduled COD date (dd/mm/yy)	
6.	Actual COD date (dd/mm/yyyy)	
7.	In case of delay in achieving scheduled COD, the reasons thereof.	

		Sr. No.	Bank/FI	Amount allocated	O/s as on dd/mm/yy
8.	Consortium details. Name of Lead Bank.				

9.	Banks reference/Borrower company's request.	
10.	Status of account in the books of the banks.	Standard or Not?
11.	Interest rate as on dd/mm/yyyy	
12.	Reset date, frequency of reset and mechanism of reset.	

		Date	Amount		
13.	Detailed repayment schedule				

14.	Project cost estimate at the time of first sanction. Final achieved cost of the project.	
15.	If increase in project cost, reasons thereof.	
16.	Means of finance (both originally envisaged and final achieved)	

17.	Latest audited financials of the SPV.	Copy to be attached.
18.	Latest external rating. Copy of same.	
19.	Terms and conditions of sanction advice.	
20.	Current status of toll collections/ tariff being charged.	

21.	In the event of non-submission of PIM, detailed implementation schedule may be provided.	Key dates and timelines concession/MOU/PPA period (in years)
		Construction period (in years)
		Operational period (in years)
		CA/MOU/PPA signing date (dd/mm/yyyy)
		Scheduled project completion date as per CA (dd/mm/yyyy)
		Debt drawdown start (dd/mm/yyyy)
		Debt repayment start (dd/mm/yyyy)
		Debt repayment end date (dd/mm/yyyy)
		Moratorium (in years)
		Repayment period (in years)
		Door-to-door maturity (in years)
		Concession/MOU/PPA end date (dd/mm/yyyy)

Annexure-A-14

Problem Loan Review Report

1. Name of the borrower:
2. IRAC Status:
3. (A) Borrower's Profile:
    i) Constitution:
    ii) Sector:
    iii) Group to which it belongs:
    iv) Since when dealing with the Bank:

   (B) Ownership and Management:
    i). Names of Directors/partners/proprietor:
    ii). Name of the Chief Executive:
    iii). Any adverse report on the owners/management:
4. Position as on ------------------ (Rs. In Crores)

Facilities	Existing Limits	DP	Outstanding
Term Loan/Working Capital			

5. Date of sanction and last renewal:

6. Date when it was recognized as problem loan:

7. Specify the adverse features observed in the running of the unit/ conduct of the accounts:

8. Key financial data for the past 2 years:
   a) Capital:
   b) Total Net Worth:
   c) Current Ratio:
   d) Debt Equity Ratio:
   e) DSCR (for term loans)
   f) Receivables:
      Total:
      Over 6 months old:
   g) Operating profit/loss:
   h) Net profit/ loss:
   i) Cash Accruals:
   j) Statutory dues:

9. Due to other Banks/Financial Institutions:

10. Security: (Rs. In Crores)

	Description	*Estimated realizable value*	*Date of last valuation/ review of the means*

11. Reasons for the account becoming a problem account:

12. Current status of the security documents held on the account and the charges created in favour of the Bank:

13. Position of accounts of any associate concerns, if banking with any of our branches:

14. Date of last inspection and of meeting with the borrowers and/or guarantors to discuss the problem observed:

15. Summary of observations/discussions:

16. Action proposed/taken, with time plan:

17. If the proposed action plan is approved and implemented, when the sickness of the account is likely to be arrested/or our dues realized. Please time-schedule the expected results, to the extent possible:

18. Recommendations of the Branch:

Dated____________ Field Officer/Manager/Branch Manager

Observation of the General Manager

Annexure-A-15

Problem Loan Progress Report

For the Month/Quarter ended-----------------

1. Name of the Borrower:

2. Refer Review Report dated:
   (Copy enclosed)

3. Date from which the approved action plan is implemented:

4. Position of Accounts: (Rs. In Crore)

Facility	*Outstandings when the implementation of the corrective action commenced*	*Outstandings as at end of the previous month/ quarter*	*Outstandings as at end of the current month/ quarter*

5. Comments on the progress in the implementation of the corrective action indicate when the account is likely to be normalized/or our dues realized:

Dated Field Officer/Manager/Branch Manager

Observation of the General Manager